English Communicative

Part VIII

For students of Grade VIII

Chandan Sengupta

Creative Learning Series

English Communicative Part VIII

Chandan Sengupta.

This workbook is prepared to address the need of fellow aspirants of different competitive examinations duly conducted time to time by various boards of studies. We also wanted to cover up the need of students having eagerness to develop their skills through self studies. It is not merely a gguide book. This workbook cannot introduce any learner simply to the mechanism of correct use of grammar related rules of speaking and writing. Primary knowledge of Grammar and Composition is required before moving through this workbook.

Types of questions asked in exams are of similar pattern. Contents, in some cases, may differ. These materials are collected from our daily use of English. It would be better if fellow students start talking in English in a group made up of few of the selected friends working in a closed user group. It would be more convenient if such group start interacting through electronic media and through other suitable means. Another fruitful initiative will be following electronic media, news channels, analytics and other sources of information and views so as to collections of vocabulary will be increased. Collection and use of new words will definitely increase the grasping of students on the process of writing and representation of facts in speech. One can even aspire for an enhancement in the linguistic skill by following stories and compositions made by famous authors. Initiatives of any kind will be accepted and quantified in accord to the coverage of selected areas of competencies. The related fields of studies are linked together in such a way that they cannot be addressed individually through focused study materials. We simply put them in a definite order to link up our efforts to gain linguistic competencies of desired types.

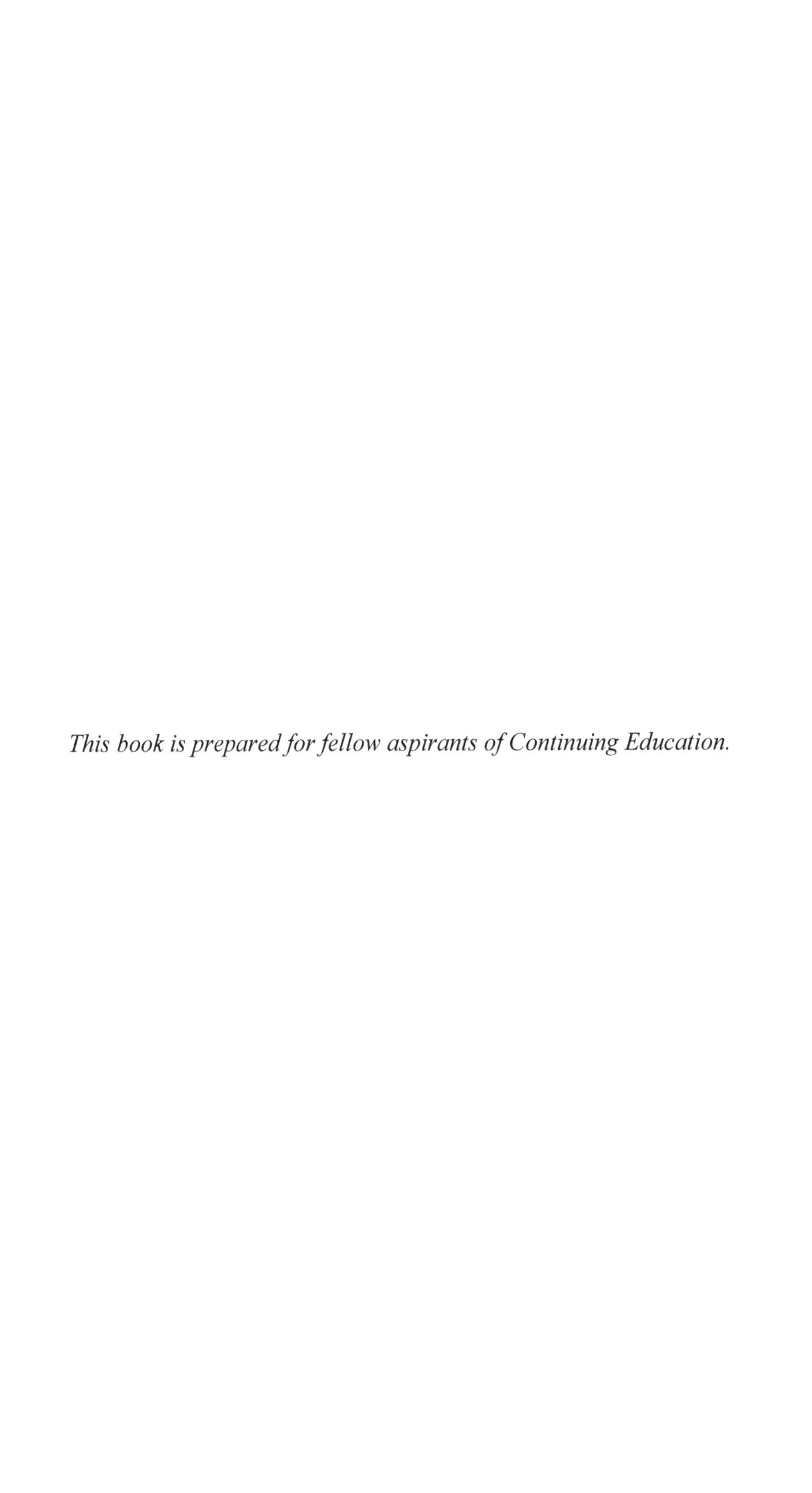

This book is prepared for fellow aspirants of Continuing Education.

Contents

Foreword

One should remember following before moving on further.

Points to Remember

1. The compound personal pronouns may be used as the objects of transitive verbs or of prepositions when the object denotes the same person or thing as the subject.
2. In this use they are called reflexive pronouns.
3. King Alfred interested himself in his subjects
4. Some words are used either as adjectives or as pronouns. Such words are called adjective pronouns.
5. The demonstratives are this (plural, these), that (plural, those). They point out persons or things for special attention
6. The indefinite pronouns point out objects less clearly or definitely than demonstratives do.
7. Most indefinites may be either pronouns or adjectives. But none is always a substantive in modern use, and every is always an adjective.
8. Each other and one another are regarded as compound pronouns. They designate related persons or things.
   - My neighbor and I like each other.
9. All, several, few, many, and similar words are often classed as indefinites. They may be used as adjectives or as substantives. Everybody, everything, anybody, anything, somewhat, aught, naught,20 etc., are called indefinite nouns.
10. Relative pronouns have a peculiar function in the sentence, since they serve both as pronouns and as connectives. Their use may be seen by comparing the two sentences that follow:—
    - 1. This is the sailor, and he saved my life.
11. Relative pronouns connect dependent clauses with main clauses by referring directly to a substantive in the main clause
12. The simple relative pronouns are who, which, that, as, and what.
13. Who is either masculine or feminine; which and what are neuter; that and as are of all three genders.
    - All who heard, approved.
14. A relative pronoun must agree with its antecedent in gender, number, and person.

- It is I who am wrong. [First person, singular number: antecedent, I.]
- The road that leads to the shore is sandy. [Third person singular: antecedent, road.]

15. A relative pronoun in the objective case is often omitted.

16. Certain questions of gender call for particular attention.

1. Which is commonly used in referring to the lower animals unless these are regarded as persons. This is true even when he or she is used of the same animals

17. In the case of things without animal life, of which and whose are both common. The tendency is to prefer of which in prose, but whose is often used because of its more agreeable sound. In poetry, whose is especially frequent.

- Jack was fishing with a bamboo rod, to the end of which he had tied a short piece of ordinary twine.

18. The clause introduced by a relative pronoun is an adjective clause, since it serves as an adjective modifier of the antecedent

19. A relative pronoun that serves merely to introduce a descriptive fact is called a descriptive relative.

20. A relative pronoun that introduces a clause confining or limiting the application of the antecedent is called a restrictive relative.

21. Before a descriptive relative we regularly make a pause in speaking, but never before a restrictive relative.

22. A descriptive relative is preceded by a comma; a restrictive relative is not.

- Three sailors, who were loitering on the pier, sprang to the rescue.

23. The relative pronoun what is equivalent to that which, and has a double construction:—(1) the construction of the omitted or implied antecedent (that); (2) the construction of the relative (which).

24. The compound relative pronouns may include or imply their own antecedents and hence may have a double construction.

25. Whoever calls, he must be admitted. [Here he, the antecedent of whoever, is the subject of must be admitted, and whoever is the subject of calls.]

- He shall have whatever he wishes.

26. The interrogative pronouns are who, which, and what. They are used in asking questions

- Whose voice is that?
- Which shall I take?
- Which is correct?

27. An adjective is said to belong to the substantive which it describes or limits.

28. An adjective which describes is called a descriptive adjective; one which points out or designates is called a definitive adjective

29. A proper noun used as an adjective, or an adjective derived from a proper noun, is called a proper adjective and usually begins with a capital letter.

30. Definitive adjectives include:—pronouns used as adjectives (as, this opportunity; those pictures; either table; what time is it?);

31. Adjectives may be classified, according to their position in the sentence, as attributive, appositive, and predicate adjectives.

32. An attributive adjective is closely attached to its noun and regularly precedes it.

- The angry spot doth glow on Cæsar's brow.

33. A predicate adjective completes the meaning of the predicate verb, but describes or limits the subject.

34. The adjectives a (or an) and the are called articles.

1. The definite article the points out one or more particular objects as distinct from others of the same kind.

35. The indefinite article a (or an) designates an object as merely one of a general class or kind.

- Lend me a pencil.

36. An adjective preceded by the may be used as a plural noun.

- The brave are honored.

37. An is used before words beginning with a vowel or silent h; a before other words. Thus,—

- an owl;

38. The degrees of comparison indicate by their form in what degree of intensity the quality described by the adjective exists.

39. There are three degrees of comparison,—the positive, the comparative, and the superlative.

40. The comparative degree of an adjective is formed by adding the termination er to the positive degree.

41. It denotes that the quality exists in the object described in a higher degree than in some other object.

42. Adjectives ending in silent e drop this letter before the comparative ending er and the superlative ending est. Thus,—

- wise, wiser, wisest;

43. Many adjectives are compared by prefixing the adverbs more and most to the positive degree.

- recent, more recent, most recent;

44. An adverb is a word which modifies a verb, an adjective, or another adverb.

- The storm ceased suddenly.

45. Adverbs are classified according to their meaning as: (1) adverbs of manner; (2) adverbs of time; (3) adverbs of place; (4) adverbs of degree

46. There is often used merely to introduce a sentence in the inverted order

- There are many strangers in town.

47. Relative adverbs introduce subordinate clauses and are similar in their use to relative pronouns.

48. I know a farmhouse {in which | where} we can spend the night.

49. The principal relative adverbs are:—where, whence, whither, wherever, when, whenever, while, as, how, why, before, after, till, until, since.

50. An interrogative adverb introduces a question.

51. Where, when, whence, whither, how, why, may be used as interrogative adverbs.

52. Most adverbs are compared by means of more and most.

- Richard came more promptly than John. [Comparative.]
- Henry came most promptly of all. [Superlative.]

53. The comparative degree, not the superlative, is used in comparing two persons or things.

54. When two adjectives or adverbs are contrasted by means of than, more is used with the first.

- Such indulgence is more kind than wise.

55. Words indicating number are called numerals. They are adjectives, nouns, or adverbs.

- There are seven days in the week. [Adjective.]

56. Cardinal numeral adjectives (one, two, three, four, etc.) are used in counting, and answer the question "How many?"

57. Ordinal numeral adjectives (first, second, third, etc.) denote the position or order of a person or thing in a series.

- Carl plays the second violin.

58. All the cardinal and ordinal numerals may become nouns and may take a plural ending in some of their senses.

- One is enough.

- The nine played an excellent game.
- Three twos are six.

59. Certain numeral adjectives (single, double, triple, etc.) indicate how many times a thing is taken or of how many like parts it consists.

- A double row of policemen stood on guard.

60. Certain numeral adverbs and adverbial phrases indicate how many times an action takes place.

- Once my assailant slipped.

61. A verb is a word which can assert something (usually an action) concerning a person, place, or thing

- 1.We jumped for joy.
- Rabbits burrow into the sides of hills.

62. Certain verbs, when used to make verb-phrases, are called auxiliary (that is, "aiding") verbs, because they help other verbs to express action or state of some particular kind

63. Verbs are either transitive or intransitive

64. Some verbs may be followed by a substantive denoting that which receives the action or is produced by it. These are called transitive verbs. All other verbs are called intransitive.

65. A verb which is transitive in one of its senses may be intransitive in another.

66. Many transitive verbs may be used absolutely,—that is, merely to express action without any indication of the direct object.

67. Is (in its various forms) and several other verbs may be used to frame sentences in which some word or words in the predicate describe or define the subject

68. A participle is said to belong to the substantive which it describes or limits.

- Rising, she opened the window. [Rising belongs to she.]
- I heard the rain falling. [Falling belongs to the object rain.]

69. A participle should not be used without some substantive to which it may belong.

- RIGHT: Entering the room, we saw a strange sight. [The participle entering belongs to the pronoun we.]

70. A participle may take an object if its meaning allows.

- Lifting the box, he moved toward the door.

71. The past participle is often used as a predicate adjective expressing state or condition.

- When the rain at last ceased, we were drenched [that is, very wet].

72. A substantive, with the participle belonging to it, is often used to make a peculiar form of adverbial modifying phrase The wind failing, we lowered the sail.

73. A substantive, with a participle, may express the cause, time, or circumstances of an action. This is called the absolute construction.

74. The substantive is in the nominative case and is called a nominative absolute.

- Two days having elapsed, we again set forward. [The phrase in italics is equivalent to when two days had elapsed: it expresses time.]
- This done, proceed to business. [The phrase this done is equivalent to the clause since (or when) this is done, and indicates cause or time.]

75. From nearly every English verb there may be formed a verbal noun in -ing.

76. Verbal nouns in -ing have the form of present participles, but the construction of nouns.

77. They are often called participial nouns.

78. Verbal nouns in -ing may take a direct or an indirect object if their meaning allows.

- Digging gold seems to the uninitiated like finding buried treasure.

79. A verbal noun in -ing may take an adverbial modifier.

80. But verbal nouns in -ing, like other nouns, may be modified by adjectives.

- Extemporaneous speaking is good practice.

81. To the verbal nouns being and having, past participles may be attached, so as to give the effect of voice and tense.

- There were grave doubts expressed as to his having seen the mastodon.
- After having been treated in so harsh a fashion, I had no wish to repeat the interview.

82. Verbal nouns in -ing are similar in some of their constructions to infinitives used as nouns

Preface

There is no end if we start incorporating different aspects related to English Grammar along with expanded exercises. Job seekers require some sort of practice materials as per the prescribed formats issued to them by board of examiners. We also consider some additional practice materials for gaining mastery upon concepts and perspectives of the rules related to writing and speaking a language. This publication is prepared accordingly to address ever growing need of fellow students of the higher levels of studies. Students of other faculties can also opt for this publication with an apprehension of gaining advancement in the allied fields of studies. There are reference materials in plenty.[1] Some of such materials are of higher importance and some are at the basic stage. Our aspirants require some practice materials which fits better with the context. Best use of the language is another aspect depending upon which we select language related practice materials.

It is also recommended that aspirants should prepare daily routine for practicing best uses of grammar and vocabulary on the basis of materials provided to them. Some of the materials obtained from old scriptures and great writings. We also worked out some self - learning modules along with suggested solutions to equip the fellow learner with background materials needed for accelerating self-study. These materials will punctuate the use of language in relation to the modern context. We also propose that students should maintain an expanded list of vocabularies so that timely need of the same can be fulfilled. It will also enhance the learning skills of the fellow student by providing them some better alternatives to be used.

---

[1] *Meiklejohn's "English Language," Longmans' "School Grammar," West's "English Grammar," Bain's "Higher English Grammar" and "Composition Grammar," Sweet's "Primer of Spoken English" and "New English Grammar," etc., Hodgson's "Errors in the Use of English," Morris's "Elementary Lessons in Historical English Grammar," Lounsbury's "English Language," Champney's "History of English," Emerson's "History of the English Language," Kellner's "Historical Outlines of English Syntax," Earle's "English Prose," and Matzner's "Englische Grammatik." Allen's "Subjunctive Mood in English," Battler's articles on "Prepositions" in the "Anglia,"*

PREFACE

One should keep in mind that language is considered as a personality booster. We learn English Grammar for gaining mastery in speaking and writing English perfectly. We also learn different rules of writing for confirming our skill of writing and speaking in the context of the modern communication system. It is also becoming evident from our systematic studies that we use only a part of speaking and writing alternatives to express our views and concerns on some of the parts of our .communication formats.

This Workbook is prepared for providing supporting content and comprehensive guidance to aspirants of different examinations, such as UPSC, PSC, SSC, RRB, Bank Probationary Officer's Examination and other competitive examinations conducted by different boards of studies. Basic framework of the syllabus is taken up from the content areas prescribed by Central Board of Secondary Educations for English Communicative Programmes. It will be equally helpful for teachers and other associates having passion of providing quality guidance along with time tested practice materials.

Equal strength is provided on both grammar rules and communication skills. Some of the fundamentals are duly incorporated to make the content area a balanced one for the fellow aspirants. Incorporation of some of the basic templates is avoided for keeping the volume of this workbook in limit. One can take support of any of the grammar and comprehension handbook for gaining mastery in all such basic formats. This workbook will imply focus on the higher levels of English Grammar and Compositions.

**

Vocabulary

Prefixes and Suffixes :

Pre means before, fix means set. Adding prefix before a word we can create new word.

For Eg: able- enable; understand – misunderstand; belief- disbelief; etc…

Suffixes are used after a word to create new words.

For Eg: Teach- Teacher; Agree- Agreement; etc…

In fact, if you study the shape of a word, you can divide into three parts- the prefix, suffix, and the root word.

Let us now study some prefixes and suffixes and see the words that can be formed by using them:

Some of the tips to learn Vocabulary;

The prefix 'RE 'means back or again.

For Eg:

rebuild -------RE build means Build again

recall------ RE call means to bring back to mind or remember.

Refold ------ RE fold means fold again.

Regain ----- RE gain means get back.

Remind ------ RE mind means mention again

Repay ------ RE pay means payback.

--- You try to write some more like this…..

The root PORT means carry

For Eg:

Port ---- PORT means a place ships may wait in.

Porter ------ PORT er means one who carries things, as baggage.

Deport ----- de PORT means to send a person away.

Report ------- re PORT means an account of something which happened.

Support ---- sup PORT means to carry along with help.

Portable --- PORT able means can be carried.

----- practice some more like this…..

The prefixes EN and EM means into/ in

For Eg:

endanger ---- EN danger means put into danger

Enroll ----- EN roll means to enter or register.

Entrust ----- EN trust means charge with a specified office or duty involving trust.

Enslave ---- EN slave means put into slavery.

Embrace ------ EM brace means to take into one's arms.

Embark ------- EM bark means get into a train or ship a for journey.

The suffix ATE means to cause or make.

For Eg:

dedicate ----- dedic ATE means to set apart for a purpose.

Advocate ----- advoc ATE means to speak for to defend.

Deviate ---- Devi ATE means to turn aside from the right way.

Liquidate ----- liquid ATE means to end a debt by payment.

educate ----- educ ATE means to lead to knowledge.

enumarate ----- enumar ATE means to count.

The Root MEM means REMEMBER.

For Eg:

memento ----- MEM ento means something to make one remember.

Memorandum ---- MEM orandum means a reminder.

Memory ------ MEM ory means the ability to recall.

Memoir ------ MEM oir means a record of a thing to remember.

Memorable ------- MEM orable means worth remembering.

In memoriam ------ In MEM oriam means In memory of.

The root UNI means ONE.

For Eg:

Unique ----- UNI que means one of a kind.

Union ---- UNI on means the joining of many into one.

Unitarianism ----- UNI tarianism means a belief in one god.

Unanimous ----- UN animous means having one opinion held by all.

Universe ----- UNI verse means all parts of the world as one.

Unimanual ---- UNI manual means done with one hand.

So, such these root words offer you an easy step – by- step approach to an understanding of thousands of words in the English Language.

Examples

The new pattern vocabulary is nothing but an Analogy. It means comparison, relation, resemblance and correlation. The Analogy s are given in exams to test the analytical ability of yours.

You will find word analogies, or verbal analogies, used in standardized tests and sometimes in job interviews where you must show the relationship between two objects or concepts using logic and reasoning. These analogies are set up in a standard format. For Eg: tree: leaf:: flower: petal. An analogy is more of a logical argument than a simple figure of speech.

Now I will explain to you the basic level of analogy s. Read all the choices before choosing your answer. Finding out a right choice from given options reveal your smartness in thinking.

In the following s, you are required to identify and assess the logical relationship between a given pair of words in the , then choose a pair of words from the options that exhibit the same logical relationship as the original pair in the s.

1. Grove: Forest : --------- : Lake.
a. pond
b .ocean
c. tree
d. boat.
Ans: a. Pond,
Explanation: A grove is a similar version of a forest, and a pond is a smaller version of a lake.

2. Spelunker: -------- : : Astronomer : Space
a. spaceship   b. light   c. cave   d. wave
Ans: c. cave
Explanation: A spelunker is someone explores caves, and an astronomer is someone who explores space.

3. Mend: Sewing:: Edit : ---------
a. darn   b. repair   c. manuscript   d. makeshift
Ans: c.Manuscript.
Explanation: one fixes sewing by mending; one fixes manuscript by editing.

4. Perfidy: -------- : : satire : Parody
a. treachery   b. humour   c. forgiveness   d. performance.
Ans: a. treachery
Explanation: Perfidy is synonym for treachery, and satire is a synonym for parody.

5. Hawali: 1959:: ------- 1912

a. Network   b. South Carolina   c. Arizona   d. Maine

Ans: c.Arizona

Explanation: Hawaii became a state in 1959, and Arizona became a state in 1912.

6. Rotation: Earth:: -------- : Top

a. planet   b. spinning   c. sun   d. expanding

Ans: Spinning

Explanation: Rotation is the movement of the earth and spinning is the movement of a top.

7. Piercing: ------ : : Hushed : Whisper

a. diamond   b. watch   c. siren   d. ears

Ans: Siren

Explanation: A siren is described as piercing, and a whisper is described as hushed.

8. Cabal: -------- : : Output : Yield.

a. Plot   b.plant   c. cable   d. stop.

Ans: a. Plot

Explanation: Cabal is a synonym for plot, and Output is a synonym for Yield.

9. Channel: Waterway :: -------- : Fabric

a. polyester   b. zipper   c. cotton   d. stone

Ans: c. Cotton

Explanation: A channel is a natural water way, and cotton is a natural fabric.

10. Penurious: -------- : : Deep : Significant

a. generous   b.stingy   c. decrepit   d. cavernous

Ans: b.stingy

Explanation: Penurious is a synonym for stingy, and deep is a synonym for significant

11. ------- : Flood :: Helmet: Injury

a. drowned   b.Coast Guard   c.river   d.levee

Ans : d. levee

Explanation: A levee prevents a flood, and a helmet prevents injury.

12. Rein : Horse :: Control panel : ------

a. Pilot   b. bit   c. plane   d. rider

Ans: plane

Explanation: A rider uses a rein to guide a horse; a pilot uses the control panel to guide a plane.

13. Spoke : : -------- Word : Sentence

a. speaker   b. paragraph   c. comma   d. wheel

Ans: d.wheel.

Explanation: A spoke is part of a wheel, and a word is part of a sentence.

14. Confederate: -------- : : Narrator: Chronicler

a. north   b. partner   c. history   d. teacher.

Ans: b.partner

Explanation: A confederate is a synonym for a partner, and a narrator is a synonym for chronicler.

15. Search : --------- :: Defeat : Vanquish

a. Peer   b. ransack   c. destroy   d. find

Ans: b. ransack

Explanation: To ransack is to search thoroughly, and to vanquish is defeat thoroughly.

16. Dolorous: ------ : : Sonorous : Loud

a. woozy   b. weepy   c. dull   d. sleepy

Ans: weepy

Explanation: Dolorous is a synonym for weepy, and Sonorous is a synonym for loud.

17. Knave: ------- : : Coward : Bravery

a. retreat.   b.beauty   c.truth   d. stoicism

Ans: c. truth

Explanation: A knave is one who does not exhibits the truth, and a coward does not exhibit bravery.

18. Cushion: Sofa : : Shelf: --------

a. Ledge   b. bookcase   c. storage   d. frame

Ans: b. bookcase

Explanation: A cushion is a part of a sofa, and a shelf is a part of a bookcase.

19. Enfeeble: Forty :: Concede : ----------
a. dispute   b.close   c.expect   d.surrender
Ans: a. dispute
Explanation: To enfeeble is an antonym of to fortify, and to concede is an antonym of to dispute.

20. Secret: Furtive :: Audible : ------
a. resonant   b.nap   c. sack   d.ring
Ans: a. resonant
Explanation: Furtive is more intensely secret, and resonant is more intensely audible.

21. Thresher : ------- :: Mastiff : Dog
a. robin   b. master   c. shark   d.policeman
Ans: c.shark
Explanation: Thresher is a type of shark, and Mastiff is a type of dog.

Key Points

Fear of Examination

Examination is a process through which some of the candidates from a large population are to be selected for fulfilling a particular purpose. Students in general are job seekers, but few of them learn for gaining personal enhancement. They also move on in search of some study materials which can equip them positively so that a considerable ace can be obtained while addressing questions of specific types in examination.

Expectation of parents from their ward resides primarily on the aspect of a gain of high score in examination. They also imply their burden of expectations on the fellow student without considering the level of emotions and bands of feelings. Choice factor, wills and wishes of fellow students should be addressed a little so as to ensure their effective participation in the process of examination and evaluation. Fear of examination is generally developed due to the kinds of expectations their parents and other associates imposed upon the ward. It also takes a shape of fear due to the pre-determined idea of the development of agony in the condition if examination results go down. Exam fear itself eats u a considerable part of memory by diverting waves of thinking towards gaining a preparedness which is required to face some sort of adverse situation during the down play duly anticipated by the ward in advance.

How to overcome?

Matter is very simple as well as easy to follow.

1.   Prepare a time bound task and maintain the same throughout the academic session.

2.   Take support of some standard books on the basis of the types of inputs you want.

3.   Consider examination as a part of life as we have to appear periodically all the time up to a prolonged span of our life.

4.   Examination also provides us a scope of assessing our own levels of understanding and we should move on through rectification process instead of crying for the performance or score of desired levels duly expected by elders.

5.   Examination cannot be considered as any mode of status with which we are to exhibit some superiority on others. It should not be taken as a status symbol or a scale of gradation in society.

6.   Examination is not the ultimate state of scaling through which we judge the performance of a student in real life situation.

7.   There are lots of other sectors of life for which there is no examination: how pa person is talking; how a person is using words while making some good sentences; the capability of a person to establish and maintain relationship with others; effort of performing a task whenever chance comes; healing others if asked for etc. are some of the hundreds of scaling through which a personality can be judged.

8.   Our school system cannot consider all the parameters of scaling to say the level of the personality of a student.

9.   There are thousands of cross-academic as well as hybrid faculties available to be opted by students in society. That is why dying for only selected faculty and hunting for money cannot be considered as any brilliant idea.

10. One should have positive mental attitude towards addressing issues and concerns in daily life.

11. Regular study is most important and effective too than compared to intensive study of a short period of time.

12. We always rely upon other non-standard process due to their cheap availability. One should not compromise with quality.

13. Treasure of knowledge never moves towards us, but we have to move towards the treasure of knowledge.

14. There are several sources available in market from which the basic modules required for a specific purpose to be fulfilled can be obtained and also can be worked out for accelerating the regularised study.

Volume of practice material is less important than the strategy with which such volume of practice materials can be used or re-arranged.

There are millions of books available in market which can introduce a learner to English language and English grammar. More discussed theme of language learning is the English Grammar. This effort came in focus due to the increasing demand of people from different walks of life regarding the type of workbook which can equip a student in a specific way in terms of the enhancement of language related skills.

This workbook is designed to provide additional study materials to fellow students of High School standards. They equip themselves differently by making them fit for forthcoming examination. Learning by doing is the best way of acquiring such kinds of skills in stipulated time frame.

A language stands upon its rules of grammar and compositions. Similar mechanism is applicable to English also. It has such kinds of sets of rules through which one can aspire for the attainment of a perfectness in writing and expressions.

English as a language is not so difficult for any non-English person. The basic structure of English language is user friendly and is also of a comprehensive type. Modern instruments are also much friendly with this language. Because of this reason and some other, English as a user friendly language is becoming popular day by day. Number of people from non-English community who can read, write and speak English quite fluently are growing in number day by day. They are also taking different roles assigned to them in the cosmopolitan environment.

Non-English learners and aspirants often feel difficulties in pronunciation English words properly with needful tunings. These difficulties often become a serious obstacle while some English people go on trying to establish communication with them. Due to such difficulties also they often become disqualified in proving their capabilities of doing something fruitful.

This workbook and practice manual will provide an ample scope of gaining adequate skill and competence in linguistic communication. Stress is implied in the portions related to grammar and composition of the language so as to enhance the related skills and competences of the fellow learner.

It is also recommended that one should go on practicing related exercises alongside the referral readings for the purpose of gaining proficiency. A discussion on the common mistakes related to the grammar and composition of this language is also included for the purpose of drawing attention of fellow students and aspirants towards the content areas of the communication techniques.

English as a language came to India along with the colonial rule. They people felt it necessary to educate a considerable part of Indian as well as Asian communities in English for ensuring their service lines in the colonies. It was more perfectly pitched in through religious propagations.

People of India accepted the language gladly and started getting adjusted with the cultural bands of English orientation. This West Germanic language is developed from Anglo-Frician dialects. This dialect is brought to Britain during 6th to 7th Century by Anglo-Saxon Migrants. In due course of time this language developed considerably and transformed into the dialect of modern time. Anglo –Saxon dialect was more commonly known as old-English. Near about 400 Latin loan Words were introduced in English alongside the advent of Christianity. During the development Middle English near about 10,000 loan words from French origin entered the English dialect and made it an enriched one. Fully developed English dictionary, the Dictionary of the English

Language, was published by Samuel Johnson in 1755. English Grammar by Pristle was an added contribution in the line of development of English Language. In modern time the total English speaking community worldwide may exceed 1.5 billion mark!   There are several other instances to ascertain the fact regarding the ever increasing popularity of the International Language. It has also secured a prominent position in the international arena as a common dialect that people can opt with an ease.

After becoming assured about the ever increasing popularity of this language we can now imply adequate focus on the development of skills and competence of our fellow students and aspirants through exposing them to the horizon of interactive parts related to perfect and advanced English dialect. We also expect a timely participation of fellow scholars in this effort. They can continue evaluating their own skills through learning continuity supplemented with self paced evaluations.

Evolution of English Pronoun is another additional advantage of the modern English. Conflated forms of pronouns are also called an objective case. Development of such name is only because it is used only for objects of verbs. Once in old English there was distinct case system for both accusative and dative purposes. Later on such system collapsed into a single system of object (oblique) case having utility for objects of either a verb or a preposition. Studies in English were introduced in different universities during 19th and 20th Century because of its continuous developments in non-European continents. Development of such study was remarkably high in USA during 1970s.   It was also due to incorporation of English as another official language in most of the countries in the world.

Different courses in English are meant for different purposes. Studies in English are further accelerated with the advent of Informatics and allied fields. We consider English as a second language (a language study meant for non-English person). Errors in English are mainly observed from the field of syntax error, vocabulary error and error related to punctuations. Rules in English are periodically introduced by different scholars time to time. Not to terminate a sentence by preposition, for an example, was the another rule introduced by Robert Lowth .

Chandan Sukumar Sengupta

How to Speak!

Will you speak properly when chances come?

It is really a difficult question. There are different types of individuals: some prefer speaking properly to explain things in a better way, some other person prefer writing in a structured way rather than speaking in public. English Grammar provides basic template for both types of aspirants and continuously providing aids for fulfilling the same purpose. Some individuals never prefer speaking even though they maintain a considerable volume of vocabulary. There are individuals who can speak fluently by using their limited collection of vocabulary. Fluency in speaking can be gained only after establishment of adequate command over vocabulary. We also facilitate the fellow learner in different possible way to gain such mastery. Passages from interesting events and popular scriptures can be used for comprehension and guided practice for increasing the duration of study of a student.

Here also we are trying to move through the same strategy by making students involved in different kinds of background study material collected periodically from different sources.

Speaking is obviously a kind of activity which requires collection and maintenance of an extended format of words and their collocations in a definite fashion to cultivate an idea of using best possible combination of words while speaking. It may be in the form of a word tree, a network of words, a collocation table or some other creative alternatives which is convenient and easy to access.

Word class table can give us a better understanding of particular category of words to be considered while speaking or writing a broad spectrum composition. We can also correlate words in framing different types of sentences on the basis of linked and correlated words. An example of such kind of linked words is advanced for providing a basic understanding of the concept..

1. Common Errors

A comprehensive list of common errors.

Incorrect	Correct
Mr. Bhatia is my English teacher	Mr . Bhatia is my Teacher of English.
I Frogive him for his faults.	I forgave him his faults.
Chiranjiv Is my cousin Brother.	Chiranjiv is my cousin.
Credit this sum to my name.	Credit this sum to my account.
He is very miser	He is very miserly.
My all friends are very helpful	All my friends are very helpful.
She does not know swimming.	She does not know how to swim.
My uncle lives at Janpath Road.	My uncle lives at Janpath.
He is family man.	He is a man with a family.
This is more batter	This is better.
One must do his duty	One must do one's duty.
He made a blunder mistake.	He made a blunder.
It is a female compartment.	It is a ladies' compartment.
Open your book on page ten.	Open your book at page ten.
He has gone to foreign	He has gone abroad
He married his daughter	He got his daughter married.
Madhu is very proudy.	Madhu is very proud.

He live in the boarding	He lives in the boarding house.
Sachin and myself helped you.	Sachin and I helped you.
Please write with ink.	Please write in ink.
He died from cancer	He died of cancer.
He died of overwork	He died from overwork.
He has no lust of money.	He has no lust for money.
My younger brother goes to the collage daily.	My younger brother goes to college daily.
What a fun!	What fun !
She was crying the glasses in a tray.	She was carrying the glasses on a tray.
He sat in a tree.	He sat on a tree.
He is taller then me.	He is taller than I (am).
He is not as tall as his brother.	He is not so tall as his brother.
I have lost my patience.	I have lost patience.
He likes cutting jokes.	He likes cracking jockes.
You have a chance to win.	You have a chance of winning.
Don't mention.	Mention not.
Are you living in Delhi?	Do you live in Delhi?
It is a true fact.	Is is a fact.
As you like.	As you like it.
Radha resembles to her mother.	Radha resembles her mother.
Please pay for your bill.	Please pay your bill.
The police is looking for the culprit.	The police are looking for the culprit.
He said a lot to lies.	He told a lot of lies.

I believe you are better now.	I hope that you are better now.
He shirks from his studies.	He shirks his studies.
I need a house to live.	I need a house to live in.
I want a pen to write.	I want a pen to write with.
I have no influence on him	I have no influence over him.
I am too happy to see you.	I am very happy to see you.
He invited me on tea.	He invited me to tea.
We go to college by foot.	We go to college on foot.
You have no excuse to be late.	You have no excuse for being late.
Public does not like it.	Public do not like it.
This is somewhat true.	This is partially true.
I do not like the poetries of keats.	I do not like the poetry of Keats.
I prefer lassi than tea.	I prefer lassi to see.
Please give key to your watch.	Please wind up your watch.
There is no harm to do so.	There is no harm in doing so.
He gave a speech.	He made a speech.
I will return just now.	I will return presently.
I will wait here until you do not return.	I will wait here until you come.
He needs not worry.	He need not worry.
He hanged his head in shame.	He hung his head in shame.
The satellite has been sent to space.	The satellite has been launched.
Mohan insisted to go there.	Mohan insisted on going there.
He lives through honest labour.	He lives by honest labour.

Mohan and sohan are fast enemies.	Mohan and Sohan are sworn enemies.
His grandmother is died.	His grandmother is dead.
Send this letter on my address.	Send this letter to my address.
I have seen him today morning	I have been his this morning.
Are you a member in the committee?	Are you a member of the committee?
He is fail in Mathematics.	He failed in Mathematics.
We reached safely.	We reached safe.
Sachin is good in English.	Sachin is good at English.
My elder brother is in the teaching line.	My elder brother is in the teaching profession.
I have read four-fifth of this book.	I have read four-fifth of this book.
Our teacher will take your test tomorrow.	Our teacher will give us a test tomorrow.
All his family members are mad.	All members of his family are mad.
She does not know swimming.	She does not know how to swim.
Our examination starts from Monday next.	Our examination starts on Monday next.
I shall return this book after one week.	I shall return this book in one week.
Thousands were injured in the war.	Thousands were wounded in the war.
He has grown into a beautiful youth.	He has grown into a handsome youth.
There is no other alternative.	There is no alternative.
What is the cost of this pen?	What is the price of this pen?

Translate this passage from English to Hindi.	Translate this passage from English into Hindi.
I have learnt this lesson word by word.	I have learnt this lesson word for word.
I am going to cut my hair.	I am going to have my hair cut.
My watch is two minutes behind .	My watch is two minutes slow.
I asked him that why he was late.	I asked him why he was late.
He pays more attention to Hindi than English.	He pays more attention to Hindi than to English.
Close your door at once.	Shut the door at once
Verbal orders will not be obeyed.	Oral orders will not be obeyed.
Burn the lamp at once.	Light the lamp at once.
Sachin has made ten goals.	Sachin has scored ten goals.
He admitted that he had committed the murder.	He confessed that he had committed the murder.
A dictator generally misuses his political power.	A dictator generally abuses his political powers.
This is the house whose roof leaks.	This is the house, the roof of which leaks.
Being a cloudy day, we did not go out.	If being a cloudy day, we did not go out.
It is possible to score cent per cent marks in Mathematics.	It is possible to score hundred per cent marks in Mathematics.
Mohan has a thirst of knowledge.	Mohan has a thirst for knowledge.
My neighbor is five years elder to me.	My neighbor is five years older than me.
His service has been terminated.	His services have been terminated.

Please see the dictionary to find out the meaning of this word.	Please consult the dictionary to find out the meaning of this word.
Mohan asked his servant to bring water.	Mohan told his servant to bring water.
He got down from his bicycle.	He got off his bicycle.
I lived in that hotel for two days.	I stayed in that hotel for two days.
Please tell us everything in brief.	Please tell us everything in short.
I shall write him tomorrow.	I shall write to him tomorrow.
We have reached the final conclusions.	We have reached the conclusions.
To make dolls is his professions.	Making dolls is his profession.
Finishing his work, he went to see a movie.	Having finished his work, he went to see a movie.
I saw a bad dream last night.	I had a bad dream last night.
If you will abuse me, I will break tour head.	If you abuse me, I shall break you head.
If you will take tae, I shall also take.	If you take tea, I shall also rake.
You need not to tell me all this.	You need not tell me all this.
My elder brother is in the teaching line.	My elder brother is in the teaching profession.
I have read four-fifth of this book.	I have read four-fifth of this book.
Our teacher will take our test tomorrow.	Our teacher will give us a test tomorrow.
All his family members are mad.	All members of his family are mad.

Our examination starts from Monday next.	Our examination starts on Monday next.
I shall return this book after one week.	I shall return this book in one week.
Thousands were injured in the war.	Thousands were wounded in the war.
He has grown into a beautiful youth.	He has grown into a handsome youth.
There is no other alternative.	There is no alternative.
What is the cost of this pen?	What is the price of this pen?
Translate this passage from English to Hindi.	Translate this passage from English into Hindi.
I have learnt this lesson word by word.	I have learnt this lesson word for word.
I am going to cut my hair.	I am going to have my hair cut.
My watch is two minutes behind.	My watch is two minutes slow.
I asked him that why he was late.	I asked him why he was late.
He pays more attention to Hindi than English.	He pays more attention to Hindi than to English.
Close the door at once.	Shut the door at once.
Verbal orders will not be obeyed.	Oral orders will not be obeyed.
Burn the lamp at once.	Light the lamp at once.
Sachin has made ten goals.	Sachin has scored ten goals.
He admitted that he had committed the murder.	He confessed that he had committed the murder.
A dictator generally misuses his political powers.	A dictator generally abuses his political powers.
This is the house whose roof leaks.	This is the house, the roof of which leaks.

Being a cloudy day, we did not go out.	It Being a cloudy day, we did not go out.
It is possible to score cent per cent marks in mathematics.	It is possible to score hundred per cent marks in mathematics.
Mohan has a thirst knowledge.	Mohan has a thirst for knowledge.
My neighbour is five years elder to me.	My neighbour is five years older than me.
His service has been terminated.	His services have been terminated.
Please see the dictionary to find out the meaning of this word.	Please consult the dictionary to find out the meaning of this word.
Mohan asked his servant to bring water.	Mohan told his servant to bring water.
He got down from his bicycle.	He got down off his bicycle.
I lived in that hotel for two days.	I stayed in that hotel for two days.
Please tell us everything in brief.	Please tell us everything in short.
I shall write him tomorrow.	I shall write to him tomorrow.
We have reached the final conclusion.	We have reached the conclusion.
To make dolls is his profession.	Making dolls is his profession.
Finishing his work, he went to see a movie.	Having finished his work, he went to see a movie.
I saw a bad dream last night.	I had a bad dream last night.
His father has resigned from his post.	His father has resigned his post.
If you will abuse me, I will break	If you abuse me, I shall break

your head.	your head.
If you will take tea, I shall also take.	If you take tea, I shall also take.
You need not to tell me all this.	You need not tell me all this.
Let us pass away our time in the canteen.	Let us pass our time in the canteen.
I cannot pull on with this man.	I cannot get on with this man.
First, I told him about his mistakes.	At First, I told him about his mistakes.
Do not interfere in my work.	Do not interfere with my work.
I want a fresh basket of flowers.	I want a basket of fresh flowers.
The students will give their test tomorrow.	The students will take their test tomorrow.
The interview will be held between 10a.m to 12 noon.	The interview will be held between 10a.m and 12 noon.
There was a hell of a rush at the tickets window.	There was a hell of a rush at the ticket- window.
My hairs are black.	My hair is black.
Now, I shall go to my quarter.	Now I shall go to my quarters.
Law and order have to be maintained.	Law and order has to be maintained.
What is the cost of this shirt?	What is the price of this shirt?
Our examination is approaching near.	Our examination is approaching .
Good Night, sir, have a cup of tea.	Good Evening, sir, have a cup of tea.

The chairman is the wholly solely in our establishment.	The chairman is the all in all in our establishment.
We must fight-poverty with tooth and nail.	We must fight-poverty tooth and nail.
The English have left India with bag and baggage.	The English have left India bag and baggage.
We go to college by foot.	We go to college on foot.
I have many works to do on Sundays.	I have much works to do on Sundays.
He secured only passing marks in Mathematics.	He secured only pass marks in Mathematics.
Please give me a ten - rupees note.	Please give me a ten - rupee note.
This pen is superior than that.	This pen is superior to that.
I am not on talking terms with Mohan.	I am not on speaking terms with Mohan.
Sachin is our mutual friend.	Sachin is our common friend.
He picks up a quarrel over petty matters.	He picks a quarrel over petty matters.
Summon could not be issued.	Summons could not be issued.
When you say so, I must believe it.	Since you say so, I must believe it.
No less than fifty soldiers were injured in the blast.	No fewer than fifty soldiers were injured in the blast.
What is the fresh news of today?	What is the latest news of today?
I have something to ask from you.	I have something to ask you.
The train left at 3 o' clock.	The train departed at 3 o' clock.

You are requested to substitute the old picture for a new one.	You are requested to replace the old picture by a new one.
Due to illness. I could not go to college.	Owing to illness. I could not go to college.
This news was broadcasted from All India Radio only yesterday.	This news was broadcast from All India Radio only yesterday.
I will teach you reading and writing English.	I will teach you how to read and writing English.
It is the first time I have said so.	This is the first time I have said so.
Failed students cannot be promoted to the next higher class.	Students who have failed in the examination cannot be promoted to the next higher class.
Please do the needful and oblige.	Please do what is necessary and oblige.
Accompanied with my friends, I went there.	Accompanied by my friends, I went there.
What to speak of English, he cannot speak even Hindi.	Not to speak of English, he cannot speak even Hindi.
The plane circled the airport two times before landing.	The plane circled the airport twice before landing.
He became a rich man by and by.	He became a rich man in course of time.
My dear respected father, you are really great.	My dear father, you are really great.
Send your reply by return post.	Send your reply by return of post.
Please speak to the concerned	Please speak to the authority

authority.	concerned.
He is a noted dacoit.	He is a notorious dacoit.
It was very wonderful.	It was really wonderful.
I am quite sorry to hear of your failure.	I am very sorry to hear of your failure.

Use of Conditionals

Conditionals:

Meaning: Condition: शर्त

We can distribute it in two parts in which the 1st part is a condition and the 2nd part is the result of that particular condition.

Condition: It can never be in future. (this is the basic rule of these type of sentences) So whenever you find a condition in future in your exam then the error will definitely in that part.

Result: It can be in past, present, and future also.

Here are four words that is used in a conditional and with the help of these words we can understand whether a sentence is a conditional sentence or not.

1. If/when
2. Suppose
3. In case
4. Provided

First of all we'll give you some examples of conditionals sentences and these sentences will help you to understand the conditionals sentences.

Example:If our government takes some strong steps to protect women, they can go anywhere freely.

Explanation:

In this sentence the first part of our sentence is a condition and the second part is the result of our conditional part.

We can see that the whole sentence is in present we haven't use any past or future form in this sentence.

Your health will remain good if you do yoga daily.

Explanation: In this sentence our first part is a result and the second part is a condition because we have a word if in our second part.

We can see in this sentence that our result is in future but our condition is still in present as I told you that our condition can never be in future.

Note: In 1st sentence if is in the beginning and in 2nd sentence if is in the center now the point is it when we use if in the beginning of a sentence we have to use a comma (,) in our sentence but when we use if in the center we don't need to use comma in our sentence.

Rule: If we have our conditional part in present, we don't need to follow any rule for 2nd part means in result. It can be in present, past and future.

If our conditional part is in past (it can be in simple past and perfect past), we have to follow this rule:

If:

2nd form of verb/had + V3rd form

Result:

Would + V1st form   /   would have + V3rd form

Could + V1st form   /   could have + V3rd form

Might + V1st form   /   might have + V3rd form

Examples:

Example 1.

In case you will fail in your exam, what will you do?

In case you fail in your exam, what will you do?

Explanation: We have to remove will from the 1st part of our sentence because we can't use a condition in future.

Example 2. If you came last night, you can also enjoy the party.

If you came last night, you could also enjoy the party.

Explanation:

In this sentence our conditional part is in simple past so we have to follow this rule: Could + V1st form

Example 3. I went there for you if it was possible for me.
I would go there for you if it was possible for me.
Explanation:
In this sentence we have result in our 1st part and 2nd part is conditional part and when we have a condition in simple past we have to follow this rule: Would + V1st form
Now the question is why we are using would in this sentence while we can use could and the reason behind it because in this sentence we are talking about the past plan, we always use would to describe our past plans and could is used for the ability.

Example 4. If you had seen yesterday's cricket, I am sure you would enjoy seeing our team bating.
If you had seen yesterday's cricket, I am sure you would have enjoyed seeing our team bating.
Explanation: In this sentence we can see that our conditional sentence is in past perfect so we have to follow this rule: would have + V3rd form

Example 5.
If I have the courage, I would have answered him back.
If I had the courage, I would have answered him back.
Explanation:
In this sentence there can be a confusion because as we told you if our conditional is in present, in our result we can use any rule but we can see that in our result we have would + have + V3rd form so we have to change our conditional in past perfect.

Example 6. I will be very happy if you will select in the hockey team.
I will be very happy if you select in the hockey team.
Explanation:
In this sentence we are using will in our conditional part which is wrong so we have to remove will and use simple present tense.

2. Adjectives

What we think that we reflect through Language. .

-    *Chandan Sengupta*

<u>Revision Works</u>

1. Combine each of the following phrases with the adjective given in brackets by changing the adjective to a pronoun, and using the word of. For example:

    an original recipe (our)
    an original recipe of ours

    these red scarves (either)
    either of these red scarves

    the old movies (no)
    none of the old movies

1. that new bicycle (my)
2. the students (each)
3. those leather briefcases (neither)
4. these two books (your)
5. her latest inventions (some)
6. that second-hand typewriter (his)
7. their unusual experiences (another)
8. these rubber boots (no)
9. that velvet dress (her)
10. those black shoes (any)

2. Place the adjectives given in brackets before the accompanying nouns, arranging the adjectives in the correct order. For example:

    cats (two, my)
    my two cats

    apples (these, three)
    these three apples

people (other, four)
four other people

chairs (more, seven)
seven more chairs

1. maps (our, ten)
2. cows (twenty-five, all)
3. book (one, that)
4. socks (other, six)
5. lamps (those, twenty)
6. icicles (two, the)
7. manuscripts (her, three)
8. folders (twelve, these)
9. mistakes (other, seven)
10. pencils (more, two)
11. questions (another, five)
12. children (three, which)

3. Place the adjectives given in brackets before the accompanying nouns, arranging the adjectives in the correct order. For example:
bags (heavy, three)
three heavy bags

windows (two, large, the)
the two large windows

1. envelopes (large, four, her)
2. tables (small, both, the)
3. birds (tiny, those, three)
4. brothers (tall, two, her)
5. quilts (six, thick, all)
6. coats (heavy, his, two)
7. rooms (these, four, huge)
8. pumpkins (ten, his, medium-sized)

4. Place the adjectives given in brackets before the accompanying nouns, arranging the adjectives in the correct order. Make sure that the general

descriptive adjectives are separated from one another by commas. For example:

    mirror (small, octagonal, the, highly-polished)
    the small, highly-polished, octagonal mirror

    horses (frisky, their, young, three)
    their three frisky, young horses

1. jacket (light, your, short-sleeved)
2. lenses (curved, small, three)
3. puppy (four-week-old, our, damp, warm)
4. discoveries (two, unexpected)
5. carpet (heavy, a, round, thick)
6. climate (humid, hot, the)
7. blankets (dry, warm)
8. table (low, oval, their)

5. Place the adjectives given in brackets before the accompanying nouns, arranging the adjectives in the correct order. For example:

    cloth (cotton, purple)
    purple cotton cloth

    vases (Chinese, blue)
    blue Chinese vases

1. tents (canvas, green)
2. houses (Victorian, crimson)
3. curtains (white, lace)
4. cheese (Swiss, yellow)
5. ladders (wooden, brown)
6. blinds (pink, Venetian)
7. hats (felt, black)
8. cabinets (Renaissance, red)

6. Place the adjectives given in brackets before the accompanying nouns, arranging the adjectives in the correct order. Make sure that the general descriptive adjectives are separated from one another by commas. For example:

    skirt (beautiful, black, new, velvet, a)
    a beautiful, new black velvet skirt

fossils (Devonian, three, white, small)
three small white Devonian fossils

box (brass, her, square, heavy)
her heavy, square brass box

1. belt (green, beautiful, leather, a)
2. hood (dry, his, warm)
3. actors (old, two, Shakespearian, famous)
4. beads (glass, round, blue, tiny)
5. baby (lively, her, six-month-old)
6. dress (satin, a, white, long)
7. steps (narrow, cement, ten)
8. basement (cool, damp, the)
9. wolfhounds (Russian, two, grey, huge)
10. carvings (delicate, sandalwood, three)

7. Rewrite the following phrases, changing the underlined words to defining adjectives. For example:
    black boots used for hiking
    black hiking boots

    a plastic cup used for holding eggs
    a plastic egg cup

    a green carton used for storing milk
    a green milk carton

1. a new beater used for beating eggs
2. a wooden ladle used for serving soup
3. a large tin used for storing cookies
4. an old brush used for scrubbing
5. a glass plate used for baking pies
6. a light shovel used for shoveling snow
7. a metal rack used for storing hats
8. leather shoes used for jogging
9. a small house used for storing boats
10. a wicker basket used for holding bread

8. Paying attention to the usual order of attributive adjectives, place the adjectives given in brackets before the accompanying fixed expressions. Insert commas between the adjectives where appropriate. For example:

cuckoo clock (brown, a, Swiss, small)
a small brown Swiss cuckoo clock

life jackets (foam, thick, orange, three, new)
three thick, new orange foam life jackets

1. watering can (round, a, heavy, metal)
2. salt shaker (white, beautiful, porcelain, her)
3. computer games (Nintendo, new, two, exciting)
4. rose bush (prickly, small, two-year-old, this)
5. table cloths (cotton, these, pink)
6. willow branches (green, trailing, long)
7. fire engines (medium-sized, red, two)
8. coffee cup (his, yellow, heavy)
9. flower beds (heart-shaped, five, beautifully-designed)
10. front door (imposing, the, blue)
11. flower pot (green, big, plastic, that)
12. bath towel (damp, a, white, warm, flannel)
13. city buses (beige, ten, efficient, large)
14. watch dog (one-year-old, fierce, small, their)

9. Explain how the following expressions differ in meaning:

the last interesting chapter
the interesting last chapter

10. Underline the attributive adjectives in the following paragraph, and insert commas where necessary.

At one end of the large old rectangular room was a long low sofa covered with an orange cotton cloth. Against the two wooden arms of the sofa rested red velvet cushions with beautiful long dangling silk tassels. Near the sofa was a small intricately-woven Persian carpet with a fascinating design. Two proud elegant peacocks with shimmering turquoise feathers were depicted against a background of short lush grass, clear reflecting pools, and white marble statues in a delightful palace garden.

11. Paying attention to the types of adjectives which immediately precede the nouns, for each of the following phrases, underline the word or words which receive the most stress in spoken English. For example:

a big black box
a big black box

a yellow straw hat   a yellow straw hat

convenient downtown shopping   convenient downtown shopping
an ordinary Monday morning   an ordinary Monday morning
a towel rack   a towel rack

1. soup bowls   2. a convenient cupboard
3. underwater photography   4. the telephone directory
5. rubber gloves   6. a bread board
7. a sunny day   8. a new kitchen sink
9. long green grass   10. a fine Sunday afternoon
11. a red pencil sharpener   12. the back door
13. a prancing horse   14. an egg beater
15. a gold watch   16. a glass jar
17. a library card   18. the evening star
19. a thick carpet   20. a butter dish

12. Using the Simple Present of the verb to be, rewrite the following phrases as sentences, changing the attributive adjectives to predicate adjectives, and making any other changes that are required. For example:

the strong wind
The wind is strong.

the thick, warm shirts
The shirts are thick and warm.

the lively, interesting, entertaining festivals
The festivals are lively, interesting and entertaining.

the long, broad, well-managed, intensively-cultivated estate
The estate is long, broad, well-managed and intensively-cultivated.

the three-day-old colts
The colts are three days old.

1. the hot water
2. the large, threatening grey clouds
3. the thin blue book
4. the Spanish recipe
5. the one-year-old park
6. the collapsible umbrellas
7. the large white basins
8. the detailed, colorful, captivating painting
9. the two-year-old child
10. the purple cloth
11. the fast, efficient service
12. the ten-month-old houses
13. the intelligent, hard-working, responsible, reliable student
14. the long, well-written, informative letters

13. Paying attention to which adjectives are normally used only attributively and which are normally used only predicatively, write phrases or sentences in which the adjectives shown in brackets modify the accompanying nouns. Write a phrase if the adjective can be used only attributively, and write a sentence if the adjective can be used only predicatively. For example:

 nonsense (utter)
 utter nonsense
 the bird (alive)   The bird is alive.

1. the children (asleep) 2. the street (main)
3. our friends (here)   4. their assistant (afraid)
5. the consideration (principal) 6. her brother (alone)
7. the performers (ready) 8. the cliffs (sheer)
9. the house (there)   10. the reason (chief)

14. Using the Simple Past tense of the verbs shown in brackets, change the following phrases into sentences in which the adjectives are used as predicate adjectives. For example:

 the beautiful music (to sound) The music sounded beautiful.
 the delicious stew (to smell) The stew smelled delicious.

1. the sour lemon (to taste)
2. the rough surface (to feel)

3. the excited child (to grow)
4. the relieved students (to seem)
5. the awkward silence (to become)
6. the sweet roses (to smell)
7. the golden wheat (to turn)
8. the confident singer (to look)

15. For each of the following sentences, insert commas where appropriate, in order to separate the interpolated adjectives from the rest of the sentence. For example:

The marshes broad and windy stretched as far as the eye could see.
The marshes, broad and windy, stretched as far as the eye could see.

Delighted and encouraged the researchers continued their efforts.
Delighted and encouraged, the researchers continued their efforts.

1. Leaping and dancing the flames lit up the lakeshore.
2. The bells deep and resonant could be heard a mile away.
3. The flowers sweet-smelling and colorful attracted many bees.
4. Sunny and warm the climate was ideal for tourists.
5. The shears heavy and awkward were difficult to use.
6. Beautiful and delicate the flowers could be found only in the high mountains.
7. Twittering and chirping the birds circled overhead.
8. The children silent and attentive watched the magician closely.

16. For each of the following sentences, fill in the blank with either the present participle or the past participle of the verb shown in brackets. Use a present participle to refer to something being done by the thing being described; and use a past participle to refer to something which has been done to the thing being described. For example:

The evidence is __________. (to convince)
The evidence is convincing.

The _______ treasure was discovered accidentally. (to hide)
The hidden treasure was discovered accidentally.

1. Yesterday she heard _________________ news. (to surprise)
2. The _______________ tools must be returned by five o'clock. (to rent)
3. The _______________ rabbit stayed perfectly still. (to frighten)

4. We had a ___________________ experience. (to frighten)
5. The play is ________________. (to entertain)
6. The ______________ picture hung on the wall. (to complete)
7. That is an ________________ story. (to interest)
8. The king sat on a ______________ chair. (to raise)
9. The situation is ________________. (to alarm)
10. An ______________ bowl covered the cake. (to invert)
11. The ______________ lullaby sent the infant to sleep. (to soothe)
12. A ______________ walkway joined the two buildings. (to cover)
13. They laid the ________________ clothes on the bed. (to fold)
14. ________________ smells floated out of the kitchen. (to entice)
15. He stacked the ________________ wood near the fireplace. (to chop)

17. Each of the following sentences contains an interpolated adjectival phrase which is separated from the noun or pronoun to be modified by another noun or pronoun. For each sentence, underline the word to be modified, and correct the sentence by moving the adjectival phrase so that it is positioned close to the word to be modified. For example:
> The bird perched in the tree, folding its wings.
> Folding its wings, the bird perched in the tree.

> Lighting a cigarette, the door was opened by a young woman.
> The door was opened by a young woman, lighting a cigarette.

> He searched for his keys, tired from the journey.
> Tired from the journey, he searched for his keys.

1. Wanting to entertain us, the story was told to us by a nurse.
2. She decided to apply for the position, attracted by the advertisement.
3. Driving a brightly colored van, the parcel was delivered by a courier.
4. He looked through the book, glancing from time to time at his watch.
5. Wilted from the sun, we replaced the flowers.
6. The fire delighted the children, crackling and throwing off sparks.
7. Our friend made us a cake, wishing to do us a favor.
8. Anticipating an entertaining evening, the arena was soon filled with eager spectators.

18. This exercise contains sentences in which the noun or pronoun to be modified by the interpolated adjectival phrase is missing. Below each sentence is a rewritten, partially corrected version of the sentence. Study

the corrections which have already been made, and complete the sentences with personal pronouns which make sense in the sentences. For example:

Incorrect: Following in his footsteps, our destination was soon reached.

Corrected: Following in his footsteps, __ soon reached our destination.

Following in his footsteps, we soon reached our destination.

Incorrect: Finding no one at home, his plans had to be changed.
Corrected: Finding no one at home, __ had to change his plans.
Finding no one at home, he had to change his plans.

1. Incorrect: Anxiously waiting for her guests to appear, the hands of the clock seemed to stand still.
Corrected: As __________ anxiously waited for her guests to appear, the hands of the clock seemed to stand still.

2. Incorrect: Wanting to make a good impression, his hair was carefully combed.
Corrected: Wanting to make a good impression, ______ carefully combed his hair.

3. Incorrect: Knowing what we did, the message was easy to interpret.
Corrected: Knowing what we did, ________ easily interpreted the message.

4. Incorrect: Quickly opening her presents, wrapping paper was scattered all over the floor.
Corrected: Quickly opening her presents, ________ scattered wrapping paper all over the floor.

5. Incorrect: Attempting to dry the dishes, one of the plates slipped out of his hand.
Corrected: As ______ attempted to dry the dishes, one of the plates slipped out of his hand.

6. Incorrect: Having been elected president, her plans could now be carried out.
Corrected: Having been elected president, ______ could now carry out her plans.

7. Incorrect: Wondering what had happened, our questions remained unanswered.
Corrected: Although _____ wondered what had happened, our questions remained unanswered.

8. Incorrect: Entering the room, all eyes were turned in her direction.
Corrected: As _____ entered the room, all eyes were turned in her direction.

9. Incorrect: Rearranging her papers, her notes fell onto the floor.
Corrected: As _____ rearranged her papers, her notes fell onto the floor.

10. Incorrect: Pretending not to mind, their disappointment was obvious.
Corrected: Although _____ pretended not to mind, their disappointment was obvious.

19. Explain the two possible meanings of each of the following sentences.

The flag was lowered at noon.
The work was finished yesterday evening.

Answers
to Exercise 1:
1. that new bicycle of mine 2. each of the students 3. neither of those leather briefcases 4. these two books of yours 5. some of her latest inventions 6. that second-hand typewriter of his 7. another of their unusual experiences 8. none of these rubber boots 9. that velvet dress of hers 10. any of those black shoes

to Exercise 2:
1. our ten maps 2. all twenty-five cows 3. that one book 4. six other socks 5. those twenty lamps 6. the two icicles 7. her three manuscripts 8. these twelve folders 9. seven other mistakes 10. two more pencils 11. another five questions 12. which three children

to Exercise 3:
1. her four large envelopes 2. both the small tables 3. those three tiny birds 4. her two tall brothers 5. all six thick quilts 6. his two heavy coats 7. these four huge rooms 8. his ten medium-sized pumpkins

to Exercise 4:
1. your light, short-sleeved jacket 2. three small, curved lenses 3. our warm, damp, four-week-old puppy 4. two unexpected discoveries 5. a thick, heavy, round carpet 6. the hot, humid climate 7. warm, dry blankets 8. their low, oval table

to Exercise 5:
1. green canvas tents 2. crimson Victorian houses 3. white lace curtains 4. yellow Swiss cheese 5. brown wooden ladders 6. pink Venetian blinds 7. black felt hats 8. red Renaissance cabinets

to Exercise 6:
1. a beautiful green leather belt 2. his warm, dry hood 3. two famous, old Shakespearian actors 4. tin, round blue glass beads 5. her lively, six-month-old baby 6. a long white satin dress 7. ten narrow cement steps 8. the cool, damp basement 9. two huge grey Russian wolfhounds 10. three delicate sandalwood carvings

to Exercise 7:
1. a new egg beater 2. a wooden soup ladle 3. a large cookie tin 4. an old scrubbing brush 5. a glass pie plate 6. a light snow shovel 7. a metal hat rack 8. leather jogging shoes 9. a small boat house 10. a wicker bread basket

to Exercise 8:
1. a heavy, round metal watering can 2. her beautiful white porcelain salt shaker 3. two exciting, new Nintendo computer games 4. this small, prickly, two-year-old rose bush 5. these pink cotton table cloths 6. long, trailing green willow branches 7. two medium-sized red fire engines 8. his heavy yellow coffee cup 9. five beautifully-designed, heart-shaped flower beds 10. the broad, imposing blue front door 11. that big green plastic flower pot 12. a warm, damp white flannel bath towel 13. ten large, efficient beige city buses 14. their small, fierce, one-year-old watch dog

to Exercise 9:
"The last interesting chapter" means that this chapter is interesting, but none of the following chapters are interesting.
"The interesting last chapter" means that this is the last chapter, and it is interesting.

to Exercise 10:
At one end of the large, old, rectangular room was a long, low sofa covered with an orange cotton cloth. Against the two wooden arms of the sofa rested red velvet cushions with beautiful, long, dangling silk tassels. Near the sofa was a small, intricately-woven Persian carpet with a fascinating design. Two proud, elegant peacocks with shimmering turquoise feathers were depicted against a background of short, lush grass; clear, reflecting pools and white marble statues in a delightful palace garden.

to Exercise 11:
1. soup bowls 2. a convenient cupboard 3. underwater photography 4. the telephone directory 5. rubber gloves 6. a bread board 7. a sunny day 8. a new kitchen sink 9. long green grass 10. a fine Sunday afternoon 11. a red pencil sharpener 12. the back door 13. a prancing horse 14. an egg beater 15. a gold watch 16. a glass jar 17. a library card 18. the evening star 19. a thick carpet 20. a butter dish

to Exercise 12:
1. The water Is hot. 2. The clouds are large, threatening and grey. 3. The book is thin and blue. 4. The recipe is Spanish. 5. The park is one year old. 6. The umbrellas are collapsible. 7. The basins are large and white. 8. The painting is detailed, colorful and captivating. 9. The child is two years old. 10. The cloth is purple. 11. The service is fast and efficient. 12. The houses are ten months old. 13. The student is intelligent, hard-working, responsible and reliable. 14. The letters are long, well-written and informative.

to Exercise 13:
1. The children are asleep. 2. the main street 3. Our friends are here. 4. Their assistant is afraid. 5. the principal consideration 6. Her brother is alone. 7. The performers are ready. 8. the sheer cliffs 9. The house is there. 10. the chief reason

to Exercise 14:
1. The lemon tasted sour. 2. The surface felt rough. 3. The child grew excited. 4. The students seemed relieved. 5. The silence became awkward. 6. The roses smelled sweet. 7. The wheat turned golden. 8. The singer looked confident.

to Exercise 15:

1. Leaping and dancing, the flames lit up the lakeshore. 2. The bells, deep and resonant, could be heard a mile away. 3. The flowers, sweet-smelling and colorful, attracted many bees. 4. Sunny and warm, the climate was ideal for tourists. 5. The shears, heavy and awkward, were difficult to use. 6. Beautiful and delicate, the flowers could be found only in the high mountains. 7. Twittering and chirping, the birds circled overhead. 8. The children, silent and attentive, watched the magician closely.

to Exercise 16:
1. surprising 2. rented 3. frightened 4. frightening 5. entertaining 6. completed 7. interesting 8. raised 9. alarming 10. inverted 11. soothing 12. covered 13. folded 14. Enticing 15. chopped

to Exercise 17:
1. The story was told to us by a nurse, wanting to entertain us. 2. Attracted by the advertisement, she decided to apply for the position. 3. The parcel was delivered by a courier driving a brightly colored van. 4. Glancing from time to time at his watch, he looked through the book. 5. We replaced the flowers, wilted from the sun. 6. Crackling and throwing off sparks, the fire delighted the children. 7. Wishing to do us a favor, our friend made us a cake. 8. The arena was soon filled with eager spectators, anticipating an entertaining evening.

to Exercise 18:
1. she 2. he 3. we 4. she 5. he 6. she 7. we 8. she 9. she 10. they

to Exercise 19:
"The flag was lowered at noon" can mean: 1) At noon, the flag was already down, or 2) At noon, someone lowered the flag.
"The work was finished yesterday evening" can mean: 1) Yesterday evening, the work was already complete, or 2) Yesterday evening, someone finished the work.

<u>Quiz 001</u>

1. Which of the following parts of speech are adjectives not able to modify?

a) Nouns   b) Pronouns   c) Adverbs
        d) B & C

2. Adjectives that appear after linking verbs are known as:

a) Attributive adjectives   b) Predicative adjectives

c) Demonstrative adjectives   d) Interrogative adjectives

3. Which of the following types of adjectives are formed from two or more words and a hyphen?

a) Compound adjectives   b) Nominal adjectives

c) Proper adjectives   d) Collective adjectives

4. What is the name for an adjective used to describe someone or something with the highest degree of a certain quality?

a) Comparable adjectives   b) Comparative adjectives

c) Superior adjectives   d) Superlative adjectives

5. Which of the following often have properties similar to adjectives?

a) Adverbs   b) Particles

c) Determiners   d) Conjunctions

Quiz 002

1. Which of the following is an example of an attributive adjective?

a) A black dog.   b) The dog is black.   c)   The   dog black.   d) The dog.

2. Which of the following is not an attributive adjective?

a) Sarah is short.   b) The blond girl went to the party.

c) My dear friend James is here.   d) Have you called your poor brother?

3. Attributive adjectives never _____.

a) come after the noun.   b) precede the noun.

c) follow a linking verb.   d) appear in the postpositive position.

4. Most adjectives that are never attributive begin with the letter "_____."

a) A   b) B   a) C   b) D

5. Which sentence is traditionally considered to be more correct?

a) The secretary-generals of the three countries are meeting today.

b) The secretaries-general of the three countries are meeting today.

Quiz 003

1. What is the function of an adjective when it describes a noun that is part of the predicate?

a) Subject complement   b) Object complement

c) Attributive adjective   d) None of the above

2. What does a predicative adjective that follows a linking verb modify?

a) The verb   b) The object of the verb

c) The subject of the clause   d) The predicate of the clause

3. When can "well" function as a predicative adjective? (Choose the answer that is most correct.)

a) When it follows a linking verb

b) When it modifies a linking verb

c) When it means "in good health"

d) When it functions as an object complement

e) A & C   f) B & D

4. Which of the following sentences does not have a predicate adjective?

a) "I don't think I heard you right."

b) "I am feeling well."

c) "My father is really nice."

d) "Does this seem different to you?"

Quiz 004

1. Which of the following is a proper adjective?

a) Blue   b) Spanish

c) Tall   d) Tired

2. Which of the following is not a proper adjective?

a) Spanish   b) Grecian

c) Intelligent   d) Muslim

3. In the sentence "I went to a private catholic school," which word or words should be capitalized?

a) catholic   b) private

c) school   d) catholic and school

4. In the sentence "The number of afro-europeans has risen steadily," which word or words should be capitalized?

a) number   b) afro

c) Europeans   d) afro and europeans

5. Proper adjectives are adjectives formed from _____.

a) proper nouns   b) common nouns

c) adjectives   d) verbs

Collective Adjectives

Definition

Collective adjectives are a subgroup of nominal adjectives, or

adjectives that act as nouns. They are used to refer to a group of people based

on a characteristic that they share. For example:

• "The rich should help the poor."

This sentence is another way of saying, "Rich people should help poor people."

Some common collective adjectives are:

the blind;   the elderly;   the hardworking;

the homeless;   the innocent;

the intelligent; the poor;   the rich;

the sick;   the strong;

the weak;   the young

In addition, a large amount of collective adjectives refer to the nationality of a group of people. For example, instead of saying "French people cook well," we can say, "The French cook well." Other nationalities for which we have collective adjectives are:

the Chinese;   the English;   the Irish   the Japanese   the Scottishthe Spanish

Notice that when we use a collective adjective for nationality, it's capitalized. Finally, collective adjectives for nationality have to be learned by heart, as we don't have collective adjectives for all nationalities. For example, to refer to a group of German people, we have to say the Germans or simply Germans, which is a plural proper noun—a corresponding collective adjective doesn't exist for German people. Other examples include (the) Canadians, (the) Russians, (the) Americans, and (the) Slovaks.

How to use collective adjectives Using collective adjectives is simple. There are only a couple of things that we need to remember:

1. We always add the article the before the adjective (except for nationalities that use plural proper nouns).

2. We always treat collective adjectives as plural nouns. This means that they have to take plural forms of verbs.

3. We do not pluralize collective adjectives by adding the suffixes -s or -es. They are already considered plural (except for nationalities that use plural proper nouns).

Let's look at some examples:

• "The rich are usually powerful." • "The French are the best chefs."

• "The elderly need proper care."

In these examples, the rich, the French, and the elderly function as the subjects of the sentences. They are treated as plurals, which is why the sentences use the plural forms of the verbs be and need.

Collective adjectives can also function as the object of a sentence, as in:

• "We are working hard to help the homeless."

In this example, the subject of the sentence is we, while the object is the collective adjective the homeless.

Collective adjectives are often confused with collective nouns, but there are key differences. While they both refer to a group of people, collective nouns (such as team, staff or class) are inherently nouns in structure and function; collective adjectives, on the other hand, are adjectives that merely

function as nouns.

Additionally, collective nouns are often treated as singular (as in, "The best team is going to win"), whereas collective adjectives, as we have mentioned,

are always treated as plural.

Quiz 005

1. Which of the following is a collective adjective?

a) the rich   b) the tenants

c) the girls   d) the German

2. Which of the following is not a collective adjective?

a) the poor   b) the meek

c) the team   d) the French

3. Collective adjectives are always ____.

a) plural   b) singular

c) verbs   d) subjects

4. In the following sentence, which word or words should be capitalized? "i want to help the poor."

a) Both "i" and "poor."   b) Only "i."

c) "I," "help," and "poor."   d) Only "poor."

5. Collective adjectives are adjectives that function as ____.

a) nouns   b) subjects

c) objects   d) verbs

Demonstrative Adjectives: Like all adjectives, demonstrative adjectives modify nouns or pronouns. We use demonstrative adjectives to specify what we are referring to, to indicate whether the person or thing is singular or plural, and to give the listener information about that person or object's proximity to the speaker (identifying whether it's nearby or far away). Because they are used to determine a specific noun, demonstrative adjectives are sometimes known as demonstrative determiners.

There are four common demonstrative adjectives in English: this, that, these, and those.

Demonstrative adjectives always come before the noun they modify. Often, they start the sentence. For example:

• "This toy is my brother's favorite."

• "These cups are very pretty."

They can also come at the middle or at the end, as long as they are followed by a noun (if they were not followed by a noun, they would become demonstrative pronouns):

• "My brother's favorite toy is this train."

• "I wish I had more of these chocolates!"

• "Can you please go buy me those books?"

In the examples above, the demonstrative adjective is placed immediately before the noun it modifies. However, if there are additional adjectives that

also modify the same noun, they should be placed between the demonstrative adjective and the noun. For example:

• "My brother's favorite toy is this blue train."
• "I wish I had more of these delicious chocolates!"
• "Can you please go buy me those school books?"

Choosing the Correct
Demonstrative Adjective

Use this table to easily reference which demonstrative adjectives to use in different contexts:

Near Far;   Singular this that   Plural these those

This/That: This and that are used when the person or thing we are talking about is singular (there is only one).

This is used for things that are nearby. The proximity is sometimes stated explicitly in the sentence. For example:

• "This toy I'm holding is my brother's favorite."
• "This chair I'm sitting on is broken."

It's also common for the demonstrative adjective to be the only information we have about how near or far the person or object is. For example, imagine that there are two cups: One is on the table next to "Jen"; the other is across the room, next to "David."

Jen says: "This cup is very pretty."

Because she used the demonstrative adjective this, it's clear that Jen is talking about the cup that is on the table next to her, and not the cup that's next to David.

That is used for a singular person or object that is farther away. Again, the proximity is sometimes stated explicitly, as in:

• "That toy on the table over there is my brother's favorite."
• "That chair across the room is broken."

But again, the distance can also be unstated and implied by the demonstrative adjective. Let's go back to our example about Jen and David.   This time, Jen says: "That cup is very pretty."

Because Jen used the demonstrative adjective that, it's clear that she is now talking about the cup that is on the table next to David, and not the one that's next to her.

These/Those

These and those work in the same way as this and that, but as you can see in the table, they are used to refer to people and objects that are plural (more than one.)

These is used for plural objects that are nearby. As we saw with this, the proximity can be explicit, as in:

• "These toys I'm holding are my brother's favorites."   • "These chairs we're sitting on are broken."

Or, the proximity can be implied:

• "These cups are very pretty." (We know the cups are near the speaker.)

Those is used for plural objects that are farther away. Again, the distance can be stated. For example:

• "Those toys on the table over there are my brother's favorites."

• "Those chairs across the room are broken."   Or, the distance can be implied: • "Those blue cups are very pretty." (We know the cups are not near to the speaker.)

Yon/Yonder:

Yon and yonder are lesser-known demonstrative adjectives. They're both considered archaic and don't exist in most modern dialects of English. However, you may encounter them in older texts or songs. For example, this famous line from Romeo and Juliet uses the demonstrative adjective yonder: • "What light on yonder window breaks?"

Yon and yonder are still used in a few dialects of English, such those spoken in certain Celtic-influenced areas like Scotland and the Southern United States. Generally, they can be used interchangeably, and are both understood to indicate that the noun is not near the speaker, but the proximity really depends on the dialect of the people using it.

Here are some examples of how yon and yonder could be used in a sentence:

• "We will have to cross yon field to get home."   •   "Something has frightened yonder horses."

<u>Demonstrative Adjectives vs. Demonstrative Pronouns</u>

Demonstrative adjectives are often confused with demonstrative pronouns, because this, that, these, and those can serve both functions. If you think about the role of an adjective and the role of a pronoun, though, you'll see that they're not so confusing after all.

Demonstrative adjectives do what all adjectives do: modify a noun or pronoun. On the other hand, demonstrative pronouns do what all pronouns do: stand in place of a noun. Some examples:
• "This toy is his favorite." (demonstrative adjective.)   • "This is his favorite toy." (demonstrative pronoun.)
• "Give that big book to me." (demonstrative adjective.) •   "Give me that." (demonstrative pronoun)
• "I want this TV for Christmas." (demonstrative adjective.)
• "This is what I want for Christmas." (demonstrative pronoun.)
Each of the demonstrative adjectives modifies a noun (toy, book, TV), while the demonstrative pronouns stand in place of nouns.

Quiz 006
1. Choose the correct demonstrative adjective to complete the sentence: "Stay away from ____ black dog next door."
a) this   b) that   c) these   d) those
2. Choose the correct demonstrative adjective to complete the sentence: "____ books here on my desk are for you."
a) This   b) That   c) These   d) Those
3. Choose the correct demonstrative adjective to complete the sentence: "Look at ____ trees over there. Aren't they beautiful?"
a) this   b) that   c) these   d) those
4. Which of the following sentences does not contain a demonstrative adjective?
a) "Please give that to me quickly."
b) "Can you hand me those books?"
c) "Do you have this movie at home?"
d) "That girl is bad news."
5. Which of the following sentences does contain a demonstrative adjective?
a) "That's my boyfriend over there."   \
b) "Can you give me a hand with this homework?"
c) "Have you seen this before?"
b) "Those are the ones that I want."

Interrogative Adjectives

Like all adjectives, interrogative adjectives (also known as interrogative determiners) modify nouns and pronouns. English has three interrogative adjectives: what, which, and whose. They are called "interrogative" because they are usually used to ask questions. For example:
• "What book are you reading?   • "Which shirt are you going to buy?"   • "Whose computer is this?"
In each of the examples, the interrogative adjective modifies the noun it immediately precedes: book, shirt, and computer.

How to Use Interrogative Adjectives: The interrogative adjectives what and which can often be used interchangeably, while whose is very different. Let's look at when to use each:
What vs. Which: Although what and which are often interchangeable, there is a subtle difference between the two.
Generally, we use what when the amount of possible answers is unknown or
unlimited, and we use which when we either know how many choices there
are, or we consider the options to be more limited. Think about the
difference between these two sentences:
• "What present do you think you'll get for Christmas?"
• "Which present do you think you'll get for Christmas?"
In the first sentence, the speaker does not have any idea how many possible
presents there are. In the second sentence, it seems that the speaker does have an idea of what the presents may be, and that the choices are limited.
Let's look at a similar example:
• "What movie do you want to see?"
• "Which movie do you want to see?"
Again, in the first sentence, it seems like the options are unlimited, while in the second sentence, the speaker may have been discussing two or three
movies with the listener, and they are trying to make a final decision.
In most instances, we can use either what or which without causing
confusion for the reader. However, if there is clearly a limited number of

options to choose from, which is the preferred interrogative adjective to use.

Whose

Whose is an adjective that denotes possession, or belonging. We can use it to ask who the owner of an object is. For example:

- "Whose socks are on the floor?"
- "Whose book is this?"
- "Whose turn is it?"

In these examples, the speaker is trying to find out who the socks, book, and turn belong to.

Direct questions

When interrogative adjectives appear in normal direct questions, they are placed at the beginning of the sentence and are immediately followed by the noun that they modify. All the examples that we have seen up until this point were direct questions. However, interrogative adjectives don't only appear in direct questions.

Indirect questions Interrogative adjectives can also appear within indirect questions. When this happens, they appear in the middle of the sentence, but they still immediately precede the modified noun. Some indirect questions are used to express politeness:

- "Could you tell me whose socks are on the floor?"
- "Would you mind telling me which way is north?"
- "Do you know what day it is?"

Other indirect questions are used to ask for clarifying information, or to convey surprise:

- "You want which computer for Christmas?"
- "You're going out with whose brother?"
- "He wants to watch what movie?"

In such cases, emphasis is put on the interrogative adjective—we can hear the stress on the words when we say the sentences aloud.

In reported questions

Interrogative adjectives also appear in the middle of reported questions. Reported questions are also indirect; they tell us about questions. For example:

- "She wants to know whose socks are on the floor."
- "He asked which way was north."
- "I asked you what day it was."

The speaker in each of the examples isn't asking a definite question, but rather is reporting or clarifying a question that has already been asked.

Other statements

Interrogative adjectives are sometimes used in other statements that aren't questions at all: they don't ask questions, either directly or indirectly, but

still modify the nouns in the same kind of way. For example:

• "I can't remember whose socks they are."

• "I don't know which way is north."

• "I know what day it is."

Common Mistakes

Interrogative Adjectives vs.

Interrogative Pronouns

The most common mistake regarding interrogative adjectives is confusing

them with interrogative pronouns. This is because all three interrogative adjectives, what, which, and whose, can also function as interrogative pronouns. An easy way to be sure whether you are dealing with an interrogative adjective or an interrogative pronoun is to check whether the

question word is immediately followed by the noun it modifies, like in all the

examples that we have seen:

• "What book is your favorite?"

In this example, what is immediately followed by the noun book. We can be sure that, in this case, what is a possessive adjective.

• "What are you reading?"

In this sentence, what is not immediately followed by a noun that it modifies, which means that in this case, it is an interrogative pronoun.

Just remember: Even though all interrogative adjectives are question words,

not all questions words are interrogative adjectives.

Whose vs. Who's

Finally, beware of the common error of confusing whose and who's. Whose is

an interrogative adjective or pronoun, while who's is the contraction of who is.

Quiz 007

1. Which of the following is not an interrogative adjective?

a) which

b) whom

c) which

d) whose

2. What comes immediately after an interrogative adjective?

a) The verb it modifies

b) Another adjective

c) The noun it modifies

d) An adverb

3. Complete the sentence: "_____ stars can we see from Earth?"

a) whose

b) which

c) what

d) either A or B

e) either B or C

4. Which of the following sentences does not contain an interrogative adjective?

a) "Tell me which car you like best."

b) "I forgot what I was going to do this evening."

c) "Do you know which dress I'm going to buy?"

d) "Would you mind telling me whose car this is?"

5. Which of the following sentences is incorrect?

a) "Who's book is this?"

b) "Do you know whose book this is?"

c) "What book do you want to read tonight?"

d) "Which book do you want to read tonight?"

Nominal Adjectives

Definition

We know that adjectives are words that modify (or describe) nouns, such as the word red in "the red jacket," or the word beautiful in "that girl is beautiful."

Nominal adjectives, on the other hand, are adjectives that perform the function of a noun in a sentence. They are preceded by the word the and can be found as the subject or the object of a sentence or clause. For example:

• "The elderly are a great source of wisdom."
• "The French have amazing restaurants."
• "The opposite of up is down."
• "The best is yet to come."

In the examples above, the nominal adjectives do not modify any other noun
—they're acting as nouns themselves. Specifically, they are performing the function of the subject of the sentences, but, as we mentioned, they can also function as objects. For example:

• "We should treat the elderly with respect."
• "This law protects the innocent."
• "We all want the best for her."

Uses of Nominal Adjectives

Nominal adjectives perform several different functions. Some nominal adjectives are used to refer to a group of people who all share a certain characteristic, which can be a physical or non-physical characteristic. Other
nominal adjectives refer to a characteristic of an individual person or thing.

We'll look at each type of nominal adjective separately.

Collective Adjectives

Collective adjectives are nominal adjectives that are used to refer to groups of people. Sometimes they refer to a shared physical characteristic, such as the blind, the deaf, the short, or the tall. Other times, they refer to non-physical characteristics, like the hardworking, the intelligent, the poor, or the rich.

In each of these cases, the nominal adjective takes the place of a lengthier
description, such as "all the people who are rich," or "all the intelligent people."

Collective adjectives can also refer to some nationalities, such as the Chinese,
the English, or the French.

If you'd like to learn more about collective adjectives, they are covered in greater depth in their own section of the chapter about the Categories of

Adjectives.

Comparative and superlative Forms

Adjectives in their comparative or superlative form can also be nominal adjectives. Comparative adjectives are those that end in "-er" or are preceded

by the word more, as in stronger, taller, cleverer, more beautiful, etc. They

are used to compare two things. Have a look at these examples of nominal

adjectives in comparative form:

• "His brother is the taller, but he is the cleverer."
• "They gave the prize to the more beautiful of the two."
• "Of the two cars, we chose the more expensive."

Superlative adjectives are those that end in "-est" or are preceded by the word most, such as strongest, tallest, most beautiful, most clever, etc. They compare three or more things, and they can function as nominal adjectives in

the same way that comparatives can. For example:

• "Dan is the strongest."
• "I want the best for you."
• "Whenever we have a job to do, you give me the most difficult."

Other adjectives

Most of the time, nominal adjectives are collective, comparative, and superlative adjectives. However, just about any adjective can be made nominal. They can make sentences shorter and more concise by avoiding repetitive use of a noun. Here are some instances in which nominal adjectives might be preferable:

• "I liked the red car but we bought the blue." (nominal adjective)
instead of

• "I like the red car but we bought the blue car." (standard adjective)
• Speaker A: "Which color did you like best?"
• Speaker B: "I thought the blue was the prettiest." (nominal adjective)
instead of • Speaker B: "I thought the blue color was the prettiest." (standard adjective)

• "You've heard the good news, now I'll tell you the bad."
instead of
• "You've heard the good news, now I'll tell you the bad news."
Other options
You may have noticed that a lot of these examples could be worded differently. For example, when using collective adjectives, we can just as easily say "French people" instead of "the French," or "poor people" instead
of "the poor."
With comparative and superlative forms, we can add a noun to provide more emphasis or clarity. For example, we could say "He was the stronger man of the two" instead of "he was the stronger" or "I want the best thing for you" instead of "I want the best for you."
Often, we can also replace a noun with the pronoun one instead of using a nominal adjective. For example, "you take the green t-shirt, I'll take the blue one" instead of "you take the green t-shirt, I'll take the blue."
In many cases, these options are less formal than using a nominal adjective.

Quiz 008
1. Nominal adjectives take the place of a ________ in a sentence.
a) verb   b) person   c) adjective   d) noun
2. Which of the following cannot function as a nominal adjective?
a) poor   b) red   c) shirt   d) French
3. Nominal adjectives are preceded by the word ________.
a) the   b) one   c) those   d) noun
4. In the sentence "You rent the green car, I'll rent the red," which word (or words) is the nominal adjective?
a) Only green
b) Green and red
c) Only red
d) car
5. Which of the following sentences does not include an example of a nominal adjective?
a) "I'm sure you've chosen the best."
b) "I wish I had bought the red."
c) "The elderly deserve respect."

d) "You really know how to find the best music."

Compound Adjectives

Definition

A compound adjective (also known as a compound modifier or a phrasal adjective) is created by two or more words that work jointly to modify the same noun; they always appear before the noun they modify, and they are usually joined together by a hyphen (or hyphens) to clarify that

the words are working as a single modifying unit.

Creating compound adjectives

Compound adjectives are made up of multiple words, and, in various combinations, they can be composed of adjectives, nouns, quantifiers, participles, and adverbs.

Sometimes, other types of words are used to join two (or more) others. For example, the conjunction and is often used between two nouns or two

adjectives to create a three-word compound adjective.

Let's look at some examples of the different combinations we can make below.

Adjective + Adjective

When multiple adjectives are used to modify the same noun, they usually appear with commas between them or simply in a row with no punctuation,

depending on the order of adjectives. If two or more adjectives are functioning together as a single unit, though, we must use hyphens. This most commonly occurs with colors or position, as in:

• "She had bright, blue-green eyes."

• "His orange-yellow skin looked very unhealthy."

• "Look in the top-right corner of the screen."

• "The scissors are in the bottom-left drawer."

More often, adjectives are paired with other parts of speech to create compound nouns, as we shall see.

Adjective + Noun

It is very common to follow an adjective with a noun to create a compound adjective:

• "They went on a wild-goose chase."

• "I can only find part-time work at the moment."

• "The dog is a short-hair breed."
• "I know this is a last-minute suggestion, but hear me out."
It is equally common to use nouns before adjectives, as in:
• "I'd love an ice-cold soda right about now."
• "Do you have any sugar-free cookies?"

Quantifiers

When we use a quantifier (a kind of determiner) with a noun to create a compound adjective, we often pair the quantifier with a noun of measurement (length, height, weight, age, or time). For example:
• "It is the only 10-storey building in the town."
• "We bought a three-foot sandwich to share."
• "The eight-pound bag fell to the floor."
• "This is a very nice 12-year whiskey."
When indicating age, we often add the adjective old to the end, as in:
• "His 11-year-old niece is coming to visit."
(Note that we also use this same hyphenation when making a compound noun from an age, as in "My 11-year-old is coming to visit.")
When we indicate cost, we normally use quantifiers with symbols of currency, such as $, £, €, etc. When the currency is spelled out, however, we must use hyphens to form compound adjectives. Likewise, we use hyphens if
the numerals are spelled out as well. For example:
• "He bought a $5,000 computer."
• "He bought a 5,000-dollar computer."
• "He bought a five-thousand-dollar computer."
We can also use quantifiers with other nouns, too:
• "There was an 11-car pileup on the highway."
• "The theater has a 400-person capacity."

Participles

Past and present participles can be paired with adjectives, nouns, and adverbs to form compound adjectives. For example:

With nouns

• "Many legends still survive about man-eating whales, but they are simply untrue."
• "It's another record-breaking race for the Kenyan runner."
• "There are many mouth-watering items on the menu."
• "I won't spend another night in this dust-ridden house."

• "The crocodile-infested waters are particularly dangerous."
With adjectives
• "The table is made from rough-hewn wood."
• "My old-fashioned aunt would never approve."
• "There are several delicious-sounding things on the menu."
• "He has an expensive-looking car."
With adverbs
• "This company runs like a well-oiled machine."
• "Our eyes had to adjust in the dimly-lit corridor."
• "There are a only few well-running cars to choose from."
• "We need some forward-thinking individuals for the job."
• "My early-rising brother always baulks at me when I sleep in late."
Prepositions
Prepositions are also used to form compound adjectives, as in:
• "You need an up-to-date computer to run this software."
• "I've lived in too many run-down apartments."
Other cases
And
When the conjunction and is used between two words (usually nouns) to join them as a single modifier, we must hyphenate all three words. For example:
• "I find her salt-and-pepper hair very attractive."
• "These old stone-and-mortar buildings have stood the test of time."
Proper nouns
We sometimes use a multi-word proper noun to identify a noun as belonging to a particular person or brand. In this case, we do not hyphenate
the words. For example:
• "Can you play any Elton John songs?"
• "Did you see the Arthur Miller play on Broadway?"
Pronouns
Occasionally it is possible to use pronouns (especially personal pronouns)
to form compound adjectives, though this is not very common. For example:
• "It turned into a he-said-she-said situation."
Adverbs before adjectives

Adverbs are often used in conjunction with adjectives to jointly modify a noun, but they are not really considered to be compound adjectives and they

usually do not require a hyphen—the fact that they work together with the

adjective is implied. For example:

• "It was a very brave thing to do."

• "She is an exceptionally talented girl."

Quiz 009

1. Which punctuation mark do we use to create compound adjectives?

a) comma

b) semicolon

c) hyphen

d) period

2. Which of the following cannot be used to form compound adjectives?

a) participles

b) verbs

c) nouns

d) prepositions

3. Which of the following are not hyphenated when functioning as compound adjectives?

a) proper nouns

b) adjectives

c) quantifiers

d) pronouns

4. Identify the combination used to create the compound adjective (in bold)

in the following sentence:

"It was my well-educated apprentice who saved the day."

a) adjective + noun

b) adverb + past participle

c) adjective + past participle

d) noun + adjective

Order of Adjectives

Definition

Adjectives are words that modify a noun or a pronoun. In other words, they describe a person, place, or thing in a sentence. Adjectives usually come

before the noun. For example:

• "The small dog jumped over the white fence."

Small is an adjective that describes the noun dog, and white is an adjective

that describes the noun fence.

Adjectives add to the richness of our descriptions of people and things. They

allow the listener or the reader to paint a mental picture of the person or object that is being described to them.

Think about some adjectives that you know. Some of the most common words are adjectives like good, bad, young, old, big, and small.

Each of these adjectives serves a purpose by describing a different aspect of the noun. Good and bad give an opinion of the noun, old and young tell us about the noun's age, while big and small describe the noun's size.

The good news is that adjectives are relatively simple in English. In some languages, the adjective changes its form depending on whether the noun it modifies is singular/plural, or feminine/masculine. In English, we don't have those complications: the adjective always remains the same.

When we speak or write, we don't want to bore our listener or reader with repetitive sentences. Imagine a description like this:

• "He is a tall man. He is a healthy man. He is a young man."

You would be so bored that you wouldn't want to listen to another word.

Luckily, we have another option. We can make such a description more concise by using all three adjectives in one sentence:

• "He is a tall healthy young man."

Using more than one adjective in a sentence makes our writing and speech richer and more concise. However, this is also where we have to be careful, because certain adjectives appear in a certain order. For example, in the

description above, which would be more correct: tall healthy young man, or young healthy tall man?

The answer is tall healthy young man, but why?

In English, the order of adjectives can sometimes be flexible, but most of the time we use a very specific order; if we don't, the sentence sounds unnatural, as in "young healthy tall man." To avoid unnatural-sounding sentences, we group adjectives by type, and we try to use them in this order:

1. Opinion
2. Measurements
3. Shape
4. Condition
5. Age
6. Color
7. Pattern
8. Origin
9. Material
10. Purpose

Obviously we never have a sentence that uses 10 adjectives to describe one noun. That would be far too long of a sentence!

In fact, it would even be rare to find a sentence that uses more than three adjectives to modify one noun. We do need to know a little about each type, though, so that when we need to use two or three adjectives in a row, we'll use them in the right order.

First, let's look at each type of adjective in detail. After that we'll see some examples of sentences that string two or more adjectives together.

Types of Adjectives

Opinion

Adjectives of opinion always come first before any other factual descriptions of the noun. There are two types of opinion adjectives. The first are general opinion adjectives and can be used with any kind of noun,

whether it is a person, place, or thing.

Some of the most common general opinion adjectives are:

| Good | bad | lovely |
| Strange | beautiful | nice |

The second type are specific opinion adjectives. These are adjectives that can

only be used with particular types of nouns. For example:

• People and animals: intelligent, friendly, unfriendly, hard-working
• Buildings and furniture: comfortable, uncomfortable
• Food: flavorful, tasty, delicious

If you want to use a general opinion adjective and a specific opinion adjective

in the same sentence, the general opinion adjective should come first. For example: • "Isn't Maria a lovely, intelligent girl?"

Lovely is a general opinion adjective because it can be used with any noun.

Therefore, it comes first. Intelligent is a specific opinion adjective because it

can only be used with people and animals, so it comes second.

Measurements

Adjectives of measurement can tell us about the size, height, length, and weight of a person or a thing. Some of the most common adjectives of measurements are:

big

small

tiny

huge

enormous

short

tall

long

heavy

light

If we were to use more than one adjective of measurement in a sentence, we would normally use the adjective that mentions the general size first, and the other measurements after. For example:

• Correct: "He's a big, tall man."

Incorrect: "He's a tall, big man."

• Correct: "I bought a huge, heavy table for the kitchen."

Incorrect: "I bought a heavy, huge table for the kitchen."

Shape

Adjectives of shape usually describe objects. The most common are round,

square, rectangular, triangular, and oval. However, there are many words that describe the shapes of objects that we see all around us but that are used

less frequently. For example:

bent
concave
convex
flat
pointy
straight
twisted
symmetrical
Condition
Adjectives of condition tell us whether something is in a good or bad state. These are generally adjectives that describe a temporary state of the person or thing in the sentence. Some common adjectives of physical condition are clean, dirty, wet, and dry. Emotions like happy, sad, angry, scared, and excited are also adjectives of condition, as are general states such as rich, powerful, shy, or clever."
Age
Adjectives of age can describe how old a person, place, or thing is. We have to be careful with adjectives of age, because some are used to describe only
people, some are used only for things, and a few are used for both people and things. For example:
• To describe people: young, youthful, elderly
• To describe things: new, antique
• To describe both: old, ancient
Color
Adjectives of color include the names of particular colors themselves,
such as yellow, red, and blue, but they can also be approximate colors, like
reddish or yellowish, or even properties of colors, such as transparent, translucent or opaque.
If you use both a color and a property of a color in one sentence, the property
should come first, and the color after, immediately before the noun. For example:
• "A translucent, yellow cup."
• "An opaque, blue curtain."
Pattern

Adjectives of pattern can describe patterns of materials or even of animals. Some of the most common pattern adjectives are checked, polkadot, striped, plaid, and flowered.

Origin

Adjectives of origin describe where something comes from. Usually, these are adjectives that refer to a specific country or region.

When we use a country adjective, like American, British, Indian, or Korean, note that we capitalize the adjective. Adjectives of origin that refer to a

general region, such as eastern or southern, are not capitalized.

Material

Adjectives of material tell us what something is made of. For example:

• "A wooden table."

• "A plastic chair."

• "A steel railroad track."

Purpose

Last in the order of adjectives are adjectives of purpose. They tell us what something is for. For example:

• "A sleeping bag."

• "A shopping cart."

Now, let's put all of this information about the different types of adjectives

together and see some examples of how it works when we modify a noun with more than one adjective:

• "Don't forget to bring your new striped jacket."

This sentence has two adjective types: New is an adjective of age and striped is an adjective of pattern.

• "Yesterday my sister gave me a blue wool sweater.

This sentence also has two adjective types: Blue is an adjective of color, and wool is an adjective of material.

• "I bought an enormous rectangular Turkish rug on my vacation."

This sentence includes three adjective types: Enormous is an adjective of measurement; rectangular is an adjective of shape; and Turkish is an adjective of origin (specifically of a country, so it's also capitalized).

We use and to link two adjectives of the same type that describe separate parts of one object. For example:

• "The child was playing with a blue and red plastic robot.

Blue and red are two adjectives of color, joined by and. They are followed by the adjective of material, plastic.

Sometimes a series of adjectives follows a linking verb, like to be. In this case, the last adjective is connected to the previous ones with the word and. For example:

• "The house is big, white, and wooden."

Using commas with adjectives

Last but not least, we need to mention commas. You have probably noticed that in some of our example sentences the adjectives are separated by

commas, and in others they're not.

Coordinate adjectives

In general, we do use commas between adjectives that belong to the same category. For example:

• "I bought a heavy, long table."

Adjectives of the same category are called coordinate adjectives. They each describe the same feature of the noun that follows them. Coordinate adjectives are separated by a comma. One way that we can check if adjectives

are coordinate is by trying to switch around the order and see if the sentence still makes sense. For example:

• "I bought a long, heavy table."

The sentence still sounds correct, so we know that we are looking at coordinate adjectives and that we need to use a comma. Another way that we can check is by inserting the word and where the comma would go:

• "I bought a heavy and long table."

Again, the sentence still sounds correct, so we know we are dealing with coordinate adjectives.

Cumulative adjectives

When the adjectives are from different categories, they are called cumulative

adjectives. This is because they accumulate as they describe the noun; that is, they build on each other to create a complete description, and so we don't separate them with commas:

• "I bought a black wooden table."

Black is describing wooden table (not just table alone), and so this sentence would sound strange if rearranged, like this:

• "I bought a wooden black table."

We can also try inserting and, with the same result:

• "I bought a black and wooden table."

The sentence doesn't sound right either rearranged or using the and test, so

we know that we are dealing with cumulative adjectives, and we should not

separate them with commas.

Exceptions

Finally, we should remember that like with most grammar rules, the order of

adjectives is not fixed, and there are exceptions. We can do our best to keep

adjectives in their natural order, but we may encounter variations.

Quiz 010

1. Which of the following is an adjective of material?

a) tall

b) silk

c) good

d) straight

2. Which of the following is an adjective of measurement?

a) long

b) beautiful

c) intelligent

d) round

3. Complete the sentence (using correct adjective order): "I bought an old ____ typewriter."

a) beautiful

b) square

c) gray

d) dirty

4. Choose the correct adjective order:

a) a big fantastic old house

b) an old big fantastic house

c) a fantastic old big house

d) a fantastic big old house

5. Choose the correct adjective order:

a) a clean pink polka-dot sweater

b) a pink clean polka-dot sweater

c) a polka-dot clean pink sweater

d) a polka-dot pink clean sweater

Degrees of Comparison

Definition

Adjectives describe a quality or characteristic of a noun or pronoun. The basic form of an adjective is sometimes known as the positive degree.

But adjectives can also be inflected (changed in form) to compare a quality

between two nouns—this form is known as the comparative degree.

Similarly, we can also inflect an adjective to identify a noun with the highest

(or lowest) degree of an attribute among a group—this is known as the superlative degree.

Forming the Comparative and

Superlative Degrees

We generally form the comparative degree by adding the suffix "-er" to the

end of the adjective, or by using the words more or less before it.

To form the superlative degree, we either add "-est" to the end of the adjective or use the words most or least before it.

In some cases, depending on how the adjective is spelled, we have to change

the spelling slightly to accommodate the addition of the suffix; there are some simple rules we can follow to know when such a change is necessary.

(To learn when and how to use these inflected degrees of comparison, go to the sections on Comparative Adjectives and Superlative Adjectives.)

"Short" Adjectives

With one-syllable adjectives, we add "-er" or "-est" and double the final consonant if preceded by one vowel. For example:

Adjective (positive

degree)

Comparative

degree

Superlative
degree
big bigger biggest
thin thinner thinnest
sad sadder saddest
slim slimmer slimmest
The final consonant is not doubled if it is preceded by two vowels or another
consonant, as in:
Adjective (positive
degree)
Comparative
degree
Superlative
degree
weak weaker weakest
strong stronger strongest
large* larger* largest*
small smaller smallest
(*If the adjective ends in an "e," then you only need to add "-r" or "-st.")
If an adjective has two syllables and ends in "-y," we replace "y" with "i" and
add "-er" or "-est," as in:
Adjective (positive
degree)
Comparative
degree
Superlative
degree
happy happier happiest
chewy chewier chewiest
"Long" Adjectives
"Long" adjectives are adjectives that have three or more syllables, or adjectives that have two syllables and do not end in "-y." Rather than changing the ending of long adjectives, we use the words more or less before the adjective to make them comparative, or most/least to make them

superlative. For example:

careful	more/less careful	most/least careful
caring	more/less caring	most/least caring
gifted	more/less gifted	most/least gifted
intelligent	more/less intelligent	most/least intelligent
beautiful	more/less beautiful	most/least beautiful
amazing	more/less amazing	most/least amazing

Irregular adjectives

As with most grammatical rules in English, there are some exceptions to the patterns above. Adjectives that do not inflect according to the normal patterns are known as irregular adjectives.

fun	more/less fun	most/least fun
bad	worse	worst
well (healthy)	better	best
good	better	best
far*	farther/further*	farthest/furthest*

(*Although farther/further and farthest/furthest are often used interchangeably, there are differences between these two forms. In American English, farther/farthest is preferred when comparing physical distances, and further/furthest is preferred when comparing figurative distances; in British English, further/furthest is preferred for both uses.)

Adjectives with multiple forms of inflection

There are also some adjectives that can be inflected using either form we looked at above.

Quiz 011

1. Which of the following suffixes is used to shift a one-syllable adjective to
the superlative degree?

a) –ed   b) –er   c) –est   d) -en

2. Which of the following pairs of words is used to shift a two-syllable "-ly"
adjective to the comparative degree?

a) more/less   b) most/least   c) much/many

    d) most/less

3. What is the comparative form of the irregular adjective well?

a) good   b) better   c) worse
       d) best

4. What is the superlative form of the adjective likely?

a) likelier   b) likeliest   c)   more/less   likely
       d) most/least likely

e) A & C   f) B & D

Comparative Adjectives

Definition

Comparative adjectives are adjectives that compare differences between the attributes of two nouns. These are often measurements, such as height,

weight, depth, distance, etc., but they don't have to be. We can also use comparative adjectives to compare non-physical characteristics.

For example:

Adjective Comparative

tall taller

fast faster

sweet sweeter

beautiful more/less beautiful

intelligent more/less intelligent

Forming Comparative Adjectives

As we can see above, we form comparative adjectives either by adding "-er" to

the end of the adjective, or by adding the word more (or less) before the adjective. So how do we know which to choose? Although there are some

exceptions, you can follow some simple general rules for forming comparative adjectives:

Short Adjectives

When we discuss comparative adjectives, we class them into two types: short and long. "Short" adjectives are adjectives that have only one syllable, or else have two syllables and end in "-y." For the majority of short

adjectives, we form the comparative according to the following rules:

Syllables Rule Examples

One syllable Add "-er" to the end of the
adjective. Tall becomes Taller
Two syllables ending
in "-y" Replace "-y" with "-ier" happy becomes
happier
Aside from the major rules in the table, there are two other things we must
keep in mind about short adjectives.
First, if the adjective ends in "-e," we just add "-r," not "-er." This is to avoid
doubling the letter "e." For example:
• Large becomes larger, not largeer.
• Cute becomes cuter, not cuteer.
• Safe becomes safer, not safeer.
Second, if the last three letters of the adjective are in the pattern consonant,
vowel, consonant, we double the final consonant before adding "-er" to the
word. For example:
• Big becomes bigger, not biger.
• Sad becomes sadder, not sader.
• Thin becomes thinner, not thiner.
Long Adjectives
"Long" adjectives are adjectives that have three or more syllables, or
adjectives that have two syllables and do not end in "-y." For these adjectives,
we can follow these rules:
Syllables Rule Examples
Two syllables not
ending in "-y"
Insert the word more/less
before the adjective.
Careful becomes
more/less careful.
Three or more
syllables
Insert the word more/less

before the adjective.

Intelligent becomes

more/less intelligent.

Irregular adjectives

As with most grammatical "rules" in English, there are some exceptions to

the patterns above. Here are a few of the adjectives that have irregular comparative forms:

Adjective Comparative form

fun more/less fun

bad worse

good better

well (not ill) better

There are also some adjectives that have two generally accepted comparative

forms. These are some of the most common:

Adjective Comparative Form 1 Comparative Form 2

clever cleverer more/less clever

likely likelier more/less likely

narrow narrower more narrow

quiet quieter more/less quiet

simple simpler more/less simple

far* farther further

*When referring to distance, farther and further can be used

interchangeably. However, in American English, farther is preferred when

comparing physical distances and further when comparing figurative

distances. For example:

• "San Francisco is farther from New York than Boston." (physical distance)

BUT

• "I was able to make further progress at work." (figurative distance)

In British English, further is more common both for physical and figurative

distances.

Using Comparative Adjectives

Now that we have discussed how to form comparative adjectives, we can look

at how they are used in sentences and within larger conversations.

Depending on the situation, you may or may not need to explicitly mention

both nouns being compared.

Explicitly mentioning both nouns

Often, the two nouns that are being compared both appear in the sentence.

This is the case if there is any chance of the listener or reader being confused

by what you're talking about. When we need to mention both nouns, we follow this structure:

Noun 1 + be + comparative

adjective + than + noun 2

For example:

• "An airplane is bigger than a car."

• "Mt. Everest is taller than Mt. Fuji."

• "Tom is faster than John."

In each of these sentences, the noun that has the characteristic to a greater

degree comes first. We can achieve the same meaning by using opposite

adjectives and switching the order that the nouns appear in. For example:

• "A car is smaller than an airplane."

• "Mt. Fuji is shorter than Mt. Everest."

• "John is slower than Tom."

If we want to achieve the same effect using "long" adjectives, instead of

inserting the word more before the adjective, we can insert the word less. For

example:

• "Tom is more studious than John."

OR

• "John is less studious than Tom."

Keep in mind that the two nouns being compared don't necessarily have to

be individual people or objects. One or both of the nouns or noun phrases

being compared can also refer to groups. For example:

• "Cats are more independent than dogs."
• "Women are shorter than men."
• "Jen is smarter than the rest of the students in her class.
We can even compare two gerunds (verbs ending in "-ing" that function as nouns). We can compare characteristics of two gerunds in the same way that we can compare any other type of noun:
• "Running is faster than walking."
• "Drawing is easier than painting."
• "Sailing is more relaxing than waterskiing."
Finally, we can use the regular patterns for making negative and interrogative sentences. For negatives, we simply add the word not, or its contracted form, "-n't," after the verb be:
• "Walking is not faster than running."
• "Women aren't taller than men."
• "Waterskiing isn't more relaxing than sailing."
To form interrogatives (questions), we simply place the conjugated form of the verb be at the beginning of the sentence:
• "Is running faster than walking?"
• "Is Jen smarter than the rest of the students in her class?"
• "Are cats more independent than dogs?"
If we are not sure which noun is taller, faster, etc., we can ask by adding a question word like who, which, or what to the beginning of the sentence,
and placing the two nouns as options at the end:
• "Who is taller, Mary or Jane?"
• "Which is tastier, pizza or pasta?"
• "What's faster, a car or a motorcycle?"
Omitting one or both nouns
Sometimes in conversation, it isn't necessary to explicitly mention one or both nouns that we're comparing. In fact, it might even sound repetitive. Take for example the following conversation:
• Speaker A: "I don't think you should be running. Swimming is easier on the knees than running."
• Speaker B: "Yes, but running is better for my heart than swimming."
That's a very repetitive conversation and probably wouldn't occur in natural speech. Instead, the two speakers can omit the parts underlined, which

avoids repetition and creates a more natural-sounding conversation:

• Speaker A: "I don't think you should be running. Swimming is easier on the knees.

• Speaker B: "Yes, but running is better for my heart."

Note that when we omit a noun, we also omit the word than.

Gradable and ungradable adjectives

We can only use gradable adjectives as comparative adjectives. Gradable adjectives are adjectives that can move up and down on a scale of intensity.

For example, tall is a gradable adjective because something can be a little tall, tall, or very tall.

We can also use expressions like a bit, a little, much, a lot, and far before the comparative adjective to indicate scale. For example:

• "Jane is much taller than Emily."

• "Giraffes have far longer necks than elephants."

• "Is your dad a little bigger than you?"

Ungradable adjectives are adjectives that can't move up and down on a scale of intensity. For example, you cannot say "I am very married." You are either married, or you aren't. The same can be said for the adjective dead: something is either dead or it isn't. These types of adjectives cannot be used in the comparative form.

Expressing Equality and Inequality using as … as

There is another way to express similarities and differences between two nouns using adjectives that aren't comparative. To describe two things as equal, we can use the construction as + adjective + as. For example:

• "The apple is as big as the orange." (The two are the same size.)

• "The table is as heavy as the desk." (The two are the same weight.)

• "Jane is as talkative as Mary." (They both like to talk the same amount.)

We can use the same construction to say that two things are unequal. We just have to add the word not:

• "The apple is not as big as the orange." (The orange is bigger.)

• "The table is not as heavy as the desk." (The desk is heavier.)

• "Jane is not as talkative as Mary." (Mary is more talkative.)

Quiz 012

1. Comparative adjectives express differences between __________ nouns.

a) Two

b) Two or three

c) Three

d) More than three

2. Which of the following comparative adjectives is misspelled?

a) bigger

b) taller

c) longer

d) smaler

3. Comparative adjectives are never ___________.

a) gradable

b) ungradable

4. Which of these sentences is incorrect?

a) "I think ice cream is better than cake."

b) "I wish I had a faster car."

c) "Are you going to buy a nicer radio than?"

d) "I'm always looking for a cheaper option."

5. Which sentence has a different meaning from the other three?

a) John is taller than Tom.

b) Tom is shorter than John.

c) Tom isn't as tall as John.

d) John isn't as tall as Tom.

Superlative Adjectives

Definition

Superlative adjectives are adjectives that describe the attribute of a person or thing that is the highest (or lowest) in degree compared to the members of the noun's group. Superlative adjectives are similar to comparative adjectives, except they express the most extreme degree of comparison, and they are only used when talking about groups of three or more people or things.

Forming Superlative Adjectives

We form superlative adjectives either by adding "-est" to the end of the adjective, or by adding the word most before the adjective.

Although there are some exceptions, we can follow some simple general rules for forming superlative adjectives.

"Short" Adjectives

With one-syllable adjectives, we add "-est" and double the final consonant if preceded by one vowel. For example:

big – biggest

thin – thinnest

sad – saddest

slim – slimmest

The final consonant is not doubled if it is preceded by two vowels or another consonant, as in:

weak – weakest

strong – strongest

large – largest

small – smallest

(If the adjective ends in an "e," then you only need to add "-st," as in the case of large – largest.)

If an adjective has two syllables and ends in "-y," we replace "y" with "i" and

add "-est," as in:

happy – happiest

chewy – chewiest

sticky – stickiest

furry – furriest

"Long" Adjectives

"Long" adjectives are adjectives that have three or more syllables, or adjectives that have two syllables and do not end in "-y." Rather than changing the ending of long adjectives to make them superlative, we use the word most before the adjective to indicate the highest degree of something, or least to indicate the lowest degree. For example:

careful – most/least careful

caring – most/least caring

gifted – most/least gifted

intelligent – most/least intelligent

beautiful – most/least beautiful

amazing – most/least amazing

Exceptions

As with most grammatical "rules" in English, there are some exceptions to the patterns above. Here are a few of the adjectives that have irregular superlative forms:

fun – most/least fun

bad – worst

good – best

far – farthest/furthest*

*When referring to distance, farthest and furthest can be used interchangeably. However, in the American English, farthest is preferred when comparing physical distances, while furthest is preferred when comparing figurative distances. For example:

• "San Francisco is farther from New York than Boston, but Hawaii is the farthest." (physical distance)

BUT

• "Of all the lies I've heard today, that one is the furthest from the truth." (figurative distance)

In British English, furthest is more common both for physical and figurative distances.

Adjectives with multiple superlative forms

There are also some adjectives that can either take the "-est" ending or be preceded by "most" to become superlative. The following are some of the most common:

Adjective Superlative Form 1 Superlative Form 2

clever cleverest most/least clever

likely likeliest most/least likely

narrow narrowest most/least narrow

quiet quietest most/least quiet

simple simplest most/least simple

Using Superlative Adjectives

We usually use superlative adjectives when comparing the attributes of someone or something to others, either in a collective group or among several individuals.

When we use a superlative adjective in a sentence, we almost always precede

it with the word the. For example:

• "John is the tallest student in his class."

• "Daniel always buys the most advanced smartphones available."

• "Mrs. Phillips is the nicest teacher among the staff."

• "It is the highest mountain in the world."

• "There are many expensive brands of watches, but these are the most

expensive kind."
• "This is the best book I've ever read."
• "Among her four sisters, Georgina has the worst eyesight."
We can also identify a superlative attribute of a person or thing compared to him-/her-/itself in other points in time. In this case, we generally do not use the word the. For example:
• "I am most alert after my morning coffee." (compared to a different time of day)
• "The car is fastest when the engine has warmed up." (compared to when
the engine is cold)
• "Flowers are prettiest in the spring." (compared to the other seasons)
Omitting the group of comparison
When we use superlatives, it is very common to omit the group that something or someone is being compared to because that group is often implied by a previous sentence, and to repeat the group would sound very repetitive. For example:
• "My brothers are all fast swimmers. John is the fastest, though."
In informal speech or writing, it is quite common for the word the to be left out when the group of comparison is omitted, as in:
• "We all were carrying big, heavy sticks with us. Mine was biggest, though." However, this should be avoided, especially in formal or professional speech or writing.
Superlatives for hyperbole
We can also omit a group of comparison when a superlative adjective is being used for hyperbolic effect. For instance:
• "I'm going to buy my daughter the most beautiful puppy for her birthday."
• "I had the biggest steak for my lunch today."
Expressing the lowest degree
As we've seen, "long" adjectives can either take most or least to indicate the highest and lowest degrees of comparison. For example:
• "Though it was the least intelligent movie that I've seen this year, it was the most exciting one I'd been to in a long time."
"Short" adjectives, on the other hand, have only one superlative form that expresses the highest degree of its characteristic. For two-syllable

adjectives ending in "-y," we can generally just use the word least with the base form of the adjective. For example:
• "He's the least tidy child I've ever met."
• "The baby's least grumpy when he's had enough naps."
We can also technically use the least with a single-syllable adjective in its normal form to express the lowest degree, but this is often awkward to read or say. For example:
• "John is the tallest student in his class, but he is the least tall on the

Quiz 013
1. Superlative adjectives express differences among a group of __________ nouns.
a) Two   b) Two or three
c) Three or more   d) Five or more
2. Which of the following suffixes is used to create the superlative form for short adjectives?
a) –er   b) –est
c) –ier   d) -ence
3. Which of the following is an incorrect superlative adjective?
a) biggest   b) least intelligent
c) longest   d) most small
4. When do we generally not use the article the with a superlative adjective?
a) When the person or thing is being compared to itself in other times
b) When the person or thing is being compared with a group in other times
c) When the superlative adjective is being used for hyperbolic effect
d) When a single-syllable adjective is being made into the superlative form

Answer Key:
001. Adjectives: 1-c, 2-b, 3-a, 4-d, 5-c

002. Attributive Adjectives: 1-a, 2-a, 3-c, 4-a, 5-b

003. Predicative Adjectives: 1-b, 2-c, 3-e, 4-a

004. Proper Adjectives: 1-b, 2-c, 3-a, 4-d, 5-a

005. Collective Adjectives: 1-a, 2-c, 3-a, 4-b, 5-a

006. Demonstrative Adjectives: 1-b, 2-c, 3-d, 4-a, 5-b

007. Interrogative Adjectives: 1-b, 2-c, 3-e, 4-b, 5-a

008. Nominal Adjectives: 1-d, 2-c, 3-a, 4-c, 5-d

009. Compound Adjectives: 1-c, 2-b, 3-a, 4-b

010. Order of Adjectives: 1-b, 2-a, 3-c, 4-d, 5-a

011. Degrees of Comparison: 1-c, 2-a, 3-b, 4-f

012. Comparative Adjectives: 1-a, 2-d, 3-b, 4-c, 5-d

013. Superlative Adjectives: 1-c, 2-b, 3-d, 4-a

Error Correction Rules
Kinds of Adjective:

Proper Adjective:
This type of Adjective qualifies proper Noun.
Example: Indian, American, etc.
Virat kohli is an Indian player.
Donald Trump is an American president.

Quantitative Adjective:
This type of Adjective qualifies quantity of material noun.
Example: A great deal of, enough, all, no, some, much etc.
He is kind enough.
All the student are safe.
There is much water in swimming pool.
The baby has drunk much milk.

Demonstrative Adjective:

It qualifies the degree of distance for Noun / Pronoun.
Example: This, That, These, Such, Any etc.
This pen is Blue.
This bike is heavier than car.
Those politicians are good.

Descriptive Adjective:
This kind of Adjective explains the size, characteristic, colour, type of Noun / Pronoun.
Example: Tall, Large, Tiny, Rectangular, Square, Blue, Black, Ugly, Heavy, Dry etc.
I am a tall boy.
He is heavy wrestler.
My playground is triangular.

Distributive Adjective:
It qualifies one object or person between two or more than two person.
Example: Each, Every, either, neither etc.
Neither pen writes well.
Every child goes school.
Either of the Laptop works.

Possessive Adjective:
This kind of Adjective qualifies the possession or relation of noun / pronoun.
Example: Your, My, Our, His, Her etc.
My jacket is red but yours is blue.
That is your car.
This is my college.

Emphasizing Adjective:
This kind of Adjective is used to make special pressure on noun / Pronoun.
Example: Own, Very, Such, Same, Very etc.
I saw her at the Railway station with my own eyes.
This is my own pen.
This is the very thief who has stolen my smart phone.

(very means same to that person who is already known)

Interrogative Adjective:
This kind of adjective is used to make sense of question.
Example: What, How, Where, When etc.
Whose bike is this?
Which book is the best?
What type of laptop do you want to buy?

Numerical adjective:
It qualifies the number of countable noun.
Example: All, Some, No, Many, A good many, A number of etc.
There are many books in the library.
A cow has four legs.
All the students are present in the class.

Note: Enough, All, No, A lot of, Some etc are quantitative and numerical adjective
both, but their uses are different. (Will be discussed in rules of adjective topic)

Kinds of Numerical Adjective:
Definite numerical adjective:
Cardinal: One, Two, Three etc.
Ordinal: First, Second, Third etc.
Multiplicative: Single, Double, Triple etc.
Indefinite Numerical Adjective:
Much, many, some, enough, a lot of, several etc.

Exclamatory Adjective:
This kind of adjective is used to express emotion of heart.
Example: What! , How! etc.
What a beautiful day!
What nonsense this is !
What a kind of man he is!
What a nice story is! etc.
Relative Adjective:

This kind of adjective is used to make sense of relation for Noun or Pronoun.

Example: Who, Which, That etc.

This is the laptop that is used for best gaming experience.

This the singer who sings spiritual songs.

Present / Past participle Adjective:

This kind of Adjective is used where past or present Participle is needed.

Example: Burning train, flying kite, Singing baby, Tiring journey, Moving car etc.

I like a flying kite.

Old woman slipped down from the moving train.

I am fond of a tiring journey.

**

3. Adverbs

Revision Works

1. Rewrite each of the following sentences, placing the adverb of frequency given in brackets in the middle position of the main clause. For example:

> She is late for work. (rarely)
> She is rarely late for work.

> We visit him on Sundays. (sometimes)
> We sometimes visit him on Sundays.

> I have read that book before. (never)
> I have never read that book before.

> Yes, I do. (usually)
> Yes, I usually do.

1. I had wanted to see the ocean. (always)
2. They do. (frequently)
3. She is very friendly. (usually)
4. They have the opportunity to travel. (seldom)
5. I am at home in the mornings. (generally)
6. He has. (always)
7. We were given free transportation to the school. (frequently)
8. Birds return to the place where they were born to build their nests. (often)
9. Albatrosses are seen close to shore. (seldom)
10. We would. (never)
11. They follow the news. (rarely)
12. Maple wood is used to make violins. (sometimes)

2. Rewrite each of the following sentences, placing the adverb of frequency given in brackets in the middle position of the main clause. For example:

Have you visited New York? (ever)
Have you ever visited New York?

I do not go to the library on the weekend. (always)
I do not always go to the library on the weekend.

1. He did not arrive on time. (ever)
2. Do you visit Boston? (often)
3. Are they surprised at the results? (frequently)
4. The children do not follow our instructions. (always)
5. Do you wonder what will happen next? (sometimes)
6. Did they find the missing information? (ever)
7. We do not stay out after dark. (usually)
8. The facts are not known. (generally)

3. For each of the following sentences, place the adverbs given in brackets in their most usual positions in the sentence. Place connecting adverbs in the beginning position, place adverbs of frequency in the middle position, and place adverbs of manner and adverbs of time in the end position. Adverbs of manner should precede adverbs of time. For example:

They left. (early, usually)
They usually left early.

We proceeded. (cautiously, therefore)
Therefore, we proceeded cautiously.

We will review our options. (tomorrow, carefully)
We will review our options carefully tomorrow.

1. We pick the flowers. (carefully, usually)
2. She . (correctly, rarely)
3. He is wrong. (however, seldom)

4. We will attend the concert. (therefore, tonight)

5. We found the hotel. (easily, nevertheless)

6. They left. (quietly, this morning)

7. She wins first prize. (always, furthermore)

8. He finished. (late, often)

9. We reached the station. (quickly, consequently)

10. You speak. (loudly, never)

11. We would have gone to the beach. (otherwise, yesterday)

12. They worked. (quickly, today)

13. I want to analyze the book. (carefully, sometime)

14. We arrive. (early, sometimes)

4. The following sentences do not contain verbs of motion. Complete each sentence by placing the adverbs and adverb phrases given in brackets in the end position, in the following order:

 Adverb of Manner
 Adverb of Location
 Adverb of Time
 Adverb of Purpose

For example:

 The tickets sold. (at the box office, quickly, this afternoon)
 The tickets sold quickly at the box office this afternoon.

 I bought some film. (to photograph the parade, at the store, yesterday)
 I bought some film at the store yesterday to photograph the parade.

1. We ate. (at the restaurant, well, yesterday evening)

2. They will be. (next month, on business, in France)

3. The children whispered. (on Christmas Eve, excitedly, in front of the tree)

4. We hung the picture. (on the wall, carefully)

5. The birds twittered. (this morning, outside the window, loudly)

6. The boys and girls waited. (for the parade to pass by, impatiently)

7. We slept. (all afternoon, on the grass, soundly)

8. The choir sang. (last week, beautifully, at the competition)
9. We watched the skaters. (to determine who might win the competition, avidly, this morning)
10. The moon shone. (over the water, long after the sun had set, brilliantly)

5. For each of the following sentences, paying attention to whether or not the sentence contains a verb of motion, place the adverbs and adverb phrases given in brackets in the correct order in the end position of the sentence. For example:

He lived. (for six years, happily, in Copenhagen)
He lived happily in Copenhagen for six years.

They returned. (from Holland, last week, unexpectedly)
They returned from Holland unexpectedly last week.

1. They stood. (at the bus stop, for twenty minutes, patiently)
2. We arrived. (here, last night, on foot)
3. The young child walked. (by herself, this morning, to school)
4. They were waiting. (at seven o'clock, eagerly, outside the fairgrounds)
5. She arrived. (in a black limousine, at the hotel)
6. Chickadees build their nests. (in dense evergreens, in the early spring, secretively)
7. The waves crashed. (against the shore, loudly)
8. I walked. (in the rain, to work, yesterday)
9. He sat. (until the announcements were finished, on the edge of his chair, expectantly)
10. We left. (this morning, home, in a hurry)
11. She went. (by bus, downtown, today)
12. They talked. (for an hour, animatedly, on the front lawn)

6. For each of the following sentences, fill in the blank with is or are, as appropriate. For example:

Here ___ one of the computations.
Here is one of the computations.

> There ___ all of the results.
> There are all of the results.

1. There _______ his brother and sister.
2. Here _______ the news.
3. There _______ several of her classmates.
4. Here _______ both of the disks.
5. There _______ a pair of pliers.
6. Here _______ a few chocolates.
7. Here _______ a box of eggs.
8. There _______ two of the books.
9. Here _______ another of the magazines.
10. Here _______ some of the .
ii. There _______ one of his brothers.
12. Here _______ the essays.

7. Rewrite the following sentences, replacing the underlined phrases with personal pronouns, and changing the word order as necessary. For example:

> Over the treetops sailed the kite.
> Over the treetops it sailed.

> Here comes our teacher.
> Here he comes.

1. Up the stairs dashed the reporter.
2. Onto the stage glided the ballerina.
3. Here is the butter.
4. There go the geese.
5. To and fro rode the girl on the horse.
6. Here come the children.
7. High in the heavens shone the lights of a million stars.
8. There goes the train.
9. Into the hotel darted the boy.
10. Here are your keys.

11. Over the grass rolled the ball.
12. There is my aunt.

8. The following sentences are incorrect, because each contains a double negative. Each sentence can be corrected by omitting or altering one of the negative expressions. Write two corrected versions for each sentence. For example:

    We have not got no sugar.

    We have got no sugar.

    or We have not got any sugar.

    I have never seen nothing like it before.

    I have seen nothing like it before.

    or I have never seen anything like it before.

1. He does not need no advice.
2. We never go nowhere interesting.
3. I did not get none of the right.
4. She does not know nothing.
5. We had not met neither of the boys before.
6. They did not do no harm.
7. He never speaks to nobody.
8. You do not have no reason to behave like that.
9. I do not know nothing about it.
10. I do not have no time for such things.

9. For each of the following sentences, add the negative expression shown in brackets at the beginning of the sentence, and make any other changes that are necessary. For example:

    I had reached home when I remembered the message. (hardly)

    Hardly had I reached home when I remembered the message.

    We had the opportunity to do whatever we wanted. (seldom)

    Seldom did we have the opportunity to do whatever we wanted.

1. We had entered the room when the telephone rang. (scarcely)
2. I have seen a more beautiful ballet than that one. (never)
3. We realized that a dangerous stretch of road lay ahead of us. (little)
4. I have worked as hard as I could. (never before)
5. A writer can express his exact feelings in words. (rarely)
6. We perceive everything that is around us. (hardly ever)
7. One can find a more striking example of erosion than the Grand Canyon. (nowhere)
8. They guessed what was about to happen. (little)
9. I am entirely satisfied with my situation. (seldom)
10. One comprehends a complex situation immediately. (rarely)

10. Paying attention to the correct word order, rewrite the underlined indirect questions as direct questions. For example:

I would like to know why you are here.
Why are you here?

I wonder how often he comes here.
How often does he come here?

Tell me where you have been.
Where have you been?

1. I want to know how much money you collected.
2. I wonder where they were.
3. Tell me why I should attend the meeting.
4. I would like to know when he finds time for his hobbies.
5. Do you know why she left school?
6. I am curious to know how many times you have seen this movie.
7. Will you tell me when you completed the assignment?
8. He will ask how long it will take.
9. Tell me where you are.
10. I wonder why she did not reply.
11. Find out when the bank opens.
12. Can you tell me where she is staying?

11. Paying attention to the correct word order, use the phrases given in brackets to rewrite the following direct questions as indirect questions. For example:

Where is the nearest store? (Please find out)
Please find out where the nearest store is.

How many boxes of paper did he order? (We need to know)
We need to know how many boxes of paper he ordered.

Why has she not finished the assignment? (I will ask her)
I will ask her why she has not finished the assignment.

1. Why is the information not here? (Please tell me)
2. When will they finish work? (Did you ask)
3. Where has she studied? (I wonder)
4. How many pounds of cherries did you sell? (Tell us)
5. Why was the meeting cancelled? (Will you tell me)
6. How long will the trip take? (I wonder)
7. How is he? (Did you hear)
8. Why do they have difficulty with the work? (I wonder)
9. When does she plan to leave? (Ask her)
10. How much time do you have? (Please let me know)
11. Where is the post office? (I am not sure)
12. Where did you buy that book? (Tell me)

Answers

to Exercise 1:

1. I had always wanted to see the ocean. 2. They frequently do. 3. She is usually very friendly. 4. They seldom have the opportunity to travel. 5. I am generally at home in the mornings. 6. He always has. 7. We were frequently given free transportation to the school. 8. Birds often return to the place where they were born to build their nests. 9. Albatrosses are seldom seen close to shore. 10. We never would. 11. They rarely follow the news. 12. Maple wood is sometimes used to make violins.

to Exercise 2:

1. He did not ever arrive on time. 2. Do you often visit Boston? 3. Are they frequently surprised at the results? 4. The children do not always follow our instructions. 5. Do you sometimes wonder what will happen next? 6. Did they ever find the missing information? 7. We do not usually stay out after dark. 8. The facts are not generally known.

to Exercise 3:

1. We usually pick the flowers carefully. 2. She rarely correctly. 3. However, he is seldom wrong. 4. Therefore, we will attend the concert tonight. 5. Nevertheless, we found the hotel easily. 6. They left quietly this morning. 7. Furthermore, she always wins first prize. 8. He often finished late. 9. Consequently, we reached the station quickly. 10. You never speak loudly. 11. Otherwise, we would have gone to the beach yesterday. 12. They worked quickly today. 13. I want to analyze the book carefully sometime. 14. We sometimes arrive early.

to Exercise 4:

1. We ate well at the restaurant yesterday evening. 2. They will be in France next month on business. 3. The children whispered excitedly in front of the tree on Christmas Eve. 4. We hung the picture carefully on the wall. 5. The birds twittered loudly outside the window this morning. 6. The boys and girls waited impatiently for the parade to pass by. 7. We slept soundly on the grass all afternoon. 8. The choir sang beautifully at the competition last week. 9. We watched the skaters avidly this morning, to determine who might win the competition. 10. The moon shone brilliantly over the water long after the sun had set.

to Exercise 5:

1. They stood patiently at the bus stop for twenty minutes. 2. We arrived here on foot last night. 3. The young child walked to school by herself this morning. 4. They were waiting eagerly outside the fairgrounds at seven o'clock. 5. She arrived at the hotel in a black limousine. 6. Chickadees build their nests secretively in dense evergreens in the early spring. 7. The waves crashed loudly against the shore. 8. I walked to work in the rain yesterday. 9. He sat expectantly on the edge of his chair until the announcements were finished. 10. We left home in a hurry this

morning. 11. She went downtown by bus today. 12. They talked animatedly on the front lawn for an hour.

to Exercise 6:
1. are 2. is 3. are 4. are 5. is 6. are 7. is 8. are 9. is 10. are 11. is 12. are

to Exercise 7:
1. Up the stairs he (or she) dashed. 2. Onto the stage she glided. 3. Here it is. 4. There they go. 5. To and fro she rode. 6. Here they come. 7. High in the heavens they shone. 8. There it goes. 9. Into the hotel he darted. 10. Here they are. 11. Over the grass it rolled. 12. There she is.

to Exercise 8:
1. He needs no advice. or He does not need any advice. 2. We go nowhere interesting. or We never go anywhere interesting. 3. I got none of the right. or I did not get any of the right. 4. She knows nothing. or She does not know anything. 5. We had met neither of the boys before. or We had not met either of the boys before. 6. They did no harm. or They did not do any harm. 7. He speaks to nobody. or He never speaks to anybody. 8. You have no reason to behave like that. or You do not have any reason to behave like that. 9. I know nothing about it. or I do not know anything about it. 10. I have no time for such things. or I do not have any time for such things.

to Exercise 9:
1. Scarcely had we entered the room when the telephone rang. 2. Never have I seen a more beautiful ballet than that one. 3. Little did we realize that a dangerous stretch of road lay ahead of us. 4. Never before have I worked as hard as I could. 5. Rarely can a writer express his exact feelings in words. 6. Hardly ever do we perceive everything that is around us. 7. Nowhere can one find a more striking example of erosion than the Grand Canyon. 8. Little did they guess what was about to happen. 9. Seldom am I entirely satisfied with my situation. 10. Rarely does one comprehend a complex situation immediately.

to Exercise 10:

1. How much money did you collect? 2. Where were they? 3. Why should I attend the meeting? 4. When does he find time for his hobbies? 5. Why did she leave school? 6. How many times have you seen this movie? 7. When did you complete the assignment? 8. How long will it take? 9. Where are you? 10. Why did she not reply? 11. When does the bank open? 12. Where is she staying?

to Exercise 11:

1. Please tell me why the information is not here. 2. Did you ask when they will finish work? 3. I wonder where she has studied. 4. Tell us how many pounds of cherries you sold. 5. Will you tell me why the meeting was cancelled? 6. I wonder how long the trip will take. 7. Did you hear how he is? 8. I wonder why they have difficulty with the work. 9. Ask her when she plans to leave. 10. Please let me know how much time you have. 11. I am not sure where the post office is. 12. Tell me where you bought that book.

Revision Works II

1. For each of the following sentences, fill in the blank with the adverb which corresponds to the adjective given in brackets. For example:

The letter was ________ legible. (scarce)
The letter was scarcely legible.

He did the work as _________ as possible. (careful)
He did the work as carefully as possible.

They won the game ______. (easy)
They won the game easily.

She handled the situation very _______. (capable)
She handled the situation very capably.

I _____ expected that to happen. (full)
I fully expected that to happen.

The view was _____ magnificent. (true)
The view was truly magnificent.

The theory has never been ______________ proved. (scientific)
The theory has never been scientifically proved.

1. I was ___________ impressed by their courage. (due)
2. The children chattered ______________. (noisy)
3 The sun shone ______________ behind the clouds. (pale)
4. They have settled in ______________. (comfortable)
5. He ______________ maintained his point of view. (dogmatic)
6. Everything is proceeding ___________. (normal)
7. Please drive ______________. (slow)
8. She worked ______________ until nine o'clock. (steady)
9. The cost of fuel has risen ______________. (dramatic)
10. He ______________ scrambled up the slope. (agile)
ii. Everything was explained clearly and ___________. (simple)
12. The train whistle blew ______________ at the crossing. (shrill)
13. ______________ , it stopped raining before we had to leave. (lucky)
14. She was signaling ______________. (frantic)
15. That was ___________ unexpected. (whole)
16. We arrived ______________. (punctual)
17. England is a ___________ populated country. (dense)
18. They are ___________ dependent on coal for fuel. (sole)
19. The material was produced ______________. (synthetic)
20. They ___________ agreed to the proposal. (ready)

2. For each of the following sentences, fill in the blank with the adverb which corresponds to the adjective given in brackets. For example:
He hit the ball ____. (hard)
He hit the ball hard.

The newspaper is delivered _____. (daily)
The newspaper is delivered daily.

She did ____ in the competition. (good)
She did well in the competition.

Please close the door _______. (quiet)
Please close the door quietly.

1. I drove ______________ home. (straight)
2. We came to work ______________. (early)
3. She ___________ filled in the . (quick)

4. He likes to drive ______________. (fast)

5. We proceeded ______________. (cautious)

6. He threw the ball ______________ into the air. (high)

7. How __________ do you know her? (good)

8. We arrived __________. (late)

9. They did the work ___________. (bad)

10. He spoke ____________. (little)

ii. The gathering is held . (annual)

12. They replied ______________. (immediate)

13. The workers met _____________ . (weekly)

14. I will deal with that problem ______________. (first)

15. They were ________________ dressed for the occasion. (suitable)

3. For each of the following sentences, pay attention to whether the word to be placed in the blank modifies a noun or a verb, and complete the sentence with either the adjective given in brackets or the corresponding adverb, as appropriate. For example:

It is necessary to wear ______ clothes in the winter. (thick)
It is necessary to wear thick clothes in the winter.

Snow fell ________ on the ground. (thick)
Snow fell thickly on the ground.

1. We ________________ concluded the deal. (successful)

2. He is a ______________ businessman. (successful)

3. There was a ____________ rain in the morning. (light)

4. She ran _____________ up the steps. (light)

5. The path was _____________ marked. (clear)

6. We gave him a _____________ signal to continue. (clear)

7. I ____________ disagree with you. (strong)

8. There is a _____________ wind from the north. (strong)

9. She waved ______________. (cheerful)

10. I gazed at the ____________ water of the lake. (tranquil)

11. The engine operates as ________________ as possible. (efficient)

12. Is that a ______________ decision? (recent)

13. He has behaved very ________________. (responsible)

14. ______________ snow is forecast for tomorrow. (heavy)

15. I opened the door ______________ and stepped outside. (quiet)

16. Icicles hung from the ______________ needles of the pine trees. (dark)

4. For each of the following sentences, pay attention to whether the word to be placed in the blank modifies a noun or an adjective, and complete the sentence with either the adjective given in brackets or the corresponding adverb, as appropriate. For example:

A _____ wooden fence surrounded the playground. (high)
A high wooden fence surrounded the playground.

A _______ skilled worker will be required for this job. (high)
A highly skilled worker will be required for this job.

1. They have a __________ front lawn. (wide)
2. He has challenged a __________ held theory. (wide)
3. Every author likes to receive __________ book reviews. (favorable)
4. __________ situated farms often produce higher yields than other farms. (favorable)
5. Many __________ incomprehensible phenomena have been explained with the help of modern science. (previous)
6. Many __________ city councils have succeeded in balancing the budget. (previous)
7. __________ weather conditions have prevailed for the past ten days. (unusual)
8. An __________ large number of variables must be taken into account. (extreme)
9. __________ few people understand the situation. (relative)
10. She wrote a __________ short story. (humorous)
11. That was a __________ occurring event. (frequent)
12. Our city boasts a __________ bus service. (frequent)
13. It was a __________ Easter Sunday. (hot)
14. It was a __________ debated issue. (hot)

5. For each of the following sentences, pay attention to whether the word to be placed in the blank modifies the verb or the subject of the verb, and complete the sentence with either the adjective given in brackets or the corresponding adverb, as appropriate. For example:

We tasted the soup __________. (suspicious)
We tasted the soup suspiciously.

The meal tasted __________. (delicious)
The meal tasted delicious.

1. The moon appeared __________ between the clouds. (brief)

2. He looked _______________. (happy)
3. He looked _______________ at the timetable. (attentive)
4. We felt ____________ after supper. (sleepy)
5. After the lights went out, we felt our way ____________ to our rooms. (sleepy)
6. The maple tree grew ____________. (quick)
7. The sky grew ____________. (dark)
8. He became _____________ at the thought of giving a speech. (excited)
9. She became a teacher _______________ after graduating. (immediate)
10. The pastries smelled ____________. (sweet)
11. We ____________ smelled the aroma of fresh bread. (eager)

6. Rewrite the following sentences as comparisons, using the comparative form of the adverb, and the word than. For each sentence, use the word or words given in brackets as the second part of the comparison. For example:

The living room was furnished elegantly. (the study)
The living room was furnished more elegantly than the study.

Because they were nervous, they performed badly. (they should have)
Because they were nervous, they performed worse than they should have.

1. The train travels fast. (the bus)
2. In the morning, the sun shone brightly. (in the afternoon)
3. The footpath runs straight. (the road)
4. Joe sings badly. (Rick)
5. I got up early. (you did)
6. The wild deer came near. (I had expected)
7. Her son plays the violin well. (her daughter does)
8. Captain Cook sailed far. (Columbus did)
9. You are late. (the others)
10. The stream flows swiftly. (the river)
11. She studies hard. (her classmates)
12. The project was completed successfully. (we had anticipated)

7. Rewrite the following sentences, using progressive comparisons instead of the adverb increasingly, and using the expression less and less instead of the adverb decreasingly. For example:

The rain fell increasingly heavily.
The rain fell more and more heavily.

The wind blew increasingly hard.
The wind blew harder and harder.

Finally, the rain drummed decreasingly loudly on the roof.
Finally, the rain drummed less and less loudly on the roof.

1. As the evening wore on, we spoke decreasingly animatedly.
2. The spectators cheered increasingly loudly.
3. The chirping of the crickets disturbed us increasingly little.
4. As he grew older, he walked increasingly far.
5. The new shuttle service functioned increasingly reliably.
6. The sun shone decreasingly intensely.
7. As I became tired, I wrote increasingly slowly.
8. The boy learned to read increasingly well.

8. Rewrite each of the following sentences, changing the positive form of the adverb to the superlative form, and using the definite article the. Use the words given in brackets as the second part of the comparison. For example:

This window opens easily. (of all the windows in the room)
This window opens the most easily of all the windows in the room.

He plays this piece well. (of anyone in the band)
He plays this piece the best of anyone in the band.

1. She understood the lesson readily. (of all the pupils in the class)
2. This kite flies badly. (of all the kites I have ever made)
3. That train leaves early. (of all the trains departing from this station)
4. Last night it snowed hard. (of any night in the year)
5. The potato field produces little. (of all the fields on the farm)
6. This highway runs straight. (of all the highways in the country)
7. She speaks quietly. (of all the people I know)
8. The bass sings low. (of all the singers)
9. Eagles fly high. (of all the birds which live in the mountains)
10. She prepares meals well. (of all the students in the class)

11. They regard his proposal favorably. (of all the proposals they have received)
12. Bill ran far. (of all the boys)
13. His arrow came near. (to the center of the target)
14. This bus travels slowly. (of all the buses)

9. Paying attention to the sentence structure, complete each of the following sentences correctly by filling in the blank with the positive, comparative, or superlative form of the adverb given in brackets. For example:

We clapped as _______ as we could. (loudly)
We clapped as loudly as we could.

They arrived _______________ than they had expected. (promptly)
They arrived more promptly than we had expected.

She swam the _________ of all the girls in the school. (far)
She swam the farthest of all the girls in the school.

The more you study, the _______ you will do on the test. (well)
The more you study, the better you will do on the test.

1. Cheetahs run the _________________ of all mammals. (fast)
2. We described our experiences as _______________ as we could. (vividly)
3. The more encores she sings, the ___________________ the audience applauds. (enthusiastically)
4. He practises the ___________________ of all the members of the team. (diligently)
5. The ___________ you study, the poorer your marks will be. (little)
6. He explains his ideas _____________________ than you do. (convincingly)
7. They wrote as _________________ as possible. (intelligibly)
8. Seagulls fly _______________ than ducks do. (well)
9. Birds of prey soar the _________________ of all birds. (impressively)
10. The _______________ you exercise, the stronger you will become. (much)
11. They have traveled as _________________ as possible. (widely)
12. She examined the material _________________ than I did. (thoroughly)

13. He explains the subject the ________________ of all the teachers in the school. (well)

14. Advanced skiers complete the course twice as ________________ as beginners. (rapidly)

15. I have written out the assignment ________________ than you have. (neatly)

16. The ________________ I walk, the more refreshed I feel. (far)

Answers

to Exercise 1:

1. duly 2. noisily 3. palely 4. comfortably 5. dogmatically 6. normally 7. slowly 8. steadily 9. dramatically 10. agilely 11. simply 12. shrilly 13. luckily 14. frantically 15. wholly 16. punctually 17. densely 18. solely 19. synthetically 20. readily

to Exercise 2:

1. straight 2. early 3. quickly 4. fast 5. cautiously 6. high 7. well 8. late 9. badly 10. little 11. annually 12. immediately 13. weekly 14. first 15. suitably

to Exercise 3:

1. successfully 2. successful 3. light 4. lightly 5. clearly 6. clear 7. strongly 8. strong 9. cheerfully 10. tranquil 11. efficiently 12. recent 13. responsibly 14. Heavy 15. quietly 16. dark

to Exercise 4:

1. wide 2. widely 3. favorable 4. Favorably 5. previously 6. previous 7. Unusual 8. extremely 9. Relatively 10. humorous 11. frequently 12. frequent 13. hot 14. hotly

to Exercise 5:

1. briefly 2. happy 3. attentively 4. sleepy 5. sleepily 6. quickly 7. dark 8. excited 9. immediately 10. sweet 11. eagerly

to Exercise 6:

1. The train travels faster than the bus. 2. In the morning, the sun shone more brightly than in the afternoon. 3. The footpath runs straighter than the road. 4. Joe sings worse than Rick. 5. I got up earlier than you did. 6. The wild deer came nearer than I had expected. 7. Her son plays the violin better than her daughter does. 8. Captain Cook sailed farther than Columbus did. 9. You are later than the others. 10. The stream flows

more swiftly than the river. 11. She studies harder than her classmates. 12. The project was completed more successfully than we had anticipated.

to Exercise 7:
1. As the evening wore on, we spoke less and less animatedly. 2. The spectators cheered more and more loudly. 3. The chirping of the crickets disturbed us less and less. 4. As he grew older, he walked farther and farther. 5. The new shuttle service functioned more and more reliably. 6. The sun shone less and less intensely. 7. As I became tired, I wrote more and more slowly. 8. The boy learned to read better and better.

to Exercise 8:
1. She understood the lesson the most readily of all the pupils in the class. 2. This kite flies the worst of all the kites I have ever made. 3. That train leaves the earliest of all the trains departing from this station. 4. Last night it snowed the hardest of any night in the year. 5. The potato field produces the least of all the fields on the farm. 6. This highway runs the straightest of all the highways in the country. 7. She speaks the most quietly of all the people I know. 8. The bass sings the lowest of all the singers. 9. Eagles fly the highest of all the birds which live in the mountains. 10. She prepares meals the best of all the students in the class. 11. They regard his proposal the most favorably of all the proposals they have received. 12. Bill ran the farthest of all the boys. 13. His arrow came the nearest to the center of the target. 14. This bus travels the most slowly of all the buses.

to Exercise 9:
1. fastest 2. vividly 3. more enthusiastically 4. most diligently 5. less 6. more convincingly 7. intelligibly 8. better 9. most impressively 10. more 11. widely 12. more thoroughly 13. best 14. rapidly 15. more neatly 16. farther

***

4. Determiners

1. Paying attention to whether reference is being made to a group of two objects, or a group of more than two objects, for each of the following sentences fill in the blank with the correct word chosen from the pair given in brackets. For example:

There are two trees on the lawn. _____ of them are spruce trees. (All, Both)

There are two trees on the lawn. Both of them are spruce trees.

I had three pencils. Have you seen ___ of them? (any, either)

I had three pencils. Have you seen any of them? (any, either)

There are four bushes in the garden, but _____ of them are rhododendrons. (neither, none)

There are four bushes in the garden, but none of them are rhododendrons.

1. I have three winter coats, but _________ of them are new. (neither, none)

2. There are two umbrellas here, but _________ of them is mine. (neither, none)

3. He owns twelve cows. _________ of them are Jerseys. (All, Both)

4. She has painted dozens of pictures. Have you seen _________ of them? (any, either)

5. Amy and Beth are twins. They _________ play the guitar. (all, both)

6. Two people said "Hello" to me, but I did not recognize _________ of them. (any, either)

7. My wife and I _________ enjoy classical music. (all, both)

8. I found all of the questions difficult. Did you answer _________ of them correctly? (any, either)

9. I asked six different people, but _________ of them knew where Walnut Street was. (neither, none)

10. My friends and I would like to thank you for your hospitality. We _________ enjoyed ourselves very much. (all, both)

11. There are two public libraries in the city, but _________ of them is located close to where I live. (neither, none)

12. Two wrist watches were left here. Is __________ of them yours? (any, either)

13. He has three nephews. ________ of them have graduated from university. (All, Both)

14. I have two violins. You are welcome to use ________ of them. (any, either)

15. My aunt and uncle are ________ coming for a visit. (all, both)

16. George and Tom like playing chess together, but _________ of them likes to lose a game. (neither, none)

17. The bush is covered with blueberries. Are _________ of them ripe yet? (any, either)

18. I have read five books on the subject, but ________ of them were very helpful. (neither, none)

2. Paying attention to whether the singular or the plural form is correct, fill in the blanks with the correct words chosen from the pairs given in brackets. For example:

Several of my friends _____ present. (was, were)
Several of my friends were present.

One of his friends ____ absent. (was, were)
One of his friends was absent.

Each of the dogs pricked up ____ ears. (its, their)
Each of the dogs pricked up its ears.

All of the dogs pricked up _____ ears. (its, their)
All of the dogs pricked up their ears.

1. Each of her friends _________ a university degree. (has, have)

2. Many of the birds in this park _________ here throughout the year. (live, lives)

3. Both of the children wanted to finish _________ work early. (his, their)

4. Every writer should learn from _________ own experiences. (his or her, their)

5. Either of my daughters can lend you _________ skis. (her, their)

6. Few of her ideas ________ as intriguing as this one. (are, is)

7. All of the visitors expressed _________ thanks. (his or her, their)

8. Each of our customers ________ important. (are, is)

9. One of the canaries ate only half _________ food. (its, their)

10. Either of the routes __________ a good choice. (are, is)
11. Neither of the boys forgot __________ books. (his, their)
12. Both of the drawings _______ beautiful. (are, is)
13. Neither of my uncles __________ to us often. (write, writes)
14. Every girl clapped __________ hands. (her, their)

3. Paying attention to whether an adjective, pronoun or adverb is required, complete the following sentences by filling in the blanks with no, none or not, as appropriate. For example:

There is __ danger.
There is no danger.

_____ of the trees are evergreens.
None of the trees are evergreens.

It was ___ raining when I left home.
It was not raining when I left home.

1. There is __________ wind this morning.
2. I have _________ finished reading the book.
3. _________ of the children were late for school.
4. We did _________ tell anyone the secret.
5. I have _________ idea what time it is.
6. _________ of the streets have been plowed.
7. _________ bicycles are allowed on the grass.
8. He is _________ ready.
9. _________ harm was done.
10. There is _________ time to lose.
11. She is _________ expected to arrive until tomorrow.
12. _________ of the stores are open.

4. Rewrite the following sentences as negative statements, in which the word some is replaced by the word any. For example:

He has sold some apples.
He has not sold any apples.

I need to buy some shoes.
I do not need to buy any shoes.

1. I will make some salad.

2. We need some onions.
3. I have met some of your friends.
4. He has photographed some of the most beautiful parts of the city.
5. She wants to take some courses in Archaeology.
6. I recognized some of the students.
7. We have visited some of the offshore islands.
8. I have read some books by that author.
9. There is some danger involved.
10. I have some reservations about your plan.
11. They have interviewed some of the contestants.
12. She bought some of the books second-hand.

5. Rewrite each of the following sentences to express a negative meaning. Each sentence contains a word beginning with some. If the word beginning with some occurs at the beginning of the sentence, change the word beginning with some to the appropriate word or phrase beginning with no. For example:

Some of the coats are expensive.
None of the coats are expensive.

Someone is at home.
No one is at home.

If the word beginning with some occurs later in the sentence, change the sentence to a negative statement, and change the word beginning with some to the appropriate word beginning with any. For example:

I have some paper.
I do not have any paper.

I saw your glasses somewhere.
I did not see your glasses anywhere.

1. He has some relatives in the city.
2. I know someone here.
3. Some of us were surprised by the announcement.
4. I plan to go somewhere on my vacation.
5. Some tickets were sold this morning.
6. I heard someone playing the bagpipes.
7. I gave her some advice.
8. Something is wrong.
9. We bought something at the flea market.

10. They had some exciting adventures.
11. Someone offered to help me.
12. She knows someone working at the Library.
13. He lives somewhere near here.
14. Somebody left early.
15. I saw someone arriving by taxi.
16. Some books are missing.
17. I have something to do this afternoon.
18. Some of the magazines are worth reading.

6. Paying attention to the grammatical structure, complete each of the following sentences by filling in the blank with another, other, others or else, as appropriate. For example:

Would you like _________ cup of tea?
Would you like another cup of tea?

The ______ guests have already arrived.
The other guests have already arrived.

Five of the books were returned on time , but three _______ were overdue.
Five of the books were returned on time, but three others were overdue.

Who _____ was at the party?
Who else was at the party?

1. I want to borrow _____________ book from the library.
2. Three people moved out, and two _____________ moved in.
3. Who _____________ knows the secret?
4. There are several _____________ possibilities.
5. Where _____________ should I look?
6. Some students enjoyed the film, but _____________ did not.
7. He lives on the _____________ side of the lake.
8. I have _____________ idea.
9. _____________ people soon followed her example.
10. Do you know anyone _____________ here?
11. We are going to move to _____________ city.
12. Some birds feed on insects, while _____________ eat berries.
13. Somebody _____________ should have a turn now.
14. Few _____________ people attended the ceremony.

15. You may borrow this eraser. I have several ______________
16. What ______________ have you decided?

7. The following five sentences, labelled A to E, are identical except for the position of the word only:

   A. My only friend drew the picture of the child yesterday.
   B. My friend drew only the picture of the child yesterday.
   C. My friend drew the only picture of the child yesterday.
   D. My friend drew the picture of the only child yesterday.
   E. My friend drew the picture of the child only yesterday.

The meanings of the preceding five sentences are given in the five sentences below. For each sentence, fill in the blank with the letter (A to E) which corresponds to the sentence above which has the same meaning.

1. ___ My friend drew the one existing picture of the child yesterday.
2. ___ My friend drew nothing except the picture of the child yesterday.
3. ___ My friend drew the picture of the child as short a time ago as yesterday.
4. ___ The one friend that I have drew the picture of the child yesterday.
5. ___ My friend drew the picture of the one child in the family yesterday.

8. Explain the differences in meaning of the sentences in the following pairs.
1. There is a little butter left.   2. There is little butter left.
3. We encountered a few difficulties. 4. We encountered few difficulties.

9. Paying attention to the grammatical structure, for each of the following sentences, fill in the blank with such, so or too, as appropriate. In some of the sentences, the word that has been omitted. For example:
I saw _____ beautiful flowers, I wished I had brought my camera with me.
I saw such beautiful flowers, I wished I had brought my camera with me.
   The sun was __ bright that we had to wear sunglasses.
   The sun was so bright that we had to wear sunglasses.
   I saw __ many flowers that I could not identify them all.
   I saw so many flowers that I could not identify them all.

By the time I received your message, it was ___ late to call you.
By the time I received your message, it was too late to call you.

1. She sang _________ soothing lullabies that the baby was soon asleep.
2. He owned _________ many books that his walls were lined with bookcases.
3. The boys were ________ excited to sit still.
4. He has _________ varied interests, one never knows what he will do next.
5. They have _________ few enemies, they are accepted wherever they go.
6. The snow was _________ deep for us to walk across the field.
7. Yesterday I walked _________ far that I fell asleep immediately after supper.
8. I had _________ a good time at the party, I did not want to leave.
9. I see her _________ often that I feel I know her quite well.
10. The visibility was _________ poor for the mountains to be seen.
11. This is _________ an interesting book, I stayed up all night to read it.
12. This puzzle is _________ easy that a child could do it.
13. There was _________ much traffic, I could not cross the street.
14. She was _________ tired to watch the video.
15. They have ________ little furniture, it will be easy for them to move.

for CHAPTER 20. DETERMINERS
to Exercise 1:
1. none 2. neither 3. All 4. any 5. both 6. either 7. both 8. any 9. none 10. all 11. neither 12. either 13. All 14. either 15. both 16. neither 17. any 18. none

to Exercise 2:
1. has 2. live 3. their 4. his or her 5. her 6. are 7. their 8. is 9. its 10. is 11. his 12. are 13. writes 14. her

to Exercise 3:
1. no 2. not 3. None 4. not 5. no 6. None 7. No 8. not 9. No 10. no 11. not 12. None

to Exercise 4:
1. I will not make any salad. 2. We do not need any onions. 3. I have not met any of your friends. 4. He has not photographed any of the most beautiful parts of the city. 5. She does not want to take any courses in

Archaeology. 6. I did not recognize any of the students. 7. We have not visited any of the offshore islands. 8. I have not read any books by that author. 9. There is not any danger involved. 10. I do not have any reservations about your plan. 11. They have not interviewed any of the contestants. 12. She did not buy any of the books second-hand.

to Exercise 5:
1. He does not have any relatives in the city. 2. I do not know anyone here. 3. None of us were surprised by the announcement. 4. I do not plan to go anywhere on my vacation. 5. No tickets were sold this morning. 6. I did not hear anyone playing the bagpipes. 7. I did not give her any advice. 8. Nothing is wrong. 9. We did not buy anything at the flea market. 10. They did not have any exciting adventures. 11. No one offered to help me. 12. She does not know anyone working at the Library. 13. He does not live anywhere near here. 14. Nobody left early. 15. I did not see anyone arriving by taxi.

to Exercise 6:
1. another 2. others 3. else 4. other 5. else 6. others 7. other 8. another 9. Other 10. else 11. another 12. others 13. else 14. other 15. others 16. else

to Exercise 7:
1. C 2. B 3. E 4. A 5. D

to Exercise 8:
Meanings:
1. There is some butter left. 2. There is a very small amount of butter left. 3. We encountered some difficulties. 4. We encountered a very small number of difficulties. [The phrase "few difficulties" implies that the difficulties were unimportant.]

to Exercise 9:
1. such 2. so 3. too 4. such 5. so 6. too 7. so 8. such 9. so 10. too 11. such 12. so 13. so 14. too 15. so

**.

5. Pronouns

<u>Revision Works I</u>
1. For each of the following general statements, change all of the pronouns and possessive adjectives to agree with the pronoun given in brackets. For example:

> We must work to keep our environment healthy. (you)
>
> You must work to keep your environment healthy.
>
> You should always pay your income tax before the deadline. (one)
>
> One should always pay one's income tax before the deadline.
>
> One should not think only of oneself. (we)
>
> We should not think only of ourselves.

1. We should work in order to realize our ambitions. (one)
2. When you are overworked, you should try to give yourself time to relax. (we)
3. One can never be sure whether one's intuitions are correct. (you)
4. If one organizes one's time properly, one can accomplish a great deal. (we)
5. If you own property, you should protect yourself with a good insurance policy. (one)
6. We should never be afraid to state our views. (you)
7. One should try to educate oneself as well as possible. (you)
8. We should try to teach our children a sense of responsibility. (one)
9. One can choose one's friends, but one cannot choose one's relatives. (we)
10. We become mature when we learn to trust our own judgement. (you)
11. You learn from your mistakes. (we)
12. You should always treat your friends well. (one)

2. For each of the following sentences, fill in the blank with this or these. Use this to refer to a single person or thing, and use these to refer to more than one person or thing. For example:

_____ is her bicycle.

This is her bicycle.

Is _____ jacket too large?

Is this jacket too large?

_____ are our books.

These are our books.

_____ boots are warm.

These boots are warm.

1. Does _____ bus go downtown?
2. _____ are their suitcases.
3. _____ is his camera.
4. _____ trees are over one hundred years old.
5. Is _____ flower a daffodil?
6. _____ women will perform the skit.
7. _____ is the main entrance.
8. _____ lakes are very deep.
9. _____ is their school.
10. Are _____ radishes?

3. For each of the following sentences, fill in the blank with that or those. Use that to refer to a single person or thing, and use those to refer to more than one person or thing. For example:

_____ is a hovercraft.

That is a hovercraft.

_____ plane flies to Geneva.

That plane flies to Geneva.

_____ are peacocks.

Those are peacocks.

Are _____ children on vacation?

Are those children on vacation?

1. _____________ is his pen.
2. _____________ girls are Australian.
3. Has _____________ chair been painted?
4. _____________ watches are not expensive.
5. Does _____________ train usually arrive on time?
6. Was _____________ your friend?
7. _____________ are my cousins.
8. _____________ is a swan.
9. Do _____________ notebooks belong to you?
10. _____________ are the places we will visit.

4. Rewrite the following sentences, changing the subjects and verbs from the singular to the plural. For example:

Is this ready?
Are these ready?

This towel is fluffy.
These towels are fluffy.

That measures the temperature.
Those measure the temperature.

That pail is made of aluminum.
Those pails are made of aluminum.

1. This was finished last week.
2. Is that radiator working?
3. This picture is ours.
4. That has been completed.
5. This was designed by his aunt.
6. That does not need to be altered.
7. This table is made of wood.
8. Has that student seen the play?
9. This umbrella is new.

10. That river flows through the mountains.

5. Rewrite the following sentences, changing the subjects and verbs from the plural to the singular. For example:

These were on sale.
This was on sale.

Are these books interesting?
Is this book interesting?

Those have been useful.
That has been useful.

Those plays were popular.
That play was popular.

1. These were necessary.
2. Those colors are beautiful.
3. Are these bells too loud?
4. Have those been polished?
5. These shirts are clean.
6. Those windows are on the west side of the house.
7. Are these correct?
8. These boys like to play soccer.
9. Those are sufficient.
10. Those curtains are crimson.

6. Paying attention to correct word order, arrange each of the following sets of words to form questions beginning with interrogative pronouns which are the objects of the verbs. If necessary, add the auxiliary do, does or did. For example:

you, prefer, which
Which do you prefer?

they, heard, what

What did they hear?

we, have found, what
What have we found?

I, should choose, which
Which should I choose?

1. they, have decided, what
2. you, want, which
3. I, should wear, what
4. she, said, what
5. he, likes, what
6. you, are reading, what
7. one, can do, what
8. they, bought, which
9. he, will be studying, what
10. I, saw, which
11. she, expects, what
12. they, had discovered, what
13. it, costs, what
14. you, would have done, what
15. he, will submit, which
16. she, received, what

7. For each of the following sentences, fill in the blank with the interrogative pronoun who or whom. Use who if the pronoun is the subject of the verb, and use whom if the pronoun is the object of the verb or the object of a preposition. For example:

____ is there?
Who is there?

____ has been notified?
Who has been notified?

_____ are we expecting?

Whom are we expecting?

For _____ did you buy the flowers?
For whom did you buy the flowers?

1. _________ has read the book?
2. To _________ did he give the letter?
3. _________ is at the door?
4. _________ was awarded the prize?
5. _________ did he tell?
6. _________ answered the question correctly?
7. _________ does she like the best?
8. _________ would be the most suitable person for the job?
9. For _________ are they waiting?
10. _________ has been informed of the situation?
11. _________ can we ask?
12. _________ will be ready by eight o'clock?
13. _________ is watering the flowers?
14. _________ did you photograph?
15. _________ attended the meeting?
16. _________ was at the party?
17. _________ could be heard most easily?
18. _______ do you believe?
19. To _________ did you sell your car?
20. _______ will be waiting for us?

8. Paying attention to grammatically correct usage, for each of the following sentences, fill in the blank with who, whom or whose. In these sentences, use whose only as a possessive adjective, preceding a noun. For example:

____ is raking the leaves?
Who is raking the leaves?

_____ did you call?
Whom did you call?

To _____ was he speaking?

To whom was he speaking?

_______ bicycle is leaning against the steps?

Whose bicycle is leaning against the steps?

1. By _______ was this written?

2. _______ gloves are lying on the table?

3. _______ lives here?

4. _______ did they help?

5. _______ child is this?

6. _______ was allowed to enter the competition?

7. _______ handwriting is the most legible?

8. With _______ was she speaking?

9. _______ sang the song?

10. _______ does she know?

11. _______ shoes are these?

12. _______ will make the cake?

13. _______ was present?

14. _______ curiosity would not be aroused by such a tale?

15. _______ will he teach?

9. For each of the following sentences, fill in the blank with either what or which. For example:

_____ is happening?

What is happening?

_______ of my coats do you like the best?

Which of my coats do you like the best?

_____ a surprise!

What a surprise!

1. _________ time does the train leave?

2. _________ of the three schools do you attend?

3. _________ is your name?

4. ___________ a wonderful idea!

5. ___________ planet is larger, Jupiter or Saturn?

6. ___________ of your children is the cleverest?

7. ___________ a mess!

8. ___________ is your favorite dessert?

9. ___________ would you prefer, tea or coffee?

10. ___________ of these bicycles is yours?

10. Using the introductory phrase Please tell me, rewrite the following direct questions as indirect questions. Make sure that the subjects precede the verbs in the indirect questions. For example:

Who will choose the winners?

Please tell me who will choose the winners.

Whom did they choose?

Please tell me whom they chose.

For whom had you bought the present?

Please tell me for whom you had bought the present.

1. Who was selected?

2. Whom have you consulted?

3. To whom will she address the letter?

4. What did you accomplish?

5. Which boy opened the door?

6. To which cities has he traveled?

7. Which music did the orchestra perform?

8. For whose sake has he come?

9. What caused the delay?

10. Whose house did they visit?

11. Whose dog chased the cat?

12. Which books have you read?

11. Using the introductory phrase We will ask, and paying attention to the correct word order, rewrite the following direct questions as indirect questions. For example:

Who is that?

We will ask who that is.

What was that noise?

We will ask what that noise was.

Who is here?

We will ask who is here.

1. What is this?
2. Who was there?
3. Who was first?
4. Which was it?
5. Which is ready?
6. Who is she?
7. Whose book is this?
8. Whose work is ready?
9. Who was right?
10. Who was that singer?
11. Which students are here?
12. Who were they?

12. Paying attention to correct word order, use the phrases given in brackets to rewrite the following direct questions as indirect questions. For example:

Who baked the cake? (They will ask)

They will ask who baked the cake.

Whom did you tell? (We want to know)

We want to know whom you told.

To which student had she given the prize? (Did you find out)

Did you find out to which student she had given the prize?

Who was that? (Please tell me)

Please tell me who that was.

1. Who are you? (I want to know)
2. Who swept the floor? (We will ask)
3. For whom did you organize the party? (Tell me)
4. Whom had they met? (I asked)
5. At what time will you reach the station? (I need to know)
6. Which horse won the race? (They will ask)
7. Whose answer is correct? (I wonder)
8. Which hill did they climb? (We will ask)
9. What do you mean? (Please tell us)
10. What made that noise? (I wonder)
11. Which students are ready? (Will you tell me)
12. For what purpose has he called the meeting? (Ask him)
13. Whom can we trust? (I am not sure)
14. Whose work was chosen? (They will ask)
15. Which book has she ordered? (We will find out)
16. Who am I? (Do you know)

13. For each of the following sentences, underline the relative clause, and indicate whether the clause is defining or non-defining. For example:

The sky, which was perfectly clear, was covered with stars.

The sky, which was perfectly clear, was covered with stars. [Non-defining]

The shoes which are by the bed are mine.
The shoes which are by the bed are mine. [Defining]

1. The new appliances, which are quite expensive, will be on sale next week.
2. The picture which is hanging on the wall was painted by our friend.
3. The people who own the hotel have a great deal of business experience.
4. His uncle, who sings in the choir, is a friend of my father.
5. The building, which is in excellent repair, is over two hundred years old.
6. The door that is open leads to the study.
7. My friend, who is coming for a visit, is anxious to meet you.
8. Did you see the exhibition which was held here last week?

14. Paying attention to grammatically correct usage, for each of the following sentences, fill in the blank with who, whom or whose. For example:

The person _____ owns the bookstore is my friend.

The person who owns the bookstore is my friend.

The singer to _____ we gave the bouquet will be performing again tonight.

The singer to whom we gave the bouquet will be performing again tonight.

The contestants _____ names were announced should prepare to start.

The contestants whose names were announced should prepare to start.

1. My best friend, _____ I see every day, always has something new to tell me.
2. Most students _____ live in residence find it easy to make friends.
3. Our neighbors, to _____ we lent our lawnmower, are conscientious and considerate.
4. The volunteers, _____ enthusiasm was obvious, finished the work quickly.
5. The musicians _____ we heard yesterday have played together for many years.
6. Parents _____ children do well in school usually consider themselves fortunate.
7. Children _____ like music are often good at mathematics.
8. The student to _____ the prize was awarded had an impressive record.
9. My friend, _____ I visited last week, is taking a holiday soon.
10. The class treasurer, to _____ we gave the money, announced the balance of the account.
11. The engineers _____ designed the building received an award.
12. The townspeople, _____ pride in their community is well-known, raised enough money to build a new town hail.

15. Paying attention to grammatically correct usage, for each of the following sentences, fill in the blank with who, whom or which. Use who or whom for antecedents which refer to persons, and use which for antecedents which refer to things. For example:

The woman ___ borrowed the books is a librarian.
The woman who borrowed the books is a librarian.
The key _____ opens this door is difficult to turn.
The key which opens this door is difficult to turn.
The children ____ we met are well-behaved.
The children whom we met are well-behaved.
The story _____ you heard is true.
The story which you heard is true.
The man to ____ you told the news is my brother.
The man to whom you told the news is my brother.

I have not yet received the letter to _____ you refer.
I have not yet received the letter to which you refer.

1. The window _________ is open is the kitchen window.
2. The girl _________ recited the poem is my niece.
3. The woman to _________ we were introduced was quite helpful.
4. The opportunity to _________ she owed her success came unexpectedly.
5. The man _________ they trusted was unreliable.
6. The book _________ you read is the best book by that author.
7. The Pacific Ocean, _________ may have been crossed by raft during the Stone Age, is the world's largest ocean.
8. His mother, _________ he visited frequently, ran her own business.
9. The boy, _________ was friendly and intelligent, soon found work.
10. Her husband, to _________ she told the story, was just as surprised as I was.
11. The pictures, _________ were taken in Algeria, were very striking.
12. The newspaper to _________ we subscribe is delivered regularly.

Answers

 to Exercise 1:

1. One should work in order to realize one's ambitions. 2. When we are overworked we should try to give ourselves time to relax. 3. You can never be sure whether your intuitions are correct. 4. If we organize our time properly, we can accomplish a great deal. 5. If one owns property, one should protect oneself with a good insurance policy. 6. You should never be afraid to state your views. 7. You should try to educate yourself as well as possible. 8. One should try to teach one's children a sense of responsibility. 9. We can choose our friends, but we cannot choose our relatives. 10. You become mature when you learn to trust your own judgement. 11. We learn from our mistakes. 12. One should always treat one's friends well.

 to Exercise 2:

1. this 2. These 3. This 4. These 5. this 6. These 7. This 8. These 9. This 10. these

 to Exercise 3:

1. That 2. Those 3. that 4. Those 5. that 6. that 7. Those 8. That 9. those 10. Those

 to Exercise 4:

1. These were finished last week. 2. Are those radiators working? 3. These pictures are ours. 4. Those have been completed. 5. These were designed by his aunt. 6. Those do not need to be altered. 7. These tables are made of wood. 8. Have those students seen the play? 9. These umbrellas are new. 10. Those rivers flow through the mountains.

 to Exercise 5:

1. This was necessary. 2. That color is beautiful. 3. Is this bell too loud? 4. Has that been polished? 5. This shirt is clean. 6. That window is on the west side of the house. 7. Is this correct? 8. This boy likes to play soccer. 9. That is sufficient. 10. That curtain is crimson.

 to Exercise 6:

1. What have they decided? 2. Which do you want? 3. What should I wear? 4. What did she say? 5. What does he like? 6. What are you reading? 7. What can one do? 8. Which did they buy? 9. What will he be studying? 10. Which did I see? 11. What does she expect? 12. What had they discovered? 13. What does it cost? 14. What would you have done? 15. Which will he submit? 16. What did she receive?

to Exercise 7:
1. Who 2. whom 3. Who 4. Who 5. Whom 6. Who 7. Whom 8. Who 9. whom 10. Who 11. Whom 12. Who 13. Who 14. Whom 15. Who 16. Who 17. Who 18. Whom 19. whom 20. Who

to Exercise 8:
1. whom 2. Whose 3. Who 4. Whom 5. Whose 6. Who 7. Whose 8. whom 9. Who 10. Whom 11. Whose 12. Who 13. Who 14. Whose 15. Whom

to Exercise 9:
1. What 2. Which 3. What 4. What 5. Which 6. Which 7. What 8. What 9. Which 10. Which

to Exercise 10:
1. Please tell me who was selected. 2. Please tell me whom you have consulted. 3. Please tell me to whom she will address the letter. 4. Please tell me what you accomplished. 5. Please tell me which boy opened the door. 6. Please tell me to which cities he has traveled. 7. Please tell me which music the orchestra performed. 8. Please tell me for whose sake he has come. 9. Please tell me what caused the delay. 10. Please tell me whose house they visited. 11. Please tell me whose dog chased the cat. 12. Please tell me which books you have read.

to Exercise 11:
1. We will ask what this is. 2. We will ask who was there. 3. We will ask who was first. 4. We will ask which it was. 5. We will ask which is ready. 6. We will ask who she is. 7. We will ask whose book this is. 8. We will ask whose work is ready. 9. We will ask who was right. 10. We

will ask who that singer was. 11. We will ask which students are here. 12. We will ask who they were.

to Exercise 12:
1. I want to know who you are. 2. We will ask who swept the floor. 3. Tell me for whom you organized the party. 4. I asked whom they had met. 5. I need to know at what time you will reach the station. 6. They will ask which horse won the race. 7. I wonder whose answer is correct. 8. We will ask which hill they climbed. 9. Please tell us what you mean. 10. I wonder what made that noise. 11. Will you tell me which students are ready? 12. Ask him for what purpose he has called the meeting. 13. I am not sure whom we can trust. 14. They will ask whose work was chosen. 15. We will find out which book she has ordered. 16. Do you know who I am?

to Exercise 13:
1. The new appliances, which are quite expensive, will be on sale next week. [Non-defining] 2. The picture which is hanging on the wall was painted by our friend. [Defining] 3. The people who own the hotel have a great deal of business experience. [Defining] 4. His uncle, who sings in the choir, is a friend of my father. [Non-defining] 5. The building, which is in excellent repair, is over two hundred years old. [Non-defining] 6. The door that is open leads to the study. [Defining] 7. My friend, who is coming for a visit, is anxious to meet you. [Non-defining] 8. Did you see the exhibition which was held here last week? [Defining]

to Exercise 14:
1. whom 2. who 3. whom 4. whose 5. whom 6. whose 7. who 8. whom 9. whom 10. whom 11. who 12. whose

to Exercise 15:
1. which 2. who 3. whom 4. which 5. whom 6. which 7. which 8. whom 9. who 10. whom 11. which 12. which

Revision Works II

1. In the sentences below, fill in the blanks with the personal pronouns which agree with the underlined antecedents. For example:

The man walked slowly, because __ was carrying a heavy parcel.
The man walked slowly, because he was carrying a heavy parcel.

Although ___ knew it was dangerous, the girl wanted to ride the horse.
Although she knew it was dangerous, the girl wanted to ride the horse.

The tree is very tall, but __ does not give much shade.
The tree is very tall, but it does not give much shade.

She and I are not coming, because __ are too busy.
She and I are not coming, because we are too busy.

Doughnuts taste best when ____ are fresh.
Doughnuts taste best when they are fresh.

1. The children are happy because _______ have a holiday today.
2. My father and I had planned to visit the park, but since it was raining _______ decided not to go.
3. This chair is valuable because _______ is so old.
4. The woman is pleased because _______ has found work.
5. Until _______ retired, their father managed a business.
6. After the apples have been cut up, _______ should be sprinkled with cinnamon.
7. Because her husband used to study music, _______ knows how to play several musical instruments.
8. My neighbor and I like to go shopping together, so that _______ can help each other choose what to buy.
9. Her daughter likes to study, because _______ finds the work interesting.
10. The car is in good condition, but _______ needs a new muffler.

2. Paying attention to the meanings of the sentences below, fill in each blank with he, she, it, we or they, and underline the antecedent of the pronoun. For example:

My grandfather does not want to retire, because __ likes his work.

My grandfather does not want to retire, because he likes his work.

His wife will be there if __ can find a baby-sitter.
His wife will be there if she can find a baby-sitter.

The bicycle must be repaired before __ can be ridden again.
The bicycle must be repaired before it can be ridden again.

My cousin and I live in different towns, but __ write to each other often.
My cousin and I live in different towns, but we write to each other often.

The bananas are quite soft, but ___ can be used in banana cake.
The bananas are quite soft, but they can be used in banana cake.

1. When the moon is full, _______ rises just as the sun sets.
2. Tracy and I like spending time together, because ________ share many interests.
3. When my uncle was young, ________ enjoyed playing soccer.
4. The students worked hard, because ________ were anxious to complete the assignment.
5. When the lady entered the hotel, _______ asked to speak with the manager.
6. The man was surprised when _______ heard the news.
7. My friend and I had to leave early so that ______ could catch the bus.
8. I liked the picture so much that I had _______ framed.
9. Your grandmother is old, but _______ is still beautiful.
10. The boats look picturesque when ________ are tied up in the harbor.

3. The underlined pronouns in the following sentences are ambiguous, since it is not obvious to which antecedents they refer. For each sentence, first underline the two possible antecedents of the pronoun. Then make the sentence unambiguous by choosing one of the antecedents and repeating it, instead of using the pronoun. When repeating the antecedent, it is also necessary to repeat any words which modify it. For example:
I invited the woman and her sister, but she could not come.
I invited the woman and her sister, but her sister could not come.
or I invited the woman and her sister, but the woman could not come.

George gave Tom a book. Then he went home.
George gave Tom a book. Then Tom went home.
or George gave Tom a book. Then George went home.

The boys challenged the girls to a game, but they did not play well.
The boys challenged the girls to a game, but the boys did not play well.
or The boys challenged the girls to a game, but the girls did not play well.

1. I used your pen to finish the assignment, but then I lost it.
2. My father told my uncle the story, but he did not believe it.
3. When the students met the teachers for the first time, they were not sure what to expect.
4. The girl was dressed like her mother, except that she was not wearing a hat.
5. The man had arranged to meet his son at four o'clock, but he was late.
6. The box was the same size as the trunk, but it was much heavier.
7. The lady wanted to visit my aunt, but she had to leave town unexpectedly.
8. The riders slowed down their horses because they were growing tired.
9. The butterfly was sitting close to the flower, but it could not be seen in the photograph.
10. The cups were supposed to match the saucers, but they were a lighter shade of blue.

4. Rewrite each of the following sentences, using the construction with the pronoun it, followed by the verb, followed by an infinitive. For example:

Traveling by ship was quite relaxing.
It was quite relaxing to travel by ship.

Finding the right path could take a long time.
It could take a long time to find the right path.

1. Paying close attention can be crucial.
2. Crossing the mountains would be very difficult.
3. Learning everything was not easy.
4. Skiing down the mountain was exciting.
5. Walking on a glacier can be dangerous.
6. Visiting Rome was a wonderful experience.

5. For each of the following sentences, fill in the blank with the personal pronoun which agrees with the underlined word. The objective case must be used, since the pronouns in these sentences are the objects of verbs. For example:

 I am looking for the post office. Can you help __?
 I am looking for the post office. Can you help me?

 Since you are new here, I will show ___ the way.
 Since you are new here, I will show you the way.

 If my father is at home, I will ask ___ what to do.
 If my father is at home, I will ask him what to do.

 My aunt and uncle invited me to visit ___ .
 My aunt and uncle invited me to visit them.

1. Because she is your friend, I offered to help _______ .
2. I wish someone would tell _______ the answer.
3. They look familiar. I am sure we have met _______ before.
4. If you are ready, we will drive _______ home.
5. We would like you to call _______ .
6. He is our neighbor. We have known _______ for years.
7. This is the book I need. May I borrow _______ ?
8. If you like, I will call _______ when we arrive.
9. We were surprised they remembered _______ .
10. That man waved to us, but I do not recognize _______ .
11. I think they expect _______ to come.
12. The piano is out of tune, but I am having _______ tuned tomorrow.
13. Will she mind if I ask _______ a question?
14. The beans will grow faster if you water _______ .

6. For each of the following sentences, fill in the blank with the personal pronoun which agrees with the underlined word. Use the subjective case if the pronoun is the subject of a verb, and use the objective case if the pronoun is the object of a verb. For example:

 They invited me to come, but __ did not have time.
 They invited me to come, but I did not have time.

 Just after we had mailed you the letter, ___ called us.

Just after we had mailed you the letter, you called us.

That boy is quite friendly. I like ___.
That boy is quite friendly. I like him.

He offered to lend me two books, but I had read ___ already.
He offered to lend me two books, but I had read them already.

1. I saw your brother after school. ______ lent me his bicycle.
2. Would you like me to help ______ ?
3. My friend and I expect the woman to call ______.
4. If I am ready in time, ______ will meet you there.
5. This woman is one of our relatives, ______ is my husband's cousin.
6. Her grandfather is a wise man. Everybody respects ______.
7. The chimney is old. ______ needs to be repaired.
8. My sister likes sports. We should invite ______ to join us.
9. Those people are your new neighbors. Have you met ______ yet?
10. She and I will call you if ______ are late.
11. I waited for you for twenty minutes, but ______ did not come.
12. The camera was heavy, but he carried ______ everywhere he went.
13. Some ducks swim underwater when ______ are searching for food.
14. I waved to you. Did you see ______ ?

7. Paying attention to the case of the personal pronouns, rewrite each of the following sentences so that the meaning is reversed. For example:
    We gave them the pen.
    They gave us the pen.

    I like you.
    You like me.

1. She helped us.
2. He asked them to come.
3. I recognized her.
4. You warned me.
5. We reminded them to call.
6. They told him the truth.
7. She invited us for tea.
8. He offered me a sandwich.

8. Fill in each blank with either the subjective case or the objective case of the pronoun given in brackets. Use the subjective case if the pronoun follows the verb to be. Otherwise, use the objective case. For example:

That is ___. (he)
That is he.

We remember ___. (he)
We remember him.

It was ___ who did it. (we)
It was we who did it.

He threw ___ the ball. (we)
He threw us the ball.

1. It was _______. (I)
2. Please hand _______ the book. (I)
3. I told _______ the secret. (she)
4. It was _______ who was here. (she)
5. It was _______ who knew the answer. (they)
6. Let _______ go. (they)
7. This is _______. (he)
8. I knew _______ before. (he)
9. Those were _______. (they)
10. It is _______ who will be there. (we)

9. For each of the following sentences, fill in the blank with the personal pronoun which agrees with the underlined word. The objective case must be used, since the pronouns in these sentences are the objects of prepositions. For example:

I want you to address the letter to ___.
I want you to address the letter to me.

This jar is the largest. Rice was stored in ___.
This jar is the largest. Rice was stored in it.

The girl was shy, but we had an enjoyable conversation with ___.
The girl was shy, but we had an enjoyable conversation with her.

We went to the post office, but there was no mail for ___.
We went to the post office, but there was no mail for us.

1. They want us to go with ______.
2. I would like you to wrap this gift for ______.
3. She thinks we are talking about ______.
4. The wall was so high that I could not see over ______.
5. Your nephew wants us to write to ______.
6. You should ask them to send it to ______.
7. Nancy and I would like you to come with ______.
8. He asked us to wait for ______.
9. I would be grateful if you would explain this to ______.
10. Because you were late, we saved some food for ______.
11. We told you that the costumes were designed by ______.
12. The swans were so beautiful that we wrote a song about ______.
13. The car is worth more than you paid for ______.
14. Your daughter wants me to read to ______.

10. For each of the following sentences, fill in the blank with the personal pronoun which agrees with the underlined word. Use the subjective case if the pronoun is the subject of a verb, and use the objective case if the pronoun is the object of a verb or the object of a preposition. For example:

They looked at me, but ___ did not recognize them.
They looked at me, but I did not recognize them.

We told you what would happen, but ___ did not listen.
We told you what would happen, but you did not listen.

We saw them, but they did not see ___.
We saw them, but they did not see us.

They asked us a question, but we could not tell ____ the answer.
They asked us a question, but we could not tell them the answer.

Their son did not know the way, but we pointed it out to ___.
Their son did not know the way, but we pointed it out to him.

The girl is so mischievous, we do not know what to do with ___.
The girl is so mischievous, we do not know what to do with her.

1. His father works hard. ______ is a doctor.
2. Because the woman seemed friendly, we asked ______ for directions.

3. The cupboards are so full, we cannot put anything else into ______.
4. You will be surprised if we beat ______ in the race.
5. Have you been looking for me? ______ had to run an errand.
6. My niece wants us to send the photographs to ______.
7. We have invited them to visit ______.
8. The store was open, but we did not have time to go into ______.
9. She will be angry if we make fun of ______.
10. You and I are good friends, ______ hardly ever argue.
11. Your son-in-law asked us to describe it to ______.
12. The windows are very stiff. We open ______ only in the summer.
13. The basket is heavy. ______ is full of oranges.
14. Your husband does not like anyone to contradict ______.
15. I hope you were not anxious about ______.
16. Would you like me to mail the information to ______
17. The leaves rustled in the breeze, ______ were already starting to change color.
18. The road was long, but we followed ______ to the end.
19. I asked him to tell ______ the time.
20. You will enjoy yourself if ______ come to the concert.
21. We want you to wait for ______.

11. Fill in each blank with the possessive adjective which agrees with the underlined antecedent. For example:

I am looking for __ keys.
I am looking for my keys.

The lady left ___ gloves on the counter.
The lady left her gloves on the counter.

Personal pronouns must agree with ______ antecedents.
Personal pronouns must agree with their antecedents.

1. I opened ______ book.
2. Did the man finish ______ work?
3. The bear is licking ______ paws.
4. Please show us to ______ seats.
5. She has already purchased ______ ticket.
6. Have you heard from ______ friends recently?
7. The students live near ______ school.
8. The gentleman would like to have ______ watch repaired.
9. We eat ______ breakfast at the same time every morning.

10. That woman always walks _________ dog in the park.
11. I would like to renew _________ subscription.
12. The eagle was holding something in _________ claws.
13. Will you give me _________ address?
14. The gymnasts asked _________ coach for advice.

12. For each of the following sentences, fill in the blank with the possessive adjective which agrees with the noun or pronoun shown in brackets. For example:

_____ barking kept us awake. (the dog)
Its barking kept us awake.

_____ arriving on time was fortunate. (we)
Our arriving on time was fortunate.

______ swooping and darting was a sign that it would rain. (the swallows)
Their swooping and darting was a sign that it would rain.

1. _________ following the guidelines was a good idea. (you)
2. _________ agreeing to forward the mail was helpful. (the students)
3. _________ answering the questions so easily was unexpected. (he)
4. _________ driving the car saved a great deal of time. (I)
5. _________ speaking so forcefully impressed the audience. (the woman)
6. _________ entering the race was intended as a gesture of goodwill. (we)
7. _________ chiming told us the time. (the clock)

13. Fill in each blank with the possessive pronoun which agrees with the underlined antecedent. For example:

If you cannot find your pen, I will lend you ____.
If you cannot find your pen, I will lend you mine.

I failed my exams, but my brother passed ___.
I failed my exams, but my brother passed his.

Their umbrellas are rather tattered, but we have mended ____.
Their umbrellas are rather tattered, but we have mended ours.

1. Your coat may be warm, but I think _________ is more elegant.

2. Because I had no gloves, my niece offered me _______.

3. I forgot to bring my camera. Did you bring _______.

4. When I lost my map, your son lent me _______.

5. They discarded their old telephone directories, but we kept _______.

6. We have not planted our peas yet, but the farmers have planted _______ already.

7. I never cut my hair, but my sister cuts _______ once a month.

8. The neighbors' children are very independent, but we have to help _______.

9. We store our bicycles in the shed, but they leave _______ outside.

10. I water my plants every day, but you never water _______.

11. Although she likes her school, I prefer _______.

12. My niece studies for all her tests, but my nephew refuses to study for _______.

14. Fill in each blank with either the possessive adjective or the possessive pronoun which agrees with the underlined antecedent. Remember that the possessive adjective must precede a noun or gerund, whereas the possessive pronoun is used independently. For example:

Last night I wrote to __ sister.
Last night I wrote to my sister.

I thought the book was yours, but in fact, it was ____.
I thought the book was yours, but in fact, it was mine.

She has ordered ___ tickets in advance.
She has ordered her tickets in advance.

Although they do not know it yet, the prize is ______.
Although they do not know it yet, the prize is theirs.

The rain continued ___ pattering on the roof.
The rain continued its pattering on the roof.

1. I always enjoy _______ vacation.

2. I mailed my letter. Did you mail _______?

3. He is eager to try out _______ skis.

4. I am sure _______ handling of the situation was correct.

5. I rarely use a car, but they drive _______ everywhere.

6. My aunt visits _______ cousins once a year.

7. We are proud of _______ record.

8. I have never met your children. Have you met _______?
9. The gate swung noiselessly on _______ hinges.
10. I have received my diploma, but she has not yet received _______.
11. Have you filled out _______ application?
12. The bird continued _______ twittering long after dusk.
13. They are going to sublet _______ apartment.
14. I got my driver's license last month, but he got _______ a year ago.
15. Most businesses try to expand, but we have kept _______ small.
16. They saw _______ friend on television.
17. I finished my assignment yesterday. Have you finished _______?

15. For each of the following sentences, fill in the blank with the reflexive pronoun which agrees with the underlined word. For example:
    I found _______ in a difficult situation.
    I found myself in a difficult situation.

    The children warmed _______ in front of the fire.
    The children warmed themselves in front of the fire.

1. He should take better care of _______.
2. You may help _______.
3. I saw it _______.
4. She likes to involve _______ in community affairs.
5. We could see _______ reflected in the mirror.
6. The bird perched _______ on the window sill.
7. The students found the solution _______.
8. You _______ must decide what to do.
9. The teenagers amused _______ by telephoning their friends.
10. We _______ were surprised at the news.
11. He likes to hear _______ talk.
12. She prides _______ on her ability to speak French.
13. I told _______ not to lose hope.
14. The fox hid _______ under a bush.

Answers
to Exercise 1:
1. they 2. we 3. it 4. she 5. he 6. they 7. he 8. we 9. she 10. it

to Exercise 2:
1. it 2. we 3. he 4. they 5. she 6. he 7. we 8. it 9. she 10. they

to Exercise 3:
1. your pen or the assignment 2. my father or my uncle 3. the students or the teachers 4. the girl or her mother 5. the man or his son 6. the box or the trunk 7. the lady or my aunt 8. the riders or their horses 9. the butterfly or the flower 10. the cups or the saucers

to Exercise 4:
1. It can be crucial to pay close attention. 2. It would be very difficult to cross the mountains. 3. It was not easy to learn everything. 4. It was exciting to ski down the mountain. 5. It can be dangerous to walk on a glacier. 6. It was a wonderful experience to visit Rome.

to Exercise 5:
1. her 2. me 3. them 4. you 5. us 6. him 7. it 8. you 9. us 10. him 11. me 12. it 13. her 14. them

to Exercise 6:
1. He 2. you 3. us 4. I 5. She 6. him 7. It 8. her 9. them 10. we 11. you 12. it 13. they 14. me

to Exercise 7:
1. We helped her. 2. They asked him to come. 3. She recognized me. 4. I warned you. 5. They reminded us to call. 6. He told them the truth. 7. We invited her for tea. 8. I offered him a sandwich.

to Exercise 8:
1. I 2. me 3. her 4. she 5. they 6. them 7. he 8. him 9. they 10. we

to Exercise 9:
1. them 2. me 3. her 4. it 5. him 6. you 7. us 8. him 9. me 10. you 11. us 12. them 13. it 14. her

to Exercise 10:
1. He 2. her 3. them 4. you 5. I 6. her 7. us 8. it 9. her 10. We 11. him 12. them 13. It 14. him 15. me 16. you 17. They 18. it 19. me 20. you 21. us

to Exercise 11:
1. my 2. his 3. its 4. our 5. her 6. your 7. their 8. his 9. our 10. her 11. my 12. its 13. your 14. their

to Exercise 12:

1. Your 2. Their 3. His 4. My 5. Her 6. Our 7. Its

to Exercise 13:
1. mine 2. hers 3. yours 4. his 5. ours 6. theirs 7. hers 8. ours 9. theirs 10. yours 11. mine 12. his

to Exercise 14:
1. my 2. yours 3. his 4. my 5. theirs 6. her 7. our 8. mine 9. its 10. hers 11. your 12. its 13. their 14. his 15. ours 16. their 17. yours

to Exercise 15:
1. himself 2. yourself or yourselves 3. myself 4. herself 5. ourselves 6. itself 7. themselves 8. yourself or yourselves 9. themselves 10. ourselves 11. himself 12. herself 13. myself 14. itself

***.

6. Naming Words

<u>Revision Works</u>

1. For each of the following phrases, change the noun indicating possession from the singular to the plural. For example:

    the man's experiences   the men's experiences
    the doctor's office   the doctors' office

1. the musician's instruments
2. the child's adventures
3. the animal's habitat
4. the workman's instructions
5. the ship's passengers
6. the pilot's vacation
7. the officer's friends

2. For each of the following phrases, change the noun indicating possession from the plural to the singular. For example:

    the owners' permission   the owner's permission
    the mice's nest   the mouse's nest

1. the surgeons' skill
2. the policemen's warning
3. the directors' decision
4. the secretaries' correspondence
5. the eagles' aerie
6. the women's errand
7. the managers' assistants

3. Show the relationships between the possessors and the things possessed by using the ending 's or the word of, as appropriate. For example:

Possessor	Thing Possessed	Indicating Possession
visitor	map	the visitor's map
stairs	top	the top of the stairs

	Possessor	Thing Possessed
1.	woman	scarf
2.	children	
3.	door	color
4.	concert	beginning
5.	instructor	advice
6.	deficit	size
7.	girl	tricycle

8.	building	height
9.	hen	cackling
10.	boy	parents
11.	chair	arm
12.	street	length

4. For each of the following sentences, fill in the blank with either the singular or the plural verb form shown in brackets. Be prepared to explain why the form you have chosen is correct. For example:

The committee _____ put forward a new proposal. (has, have)
The committee has put forward a new proposal.

In this example the committee is acting as a whole. Therefore a singular verb is used.

The committee _____ disagreed on what policy to adopt. (has, have)
The committee have disagreed on what policy to adopt.

In this example, the members of the committee are acting as individuals. Therefore a plural verb is used.

Two tons of coal __ required. (is, are)
Two tons of coal is required.

In this example, the amount two tons is considered as a whole. Therefore a singular verb is used.

1. The crew _______ preparing the ship to go to sea. (is, are)
2. The crew _______ different levels of experience. (has, have)
3. Two pounds of butter _____ too much. (is, are)
4. The class _____ not agree on what should be done. (does, do)
5. The class _____ contributed eighty dollars to the cause. (has, have)
6. Three ounces of gold _____ worth more than three ounces of copper. (is, are)
7. The group _____ decided to hold a meeting once a month. (has, have)
8. The group _____ varied backgrounds. (has, have)
9. Fifty cents _____ the regular price. (was, were)
10. Six dollars _____ been collected. (has, have)

5. For each of the following sentences, fill in the blank with either the singular or the plural verb form shown in brackets. Be prepared to explain why the form you have chosen is correct. For example:

Both the sky and the water ___ blue. (is, are)
Both the sky and the water are blue.
The two nouns of a compound subject with and refer to two different things. Therefore a plural verb is used.

Wilson and Brothers __ a company dealing in antiques. (is, are)
Wilson and Brothers is a company dealing in antiques.
The two nouns of a compound subject with and refer to one thing. Therefore a singular verb is used.

Either Richard or his uncle __ sure to be there. (is, are)
Either Richard or his uncle is sure to be there.
A singular noun is nearest the verb in a compound subject with or. Therefore a singular verb is used.

Neither the main office nor the branch offices ___ open. (is, are)
Neither the main office nor the branch offices are open.
A plural noun is nearest the verb in a compound subject with nor. Therefore a plural verb is used.

1. Either a large jar or two small jars ______ required. (is, are)
2. Neither the road nor the highway _______ to Pictou. (leads, lead)
3. A duck and a heron ______ in the pond. (is, are)
4. Either spring or summer ______ a good time to visit our region. (is, are)
5. Both the bow and the arrows _______ to the instructor. (belongs, belong)
6. Neither the boats nor the raft ______ in good repair. (was, were)
7. Milk and porridge ______ a nutritious breakfast. (is, are)
8. Either his brother or his sister _______ here. (lives, live)
9. Both boys and girls ______ eligible to apply. (is, are)
10. Neither threats nor persuasion ______ proved effective. (has, have)
11. Bread and potatoes ______ staple foods in many parts of North America. (is, are)
12. Either the twins or their friend ______ in the class. (is, are)
13. The Picts and the Martyrs ______ a book I would like to read again. (is, are)
14. Both feathers and fur _______ to keep animals warm. (helps, help)
15. Rope or string ______ required. (is, are)
16. Either plates or saucers ______ suitable. (is, are)
17. Smith and Smith ______ a family business. (is, are)
18. Neither the apples nor the plums ______ ripe. (was, were)

6. For each of the following sentences, place brackets around the phrase which describes the noun subject. Then, using the Simple Present tense, fill in the blank with the correct form of the verb shown in brackets. For example:

The tools, including the hammer, ___ made of iron. (to be)
The tools, [including the hammer,] are made of iron.
The ferry, as well as the other boats, ___ at anchor. (to be)
The ferry, [as well as the other boats,] is at anchor.

1. The letter, as well as the postcards, ______ on the table. (to be)
2. The windows at the front of the house ______ to be repaired. (to need)
3. His friends, as well as his sister, ______ about to leave. (to be)
4. The meadow, filled with flowers, ______ a beautiful sight. (to be)
5. The children in the class ______ eager to learn. (to be)
6. The kettle, in contrast to the saucepans, ______ pitch black. (to be)
7. The books, although purchased only last year, already ______ worn. (to look)
8. The leader of the musicians ______ responsible for the arrangements. (to be)
9. The table, together with the chairs, ______ quite old. (to be)
10. The members of the club ________ attending the meetings. (to enjoy)

Answers
to Exercise 1:
1. the musicians' instruments 2. the children's adventures 3. the animals' habitat 4. the workmen's instructions 5. the ships' passengers 6. the pilots' vacation 7. the officers' friends

to Exercise 2:
1. the surgeon's skill 2. the policeman's warning 3. the director's decision 4. the secretary's correspondence 5. the eagle's aerie 6. the woman's errand 7. the manager's assistants

to Exercise 3:
1. the woman's scarf 2. the children's 3. the color of the door 4. the beginning of the concert 5. the instructor's advice 6. the size of the deficit 7. the girl's tricycle 8. the height of the building 9. the hen's cackling 10. the boy's parents 11. the arm of the chair 12. the length of the street

to Exercise 4:
1. is [acting as a whole] 2. have [considered individually] 3. is [considered as a whole] 4. do [acting individually] 5. has [acting as a whole] 6. is [considered as a whole] 7. has [acting as a whole] 8. have [considered individually] 9. was [considered as a whole] 10. has [considered as a whole]

to Exercise 5:
1. are [or: noun nearest the verb is plural] 2. leads [nor: noun nearest the verb is singular] 3. are [and: subject refers to more than one thing] 4. is [or: noun nearest the verb is singular] 5. belong [and: subject refers to more than one thing] 6. was [nor: noun nearest the verb is singular] 7. is [and: subject refers to a single type of breakfast] 8. lives [or: noun nearest the verb is singular] 9. are [and: subject refers to more than one thing] 10. has [or: noun nearest the verb is singular] 11. are [and: subject refers to more than one thing] 12. is [or: noun nearest the verb is singular] 13. is [and: title of a book] 14. help [and: subject refers to more than one thing] 15. is [or: noun nearest the verb is singular] 16. are [or: noun nearest the verb is plural] 17. is [and: name of a company] 18. were [nor: noun nearest the verb is plural]

to Exercise 6:
1. The letter, [as well as the postcards,] is on the table. 2. The windows [at the front of the house] need to be repaired. 3. His friends, [as well as his sister,] are about to leave. 4. The meadow, [filled with flowers,] is a beautiful sight. 5. The children [in the class] are eager to learn. 6. The kettle, [in contrast to the saucepans] is pitch black. 7. The books, [although purchased only last year] already look worn. 8. The leader [of the musicians] is responsible for the arrangements. 9. The table, [together with the chairs,] is quite old. 10. The members [of the club] enjoy attending the meetings.

Revision Works II

1. For the following sentences, fill in the blanks with a or an or leave the blanks empty, as appropriate. Fill in the blanks with a or an before countable nouns, and leave them empty before uncountable nouns. For example:

 __ bird is singing outside the window.
 A bird is singing outside the window.

 ___ copper is used in making electrical wiring.
 Copper is used in making electrical wiring.

1. ___ air is made up of elements such as ___ oxygen and ___ nitrogen.
2. ___ book is lying on the floor.
3. ___ Russian is a difficult language.
4. ___ onion is ___ vegetable.
5. ___ butter and ___ cream are made from ___ milk.
6. ___ letter has been delivered to the wrong house.
7. ___ child is playing on the sidewalk.
8. ___ asbestos is a fireproof material.
9. ___ tree is growing outside the house.
10. ___ curiosity is considered a sign of ___ intelligence.
11. They want to buy ___ camera.
12. ___ egg was added to the soup.
13. ___ rain is expected this evening.
14. The farmers wished for ___ peace and ___ prosperity.
15. ___ bicycle is parked in front of the store.

2. Paying attention to whether the nouns in the following paragraphs are countable or uncountable, and to whether or not the nouns refer to things which have been mentioned before, fill in the blanks with a or the, or leave the blanks empty, as appropriate.

Phil Jones was ____ prospector, who was looking for ____ gold. He had to travel a long way, crossing ___ mountains and ____ streams to reach his destination.

Previously, he had been ____ miner and had mined ___ copper and ___ coal. But ____ copper had given out, and mining ____ coal was dangerous work. When he had heard about ___ gold in ____ mountains,

Phil had left his job and traveled west. He knew he would need ___ courage and ___ determination to reach his goal.

One evening he camped beside ___ stream. When he tested ____ stream, he found there was a small amount of glittering gold dust in it. As usual, Phil made ___ fire to prepare his evening meal. He took ____ ___ flour and ___ salt from his knapsack, and got ___ water from ____ stream. Then he mixed ___ salt with ___ flour, and gradually added ___ water, to make ___ pancakes over ___ fire.

As ___ fire died away, Phil looked up and down ___ stream. Expecting to see only ___ darkness, to his surprise, he saw ____ lights from many small fires. He knew they must be ____ fires of other prospectors. "I've reached end of my journey", he thought. Now he was in the goldfields, and with ___ luck, he would find ___ gold he had come to seek.

3. For each of the following sentences, change the word one to two, put the subject of the verb into the plural, and make sure that the verb agrees with its subject. For example:
   One bar of soap will be provided.
   Two bars of soap will be provided.

   One bag of flour is on the counter.
   Two bags of flour are on the counter.

1. One piece of luggage is allowed per passenger.
2. One bottle of water is enough.
3. One jar of honey is larger than the others.
4. One piece of furniture will be delivered.
5. One grain of rice has fallen onto the table.
6. One bucket of sand was needed to build the sand castle.
7. One cup of sugar should be mixed with the flour.
8. One game of chess will be played at four o'clock.

4. Fill in each blank with a or an if the noun following the blank is used as a countable noun, or leave the blank empty if the noun following the blank is used as an uncountable noun. For example:
   The bowl is made of ___ glass.
   The bowl is made of glass.

Would you like __ glass of water?
Would you like a glass of water?

1. The sun gives off ___ heat and ___ light.
2. There is ___ light suspended from the ceiling.
3. She will buy ___ paper to find out what movies are being shown.
4. ___ paper can be made from ___ wood or ___ cloth.
5. She has a keen sense of ___ honor.
6. It is ___ honor to be invited to speak.
7. There is ___ bed near the window.
8. He has gone to ___ bed early because he is tired.
9. ___ iron used in making ___ steel.
10. If I had ___ iron, I would press my new suit.
11. They always eat ___ lunch at twelve o'clock.
12. We will pack you ___ lunch to take with you.

5. Paying attention to which verbs can be followed by an infinitive and which can be followed by a gerund, for each sentence, fill in the blank with the infinitive or gerund of the verb shown in brackets. For example:
    Please stop ______ that! (to do)
    Please stop doing that!

    He has decided ________ a holiday. (to take)
    He has decided to take a holiday.

1. Has he finished __________ the report? (to read)
2. We plan __________ the concert. (to attend)
3. They will discuss __________ a club. (to organize)
4. She offered __________ the letter. (to write)
5. They asked __________ us. (to accompany)
6. You should practise __________ the speech. (to give)
7. I would suggest __________ the work by next week. (to finish)
8. He has not dared __________ you. (to contradict)
9. They delayed __________ us. (to call)
10. She deserves __________. (to succeed)
11. We forgot __________ the letter. (to mail)
12. He enjoys __________. (to ski)
13. They would not risk __________ the bus. (to miss)
14. Do you want __________ the book? (to borrow)
15. I don't mind __________. (to wait)
16. Her daughter is learning __________ a bicycle. (to ride)

17. It has stopped ___________. (to snow)
18. He is preparing ___________ a business. (to open)
19. They hesitated ___________ the invitation. (to accept)
20. I miss ___________ from them. (to hear)

for CHAPTER 16. UNCOUNTABLE NOUNS
to Exercise 1:
1. __ Air, __ oxygen, __ nitrogen 2. A book 3. __ Russian 4. An onion, a vegetable 5. __ Butter, __ cream, __ milk 6. A letter 7. A child 8. __ Asbestos 9. A tree 10. __ Curiosity, __ intelligence 11. a camera 12. An egg 13. __ Rain 14. __ peace, __ prosperity 15. A bicycle

to Exercise 2:
a prospector, __ gold. __ mountains, __ streams. a miner, __ copper, __ coal. the copper, the coal. the gold, the mountains, __ courage, __ determination. a stream. the stream. a fire. __ flour, __ salt, __ water, the stream. the salt, the flour the water, __ pancakes, the fire. the fire, the stream. __ darkness, __ lights. the fires. the end. __ luck, the gold.

to Exercise 3:
1. Two pieces of luggage are allowed 2. Two bottles of water are 3. Two jars of honey are 4. Two pieces of furniture will be delivered. 5. Two grains of rice have fallen 6. Two buckets of wand were needed 7. Two cups of sugar should be mixed 9. Two games of chess will be played

to Exercise 4:
1. __ heat, __ light 2. a light 3. a paper 4. __ Paper, __ wood, __ cloth 5. __ honor 6. an honor 7. a bed 8. __ bed 9. __ Iron, __ steel 10. an iron 11. __ lunch 12. a lunch

to Exercise 5:
1. reading 2. to attend 3. organizing 4. to write 5. to accompany 6. giving 7. finishing 8. to contradict 9. calling 10. to succeed 11. to mall 12. skiing 13. missing 14. to borrow 15. waiting 16. to ride 17. snowing 18. to open 19. to accept 20. hearing

Revision Works III

1. Rewrite the following general statements using singular nouns. Make sure that the verbs agree with their subjects. For example:

Engineers must be familiar with computers.

An engineer must be familiar with computers.

Trees produce oxygen.

A tree produces oxygen.

1. Automobiles should be kept in good repair.
2. Bats locate insects by means of sonar.
3. Diplomats should, if possible, be multilingual.
4. Hats are useful in cold weather.
5. Physicists must study a great deal.
6. Elephants can be dangerous.

2. Rewrite the following general statements using plural nouns. Make sure that the verbs agree with their subjects. For example:

A bicycle is a convenient means of transportation.

Bicycles are a convenient means of transportation.

A secretary should be proficient in spelling and grammar.

Secretaries should be proficient in spelling and grammar.

1. A sportsman needs to remain calm under pressure.
2. An eagle has good eyesight.
3. A conference requires careful planning.
4. A rock is composed of minerals.
5. A potato is rich in starch.
6. An omelette is made of eggs and other ingredients.

3. Rewrite the following general statements using singular nouns. Make sure that the verbs agree with their subjects. For example:

Frogs are amphibians.

A frog is an amphibian.

Wrenches are tools.
A wrench is a tool.

1. Pines are evergreens.
2. Otters are mammals.
3. Computers are machines.
4. Crabs are crustaceans.
5. Crickets are insects.
6. Oaks are hardwoods.

4. Rewrite the following general statements using plural nouns. Make sure that the verbs agree with their subjects. For example:

A robin is a bird.
Robins are birds.

A refrigerator is an appliance.
Refrigerators are appliances.

1. A schooner is a ship.
2. A mallard is a duck.
3. A rhododendron is a bush.
4. A beech is a tree.
5. A kangaroo is a marsupial.
6. An emerald is a gem.

5. Paying attention to whether the people and things referred to have been mentioned previously, fill in each blank with a, an or the, or leave the blank empty if no determiner is required.

I once had the chance to see ___ Chinese opera. It was very exciting. As well as ___ singers, there were ___ dancers and ___ acrobats. ___ acrobats staged ___ fights. During ___ fights, some of ___ acrobats wielded ___ swords, and others leaped over ___ swords. Many of ___ dancers carried scarves. ___ dancers ___ flourished ___ scarves to make ____ patterns in the air.

Behind ___ screen was a group of ___ musicians. ___ musicians played various oriental instruments. ___ instruments included ___ drums, ___ cymbals, ___ flutes and ___ gong. ___ flutes usually played the melody, and ___ gong was sounded at particularly exciting moments.

Of course there were ___ hero and ___ heroine. ___ hero had to rescue ___ heroine from ___ magician. ___ hero and ___ heroine had both proved their courage by the end of ___ opera.

6. Fill in each blank with the or leave it empty, as appropriate. Be prepared to justify your choices. For example:

    Those participants are _____ lawyers.
    Those participants are lawyers.

    _____ eagles are birds of prey.
Eagles are birds of prey.

    ___ deaf have their own language.
The deaf have their own language.

    ___ Dutch are members of the European Union.
The Dutch are members of the European Union.

    _____ planets circle the sun.
The planets circle the sun.

1. _____ English have a reputation for being animal lovers.
2. _____ wounded were treated immediately.
3. His friends are _____ scientists.
4. _____ crows are black.
5. _____ stars are covered by clouds.
6. _____ French make excellent pastries.
7. Two of the women are _____ reporters.
8. _____ turtles are reptiles.
9. _____ wealthy generally have a good knowledge of finance.

10. _____ Americans like to watch television.

11. They are _____ businessmen.

7. Paying attention to the rules for the use of the with proper nouns, fill in the blanks with the or leave them empty, as appropriate. For example:

_____ Rick is one of _____ Smiths who live on our street.

Rick is one of the Smiths who live on our street.

_____ Channel Islands lie south of _____ England.

The Channel Islands lie south of England.

_____ Rhine River flows through _____ Lake Constance.

The Rhine River flows through Lake Constance.

_____ Isle of Man lies in _____ Irish Sea.

The Isle of Man lies in the Irish Sea.

Part of _____ New York City is situated on _____ Long Island.

Part of New York City is situated on Long Island.

1. _____ Hawaiian Islands are in the middle of _____ Pacific Ocean.

2. _____ Salt Lake City is the capital of Utah.

3. _____ London lies on _____ Thames River.

4. _____ Suez Canal connects _____ Mediterranean Sea with Red Sea.

5. _____ Lake Huron and _____ Lake Erie are two of _____ Great Lakes.

6. _____ Calcutta lies north of _____ Bay of Bengal.

7. _____ North Sea separates British Isles from _____ Norway and _____ Denmark.

8. _____ Bay of Biscay lies to the west of _____ France.

9. _____ Orkney Islands are in the north of _____ Scotland.

10. _____ Anticosti Island lies in _____ Gulf of St. Lawrence.

11. Part of _____ Sahara Desert lies in _____ Algeria.

12. _____ Gerry, one of _____ Johnsons, lives on _____ Belleview Street.

13. _____ Mount Kilimanjaro is south-east of _____ Lake Victoria.

14. _____ Vancouver Island lies off the west coast of _____ Canada.

15. _____ Serengeti National Park lies in _____ Tanzania.

8. Paying attention to whether a singular or plural verb should be used, complete each of the following sentences by filling in the blank with is or are. For example:

My scissors ____ very sharp.
My scissors are very sharp.

One pair of scissors __ not enough for the whole class.
One pair of scissors is not enough for the whole class.

Five pairs of scissors ____ sufficient for a small class.
Five pairs of scissors are sufficient for a small class.

1. Her jeans _______ white.
2. Only one pair of jeans _______ clean.
3. Three pairs of jeans _______ being washed.
4. A good pair of pliers _______ handy for repairing a bicycle.
5. His pliers _______ equipped with a sharp edge for cutting wire.
6. Several pairs of pliers _______ on sale.

Answers

to Exercise 1:

1. An automobile should be kept 2. A bat locates 3. A diplomat should be 4. A hat is 5. A physicist must study 6. An elephant can be

to Exercise 2:

1. Sportsmen need 2. Eagles have 3. Conferences require 4. Rocks are composed 5. Potatoes are 6. Omelettes are made

to Exercise 3:

1. A pine is an evergreen. 2. An otter is a mammal. 3. A computer is a machine. 4. A crab is a crustacean. 5. A cricket is an insect. 6. An oak is a hardwood.

to Exercise 4:

1. Schooners are ships. 2. Mallards are ducks. 3. Rhododendrons are bushes. 4. Beeches are trees. 5. Kangaroos are marsupials. 6. Emeralds are gems.

to Exercise 5:
a Chinese opera. __ singers, __ dancers, __ acrobats. The acrobats, __ fights. the fights. the acrobats, __ swords, the swords, the dancers, __ scarves. The dancers, the scarves, __ patterns. a screen, __ musicians. The musicians. The instruments, __ drums, cymbals, __ flutes, a gong. The flutes, the gong. a hero, a heroine. The hero, the heroine, a magician. The hero, the heroine the opera.

to Exercise 6:
1. The [nationality ending in sh] 2. The [considered as a class] 3. __ [a profession] 4. __ [general statement] 5. The [obvious what is meant] 6. The [nationality ending in ch] 7. __ [profession] 8. __ [general statement] 9. The [considered as a class] 10. __ [nationality not ending in ch, se or sh] 11. __ [profession]

to Exercise 7:
1. The Hawaiian Islands, the Pacific Ocean 2. __ Salt Lake City, __ Utah 3. __ London, the Thames River 4. The Suez Canal, the Mediterranean Sea, the Red Sea 5. __ Lake Huron. __ Lake Erie, the Great Lakes 6. __ Calcutta, the Bay of Bengal 7. The North Sea, the British Isles, __ Norway, __ Denmark 8. The Bay of Biscay, __ France 9. The Orkney Islands, __ Scotland 10. __ Anticosti Island the Gulf of St. Lawrence 11. the Sahara Desert, __ Algeria 12. __ Gerry, the Johnsons, __ Belleview Street 13. __ Mount Kilimanjaro, __ Lake Victoria 14. __ Vancouver Island, __ Canada 15. __ Serengeti National Park, __ Tanzania

to Exercise 8:
1. are 2. is 3. are 4. is 5. are 6. are

7. Plurals

1. For each of the following sentences, change the subject of the verb to the plural, and change the verb so that it agrees with its subject. For example:

   The room is large.
   The rooms are large.

   The letter was delivered yesterday.
   The letters were delivered yesterday.

   The tourist has a map.
   The tourists have a map.

   The girl studies hard.
   The girls study hard.

1. The book was heavy.
2. The train has left.
3. The bird was singing.
4. The door was closed by the superintendent.
5. The shoe fits well.
6. The parcel is being opened.
7. The newspaper is read by many people.
8. The flame is flickering.
9. The ship has been sighted.
10. The street was being cleaned.

2. For each of the following sentences, change the subject of the verb to the plural, and change the verb so that it agrees with its subject. For example:

   The beach is supervised by lifeguards.

The beaches are supervised by lifeguards.

The singer performs twice a week.
The singers perform twice a week.

The class was visiting the museum.
The classes were visiting the museum.

The vase has been filled with flowers.
The vases have been filled with flowers.

1. The box was empty.
2. The river flows to the sea.
3. The bush has grown in the last two months.
4. The hat was on sale.
5. The bench is made of stone.
6. The plant has been watered.
7. The hedge is being trimmed.
8. The process was invented last year.
9. The sketch is nearly finished.
10. The breeze was warm.
11. The wall is being painted.
12. The church is two hundred years old.
13. The bridge will soon be completed.
14. The carpet has been cleaned.
15. The branch is covered with ice.

3. For each of the following sentences, change the subject of the verb to the plural, and change the verb so that it agrees with its subject. For example:

The party was held downtown.
The parties were held downtown.

The society accomplishes a great deal.
The societies accomplish a great deal.

The day seemed long.
The days seemed long.

1. The berry was red.
2. The key was difficult to use.
3. The valley is very beautiful.
4. The eddy can be dangerous for swimmers.
5. The journey was undertaken by pilgrims.
6. The daisy was picked by the child.
7. The monkey is considered to be sacred.
8. The gully is full of water.
9. The boy ran to school.
10. The facility is open to the public.
11. The secretary works overtime.
12. The toy was being sold at a discount.
13. The tray is being piled high with dishes.
14. The dairy opens at nine o'clock.
15. The chimney has been repaired.

4. Rewrite each of the following sentences, adding the word two before the proper noun. Change the proper noun to the plural, and change the verb so that it agrees with its subject. For example:

Smith lives in this building.
Two Smiths live in this building.

Harry was nominated for the position.
Two Harrys were nominated for the position.

Alex is here.
Two Alexes are here.

1. Maurice is volunteering.
2. Jones was ordered to leave.
3. Harrison owns land.
4. Sandy has telephoned us.
5. Susan met us.

6. Trish is studying French.
7. Pat does well in school.
8. Liz has arrived early.
9. Jacky was making the cake.
10. Russ knows all the .
11. Eric is planning the party.
12. Terry has difficulty understanding Spanish.

5. For each of the following sentences, change the subject of the verb to the plural, and change the verb so that it agrees with its subject. For example:

The knife has been sharpened.
The knives have been sharpened.

The reef attracts tourists.
The reefs attract tourists.

The thief will be caught.
The thieves will be caught.

1. The leaf has turned red.
2. The fife had the solo.
3. The calf is hungry.
4. The scarf kept him warm.
5. The knife will be useful.
6. The giraffe was eating leaves.
7. The cliff is being explored by geologists.
8. The wolf howls every night.
9. The loaf is rising.
10. The chief will decide.
11. The shelf is being used.
12. The proof is convincing.

6. For each of the following sentences, change the subject of the verb to the plural, and change the verb so that it agrees with its subject. For example:

The hero was enthusiastically welcomed.
The heroes were enthusiastically welcomed.

The studio is used by many artists.
The studios are used by many artists.

1. The radio is broadcasting news every hour.
2. The tomato was being baked.
3. The mosquito woke us up.
4. The soprano performed with the orchestra.
5. The solo was played by the violinist.
6. The archipelago lies off the coast of South America.
7. The silo is used for storing corn.
8. The potato has been boiled.
9. The volcano is not active.
10. The casino was open until one o'clock in the morning.
11. The innuendo should be ignored.
12. The ratio has been favorable.

7. For each of the following sentences, change the subject of the verb to the plural, and change the verb so that it agrees with its subject. For example:

The hypothesis is still tentative.
The hypotheses are still tentative.

The nebula has been studied by many scientists.
The nebulae have been studied by many scientists.

The thesis will have been reviewed by experts.
The theses will have been reviewed by experts.

1. The synopsis is accurate.
2. The phenomenon surprised us.

3. The stratum contains fossils.
4. The analysis was proved correct.
5. The crisis has caused concern.
6. The spectrum includes many different colors of light.
7. The axis of rotation will be investigated.
8. The stimulus has been found to be effective.
9. The criterion was used to judge which proposals should be accepted.
10. The oasis is visited by many travelers.
11. The honorarium is being presented today.
12. The parenthesis was omitted.

8. For each of the following sentences, change the subject of the verb to the plural, and change the verb so that it agrees with its subject. For example:

The goose likes to eat daisies.
The geese like to eat daisies.

The ox was being led to the barn.
The oxen were being led to the barn.

The salmon has been caught by the bear.
The salmon have been caught by the bear.

1. The child is happy.
2. The sheep has been sheared.
3. The man was being given directions.
4. The deer is eating the hay.
5. The woman has visited us.
6. The mouse makes a great deal of noise at night.
7. The gentleman would like to have breakfast early.
8. The louse is a nuisance.
9. Your foot is size ten.
10. The fisherman has had a good season.
11. The tooth needs to be filled.
12. The policewoman was directing traffic.

Answers

to Exercise 1:

1. The books were heavy. 2. The trains have left. 3. The birds were singing. 4. The doors were closed by the superintendent. 5. The shoes fit well. 6. The parcels are being opened. 7. The newspapers are read by many people. 8. The flames are flickering. 9. The ships have been sighted. 10. The streets were being cleaned.

to Exercise 2:

1. The boxes were empty. 2. The rivers flow to the sea. 3. The bushes have grown in the last two months. 4. The hats were on sale. 5. The benches are made of stone. 6. The plants have been watered. 7. The hedges are being trimmed. 8. The processes were invented last year. 9. The sketches are nearly finished. 10. The breezes were warm. 11. The walls are being painted. 12. The churches are two hundred years old. 13. The bridges will soon be completed. 14. The carpets have been cleaned. 15. The branches are covered with ice.

to Exercise 3:

1. The berries were red. 2. The keys were difficult to use. 3. The valleys are very beautiful. 4. The eddies can be dangerous for swimmers. 5. The journeys were undertaken by pilgrims. 6. The daisies were picked by the child. 7. The monkeys are considered to be sacred. 8. The gullies are full of water. 9. The boys ran to school. 10. The facilities are open to the public. 11. The secretaries work overtime. 12. The toys were being sold at a discount. 13. The trays are being piled high with dishes. 14. The dairies open at nine o clock. 15. The chimneys have been repaired.

to Exercise 4:

1. Two Maurices are volunteering. 2. Two Joneses were ordered to leave. 3. Two Harrisons own land. 4. Two Sandys have telephoned us. 5. Two Susans met us. 6. Two Trishes are studying French. 7. Two Pats do well in school. 8. Two Lizes have arrived early. 9. Two Jackys were making the cake. 10. Two Russes know all the . 11. Two Erics are planning the party. 12. Two Terries have difficulty understanding Spanish.

to Exercise 5:

1. The leaves have turned red. 2. The fifes had the solo. 3. The calves are hungry. 4. The scarfs kept him warm. or The scarves kept him warm. 5. The knives will be useful. 6. The giraffes were eating the leaves. 7. The cliffs are being explored by geologists. 8. The wolves howl every night. 9. The loaves are rising. 10. The chiefs will decide. 11. The shelves are being used. 12. The proofs are convincing.

to Exercise 6:

1. The radios are broadcasting news every hour. 2. The tomatoes were being baked. 3. The mosquitoes woke us up. 4. The sopranos performed with the orchestra. 5. The solos were played by the violinist. 6. The archipelagoes lie off the coast of South America. 7. The silos are used for storing corn. 8. The potatoes have been boiled. 9. The volcanoes are not active. 10. The casinos were open until one o'clock in the morning. 11. The innuendoes should be ignored. 12. The ratios have been favorable.

to Exercise 7:

1. The synopses are accurate. 2. The phenomena surprised us. 3. The strata contain fossils. 4. The analyses were proved correct. 5. The crises have caused concern. 6. The spectra include many different colors of light. 7. The axes of rotation will be investigated. 8. The stimuli have been found to be effective. 9. The criteria were used to judge which proposals should be accepted. 10. The oases are visited by many travelers. 11. The honoraria are being presented today. 12. The parentheses were omitted.

to Exercise 8:

1. The children are happy. 2. The sheep have been sheared. 3. The men were being given directions. 4. The deer are eating the hay. 5. The women have visited us. 6. The mice make a great deal of noise at night. 7. The gentlemen would like to have breakfast early. 8. The lice are a nuisance. 9. Your feet are size ten. 10. The fishermen have had a good season. 11. The teeth need to be filled. 12. The policewomen were directing traffic.

8. Passive Voice

1. Change the following affirmative statements into questions. For example:

    You are required to attend the meeting.
    Are you required to attend the meeting?

    She is being ignored.
    Is she being ignored?

1. They should be notified.
2. He might have been allowed to come.
3. You had been told about it.
4. They will be needed.
5. It has been adjourned.
6. They were being prepared.

2. Change the following affirmative statements into negative statements. For example:

    They would have been instructed to join us.
    They would not have been instructed to join us.

    It was sent on time.
    It was not sent on time.

1. We could have been seen from the island.
2. It is being dealt with satisfactorily.
3. They were being kept under observation.
4. You will be held responsible.
5. They were expected at six o'clock.
6. He will be asked to participate.

3. Change the following affirmative statements into negative questions. Do not use contractions in this exercise. For example:

    He is respected by everyone.
    Is he not respected by everyone?

She should be consulted.
Should she not be consulted?

1. They were recognized immediately.
2. We were being assisted by volunteers.
3. It had been delivered.
4. They should have been guarded more carefully.
5. We will be given financial assistance.
6. It had been organized by the club members.

4. For each of the following sentences, first indicate the tense of the underlined verb, and then change the verb from the Active Voice to the corresponding tense in the Passive Voice. Take note of the resulting change in the meaning of the sentence. For example:
They drive to work at seven o'clock every morning.
Simple Present: They are driven to work at seven o'clock every morning.

Did he notice?
Simple Past: Was he noticed?

She is not telling the truth.
Present Continuous: he is not being told the truth.

We have sent a message.
Present Perfect: We have been sent a message.

I will pay.
Simple Future: I will be paid.

1. Do they expect to leave? _______________
2. He is giving instructions. _______________
3. They have moved to a new location. _______________
4. She will fly to London. _______________
5. He has offered a discount. _______________
6. They have stopped. _______________
7. Will you have given the order? _______________
8. We sent a favorable reply. _______________
9. We were teaching German. _______________
10. I understand. _______________
11. He is offering free advice. _______________

12. She will rush to the reception. _______________________

5. For each of the following sentences, first indicate the tense of the underlined verb, and then change the verb from the Passive Voice to the corresponding tense in the Active Voice. Take note of the resulting change in the meaning of the sentence. For example:

We are paid regularly.
Simple Present: We pay regularly.

She is not assisted every day.
Simple Present: She does not assist every day.

Was he not being flown to Boston?
Past Continuous: Was he not flying to Boston?

It has been grown here for the past twenty years.
Present Perfect: It has grown here for the past twenty years.

Might they be called at nine o'clock?
Simple conjugation with might: Might they call at nine o'clock?

1. We can be heard easily. _______________________
2. She is being given advice. _______________________
3. Were they not flown over the lake? _______________________
4. I had been transferred to another department.
5. He is being stopped. _______________________
6. We have been sent a letter. _______________________
7. He is not being taught music theory. _______________________
8. Should they have been flown to their next destination?
____
9. They will be watched constantly. _______________________
10. We had been driven to the beach this morning. _______________________
11. Has he been checked into the hotel? _______________________
12. Could I have been told the news yesterday? _______________________

6. Change the underlined verbs in the following sentences from the Active Voice to the corresponding tenses in the Passive Voice. Preserve the meaning of the sentences by using the preposition by and making the necessary changes in word order. For example:

The teenager rowed the boat.

The boat was rowed by the teenager.

The girl is riding the horse.
The horse is being ridden by the girl.

The student has prepared the lunch.
The lunch has been prepared by the student.

The president will thank the members.
The members will be thanked by the president.

The children can understand the poem.
The poem can be understood by the children.

1. The woman founded the club.
2. This entry took the prize.
3. The girl is playing the guitar.
4. The mailman has delivered the letter.
5. The chauffeur can drive the car.
6. The child chose the hat.
7. The cat chased the mouse.
8. The workers will weave the carpet.
9. The stranger could have bought the hiking boots.
10. The dealer has sold the car.
11. The dog splashed the water.
12. The man has watered the garden.

7. Change the underlined verbs in the following sentences from the Passive Voice to the corresponding tenses in the Active Voice. Preserve the meaning of the sentences by omitting the preposition by and making the necessary changes in word order. For example:
The news was heard by everyone.
Everyone heard the news.

The orders were followed by the officials.
The officials followed the orders.

The money is being counted by the cashier.
The cashier is counting the money.

The ducks have been fed by the tourists.

The tourists have fed the ducks.

The flowers will be photographed by the naturalist.
The naturalist will photograph the flowers.

1. The bill was paid by the manager.
2. The bread was made by the baker.
3. The wiring must be checked by the electrician.
4. The crow was being scolded by the squirrel.
5. The book was written by a doctor.
6. The house was painted by a student.
7. The seeds were taken by the chickadee.
8. The cider has been drunk by the guest.
9. The mail is opened by the secretary.
10. The ingredients have been measured by the cooks.
11. The bird was seen by the photographers.
12. His work will be published by the magazine.

8. Complete the following sentences using the Simple Present Subjunctive of the Passive Voice of the verbs shown in brackets. For example:
She ordered that the most important details ________ known. (to make)
She ordered that the most important details be made known.

He advises that the plane ________ at a high altitude. (to fly)
He advises that the plane be flown at a high altitude.

1. They demand that the change of plans ______________ at nine o'clock. (to announce)
2. We ask that permission to compete ____________ to everyone. (to grant)
3. It is important that their accomplishments ____________. (to recognize)
4. It is crucial that we ______________ of any change. (to advise)
5. He asks that his affairs ____________ in order. (to put)
6. They requested that their qualifications ________________. (to accept)
7. We insist that he not _____________ his rights. (to deny)
8. It is necessary that the requirements ____________. (to meet)
9. She requests that the most experienced candidate ___________. (to choose)

10. It is recommended that care ___________ in making the repairs. (to take)

11. He insists that smoking _____________. (to forbid)

12. It is essential that supplies ____________ well in advance. (to order)

Answers

to Exercise 1:

1. Should they be notified? 2. Might he have been allowed to leave? 3. Had you been told about it? 4. Will they be needed? 5. Has it been adjourned? 6. Were they being prepared?

to Exercise 2:

1. We could not have been seen from the island. 2. It is not being dealt with satisfactorily. 3. They were not being kept under observation. 4. You will not be held responsible. 5. They were not expected at six o'clock. 6. He will not be asked to participate.

to Exercise 3:

1. Were they not recognized immediately? 2. Were we not being assisted by volunteers? 3. Had it not been delivered? 4. Should they not have been guarded more carefully? 5. Will we not be given financial assistance? 6. Had it not been organized by the club members?

to Exercise 4:

1. Simple Present: Are they expected to leave?

2. Present Continuous: He is being given instructions.

3. Present Perfect: They have been moved to a new location.

4. Simple Future: She will be flown to London.

5. Present Perfect: He has been offered a discount.

6. Present Perfect: They have been stopped.

7. Future Perfect: Will you have been given the order?

8. Simple Past: We were sent a favorable reply.

9. Past Continuous: We were being taught German.

10. Simple Present: I am understood.

11. Present Continuous: He is being offered free advice.

12. Simple Future: She will be rushed to the reception.

to Exercise 5:

1. Simple conjugation with can: We can hear easily.

2. Present Continuous: She is giving advice.

3. Simple Past: Did they not fly over the lake?
4. Past Perfect: I had transferred to another department.
5. Present Continuous: He is stopping.
6. Present Perfect: We have sent a letter.
7. Present Continuous: He is not teaching music theory.
8. Perfect conjugation with should: Should they have flown to their next destination?
9. Simple Future: They will watch constantly.
10. Past Perfect: We had driven to the beach this morning.
11. Present Perfect: Has he checked into the hotel?
12. Perfect conjugation with could: Could I have told the news yesterday?

to Exercise 6:
1. The club was founded by the woman. 2. The prize was taken by this entry. 3. The guitar is being played by the girl. 4. The letter has been delivered by the mailman. 5. The car can be driven by the chauffeur. 6. The hat was chosen by the child. 7. The mouse was chased by the cat. 8. The carpet will be woven by the workers. 9. The hiking boots could have been bought by the stranger. 10. The car has been sold by the dealer. 11. The water was splashed by the dog. 12. The garden has been watered by the man.

to Exercise 7:
1. The manager paid the bill. 2. The baker made the bread. 3. The electrician must check the wiring. 4. The squirrel was scolding the crow. 5. A doctor wrote the book. 6. A student painted the house. 7. The chickadee took the seeds. 8. The guest has drunk the cider. 9. The secretary opens the mail. 10. The cooks have measured the ingredients. 11. The photographers saw the bird. 12. The magazine will publish his work.

to Exercise 8:
1. be announced 2. be granted 3. be recognized 4. be advised 5. be put 6. be accepted 7. be denied 8. be met 9. be chosen 10. be taken 11. be forbidden 12. be ordered

9. Verbs

1. In each of the following sentences, underline the direct object of the verb. For example:

    She forgot the pencils.   She forgot the pencils.
    Was he writing a letter?   Was he writing a letter?
    You did not answer the question.
    You did not answer the question.

1. I watched the birds.
2. He did not close the window.
3. She rang the bell.
4. Did you find the answer?
5. I opened the door.
6. Did she play the violin?
7. You will need an umbrella.
8. They are not carrying the parcels.
9. You organized the race.
10. Were they using the blankets?

2. In the following sentences, the direct objects of the verbs are printed in bold type. In addition, each sentence contains an adverb or adverb phrase indicating time. Depending upon whether or not there is a direct object, complete each sentence using either to lay or to lie, as appropriate. Use the Present Continuous tense if the action takes place in the present, and use the Simple Past tense if the action took place in the past. For example:

    They ____________ the bricks now.
    They are laying the bricks now.

    I ________ the money on the counter last night.
    I laid the money on the counter last night.

    Right now, the dogs __________ in the middle of the road.
    Right now, the dogs are lying in the middle of the road.

Yesterday, he ___ in bed until ten o'clock.
Yesterday, he lay in bed until ten o'clock.

1. Now I _______________ too close to the fire.
2. Last night he _______________ twenty dollars on top of the bookcase.
3. Right now she _______________ a fire.
4. Until last year, the treasure _______________ hidden under the earth.
5. Yesterday she _______________ her coat on the bed.
6. His books _______________ on the floor all last week.
7. Right now he _______________ low in order to stay out of danger.
8. Yesterday morning he _______________ the parcel close to the door.
9. Last night they _______________ in wait for the thieves.
10. Now they _______________ their cards on the table.

3. In the following sentences, the direct objects of the verbs are printed in bold type. In addition, each sentence contains an adverb or adverb phrase indicating time. Depending upon whether or not there is a direct object, complete each sentence using either to raise or to rise, as appropriate. Use the Present Continuous tense if the action takes place in the present; and use the Simple Past tense if the action took place in the past. For example:

Right now, he __________ sheep.
Right now, he is raising sheep.

Last night he _______ their expectations.
Last night he raised their expectations.
The price of housing __________ now.
The price of housing is rising now.
Last year she _______ at six o'clock every morning.
Last year she rose at six o'clock every morning.
1. Last night, when we heard the news, our hopes _______________.
2. Last year they __________ six hundred dollars by selling chocolate bars.
3. Now they _______________ the price of gasoline.
4. The price of gold _______________ yesterday.
5. At the moment, he _______________ corn.
6. Right now mist _______________ from the water.

7. Last week, you _______________ a difficult question.

8. The temperature _____________ at the moment.

9. Now he _____________ his hat.

10. The water level _______________ last week.

4. In the following sentences, the direct objects of the verbs are printed in bold type. In addition, each sentence contains an adverb or adverb phrase indicating time. Depending upon whether or not there is a direct object, complete each sentence using either to set or to sit, as appropriate. Use the Present Continuous tense if the action takes place in the present; and use the Simple Past tense if the action took place in the past. For example:

Now they ____________ the table.

Now they are setting the table.

Last night we ___ our alarm clock for six o'clock.

Last night we set our alarm clock for six o'clock.

At the moment, the cat ___________ on top of the car.

At the moment, the cat is sitting on top of the car.

Yesterday he ___ at his desk all afternoon.

Yesterday he sat at his desk all afternoon.

1. Right now they _______________ down to a good meal.

2. Yesterday they _______________ the empty bottles on the front step.

3. At the moment, she _________________ in front of the fire.

4. Now we ________________ the suitcases on the moving belt.

5. In ancient times, King Arthur's knights _____________ at the Round Table.

6. Yesterday morning the doctor _______________ the broken bone.

7. Right now, we _________________ around the table.

8. He _______________ a good example last week, by studying hard.

9. Now she _______________ her watch to the correct time.

10. Yesterday afternoon we ___________ at the end of the dock, in the sun.

5. In the following sentences, the direct objects of the verbs are printed in bold type. Paying attention to whether or not there is a direct object, for each sentence, choose the correct verb from the pair given in brackets,

and complete the sentence using the Present Perfect tense of the verb. For example:

I __________ two blankets on the bed. (to lay, to lie)
I have laid two blankets on the bed.

He __________ down for half an hour. (to lay, to lie)
He has lain down for half an hour.

They ______________ the flag. (to raise, to rise)
They have raised the flag.
Our opinion of them __________. (to raise, to rise)
Our opinion of them has risen.
We __________ the electric train in motion. (to set, to sit)
We have set the electric train in motion.
She ___ just ___ down. (to set, to sit)
She has just sat down.

1. They ______________ a limit of four cartons per customer. (to set, to sit)
2. We ______________ our plans carefully. (to lay, to lie)
3. You ______________ very early for the past three weeks. (to raise, to rise)
4. We ______________ in the car all afternoon. (to set, to sit)
5. They ______________ four children. (to raise, to rise)
6. He ______________ a record for endurance. (to set, to sit)
7. I ______________ awake half the night. (to lay, to lie)
8. They ______________ the table. (to lay, to lie)
9. She ______________ still for fifteen minutes. (to set, to sit)
10. You ______________ your standards. (to raise, to rise)
11. Your standards ______________. (to raise, to rise)
12. Your gloves ______________ on the table all week. (to lay, to lie)

6. Rewrite each of the following sentences, omitting the underlined preposition which precedes the indirect object, and making the necessary changes in word order. For example:

I bought a rose for the singer.
I bought the singer a rose.
She gave an apple to the boy.

She gave the boy an apple.
1. I handed the book to the student.
2. He wrote a letter to the twins.
3. She made a scarf for the girl.
4. I told the story to the audience.
5. We paid the money to the dentist.
6. He sent a reply to the doctor.
7. We offered the job to the students.
8. She told the news to her friends.

7. Rewrite each of the following sentences, inserting the preposition to before the indirect object, and making the necessary changes in word order. For example:

I wrote the president a letter.
I wrote a letter to the president.

They showed the visitor the garden.
They showed the garden to the visitor.

1. We sent the reporters a photograph.
2. They mailed the agency a postcard.
3. I paid the manager the fee.
4. We sold the students the doughnuts.
5. You read the teacher the story.
6. She mailed the seamstress the material.
7. I sent the workers a message.
8. He offered his guest the wine.

Answers
to Exercise 1:
1. birds 2. window 3. bell 4. answer 5. door 6. violin 7. umbrella 8. parcels 9. race 10. blankets

to Exercise 2:
1. am lying 2. laid 3. is laying 4. lay 5. laid 6. lay 7. is lying 8. laid 9. lay 10. are laying

to Exercise 3:

1. rose 2. raised 3. are raising 4. rose 5. is raising 6. is rising 7. raised 8. is rising 9. is raising 10. rose

to Exercise 4:

1. are sitting 2. set 3. is sitting 4. are setting 5. sat 6. set 7. are sitting 8. set 9. is setting 10. sat

to Exercise 5:

1. have set 2. have laid 3. have risen 4. have sat 5. have raised 6. has set 7. have lain 8. have laid 9. has sat 10. have raised 11. have risen 12. have lain

to Exercise 6:

1. I handed the student the book. 2. He wrote the twins a letter. 3. She made the girl a scarf. 4. I told the audience the story. 5. We paid the dentist the money. 6. He sent the doctor a reply. 7. We offered the students the job. 8. She told her friends the news.

to Exercise 7:

1. We sent a photograph to the reporters. 2. They mailed a postcard to the agency. 3. I paid the fee to the manager. 4. We sold the doughnuts to the students. 5. You read the story to the teacher. 6. She mailed the material to the seamstress. 7. I sent a message to the workers. 8. He offered the wine to his guest.

Modal Verbs

1. Change the following affirmative statements into questions. For example:

I may go.
May I go?

We could have found it.
Could we have found it?

1. I must leave at four o'clock.
2. He might be leaving for work now.
3. We can solve the puzzle.
4. You should have called him.
5. They could have been waiting for the bus.
6. I shall go out now.
7. You will have finished the book.
8. We should be making the arrangements.
9. She would like to know the answer.
10. They can explain what happened.

2. Change the following affirmative statements into negative statements. For example:

I can answer the question.
I cannot answer the question.

He shall be sorry.
He shall not be sorry.

1. You must come with us.
2. It may be sunny tomorrow.
3. She could have won the race.
4. We might be right.
5. You would have liked that movie.

6. They can swim very well.
7. She might be finishing school now.
8. He should have been walking to work.
9. I shall be happy to see him.
10. You will have been working all night.

3. Change the following affirmative statements into negative questions.
Do not use contractions in this exercise. For example:

He must be at work now.

Must he not be at work now?

They might call us later.

Might they not call us later?

1. You should be wearing a warm hat.
2. He could have decided to stay at home.
3. They might have forgotten the message.
4. She will see you again next week.
5. They would enjoy riding on the ferry.
6. He may decide to go camping.
7. They could have been playing football yesterday.
8. We shall visit our friends.
9. She must have wanted to join us.
10. He should be getting more sleep.

4. For each of the following sentences, change the verb in the main clause from the Simple Present to the Simple Past; and change the modal auxiliary from the present to the past. For example:

He says he can do it.

He said he could do it.

Do you think she will manage it?

Did you think she would manage it?

1. She says he may go.

2. I think we can finish on time.

3. They know we will help them.

4. He says he must leave.

5. We believe she will be there.

6. Do you hope they will reply soon?

7. Does he not realize we may meet him there?

8. You think we can reach our destination by nightfall.

9. I suppose he must be at home.

10. I predict I shall succeed.

5. For each of the following sentences, change the verb in the main clause from the Simple Past to the Simple Present; and change the modal auxiliary from the past to the present. For example:

They felt they could not win.

They feel they cannot win.

He believed he would reach the Amazon River in a few days.

He believes he will reach the Amazon River in a few days.

1. He thought he might arrive early.

2. She felt she must make a phone call.

3. I maintained they would not have any difficulty.

4. They realized they could not do all the work in one day.

5. We knew we should not be able to return home for Christmas.

6. They hoped they could find their way.

7. He imagined he would be able to convince us.

8. She suspected they must be living nearby.

9. I hoped you would enjoy the play.

10. We thought you might know him.

6. Complete the following sentences, using the indicated verbs in the Simple conjugation with the auxiliary could. For example:

I wish I ____________ Portuguese. (to speak)

I wish I could speak Portuguese.

They will wish they _______________ the questions. (to answer)
They will wish they could answer the questions.

You wished you __________ some chocolate. (to buy)
You wished you could buy some chocolate.

1. He wishes he _______________ them. (to call)
2. We wish we _______________ more time sightseeing. (to spend)
3. She wished she _________________ you. (to visit)
4. They will wish they _______________ to the concert. (to go)
5. I wished I _______________ my way home. (to find)
6. He wishes he _______________ famous. (to become)
7. I wish I _______________ it to you. (to describe)

7. Complete the following sentences, using the indicated verbs in the Simple conjugation with the auxiliary could. For example:
    If he wanted to, he _____________ how to sail a boat. (to learn)
    If he wanted to, he could learn how to sail a boat.

    If we _______________ anywhere, we would visit Greece. (to travel)
    If we could travel anywhere, we would visit Greece.

1. If I _______________ you, I would be glad to do it. (to help)
2. If she played the piano, she _______________ your singing. (to accompany)
3. We _______________ before dawn if we made all our preparations tonight. (to depart)
4. He would be thrilled if he _____________ to ride a horse. (to learn)
5. If she came with us, we _______________ her all the sights. (to show)
6. If they gave us their address, we _______________ them a card. (to send)
7. He would move at once if he _______________ a better place to live. (to find)

8. Complete the following sentences, using the indicated verbs in the Perfect conjugation with the auxiliary could. For example:

Had I studied harder, I _________________ every question. (to answer)

Had I studied harder, I could have answered every question.

_______ she _________ you earlier, she would have spoken to you. (to see)

Could she have seen you earlier, she would have spoken to you.

1. If you _________________ him trying to skate, you would have laughed. (to see)
2. If I had experienced difficulties, I _________________ him for help. (to ask)
3. It would have been better if we _________________ everything to her. (to explain)
4. Had they had permission, they _____________ the arrangements themselves. (to make)
5. We _______ easily our way if we had not brought a compass with us. (to lose)
6. _______ they _____________ what he had in mind, they would not have been so complacent. (to know)
7. Had a flying saucer landed on the roof, he _______ not ___________ more surprised. (to be)
8. If only I _________________ them of the truth, much time and trouble would have been saved. (to convince)
9. If you _________________ what might happen, would you have acted differently? (to guess)
10. Had I realized he was in town, I _________________ him. (to contact)

9. Fill in the blanks, indicating whether each of the following sentences is somewhat polite (S), quite polite (Q), or very polite (V). Notice the indirect phrasing of the most polite requests and suggestions. For example:

Could you pass the butter? S

Would you please pass the butter? Q
Might I trouble you to pass the butter? V

1. Could you help me? ___
2. Would you like some help? ___
3. Might I be of assistance? ___
4. You could come with us. ___
5. You might wish to accompany us. ___
6. Would you like to come with us? ___
7. Might I trouble you for two pounds of fish? ___
8. I would like to buy two pounds of fish, please. ___
9. Could you give me two pounds of fish? ___
10. Could I have your opinion on this? ___
11. Would you please tell me what you think? ___
12. Might I know your feelings on the matter? ___

10. Complete each of the following sentences with the auxiliary may, might or must. Use may or might when the event described seems somewhat probable, and use must when the event described seems very probable. For example:

You ___ be right; we shall have to wait and see.

You may be right; we shall have to wait and see. or You might be right; we shall have to wait and see.

That ____ be our landlord; I would recognize him anywhere.
That must be our landlord; I would recognize him anywhere.

1. Although it _________ be true, it seems unlikely.
2. That _________ have been the number 10 bus, because no other bus runs on this street.
3. We __________ have to wait a long time for a bus, because they do not run very frequently.
4. That ________ be the right answer; there is no other possibility.
5. Tell me your problem; I _________ be able to help you.
6. It _________ have been he who answered the phone, because no one else was at home.

7. Since we have never been to this store before, we __________ have difficulty finding what we want.

8. You __________ be pleased that you are doing so well in your new job.

9. I __________ go downtown tomorrow; it depends on the weather.

10. Although he is a very careful worker, it is possible that he __________ have made a mistake.

11. Rewrite the following sentences, putting the underlined verbs into the future. For example:

They can explain the situation to us.
They will be able to explain the situation to us.

May they leave whenever they wish?
Will they be allowed to leave whenever they wish?

She must obtain a license.
She will have to obtain a license.

1. She can describe it to you.
2. You must lock the doors when you leave.
3. He can follow the instructions.
4. May they stay overnight?
5. We must remember to buy groceries.
6. She can finish the work on time.
7. Must he take his glasses with him?
8. Can they buy the tickets in advance?
9. She must learn to be more careful.
10. You may choose your own seat.

12. Add negative tag questions to the following affirmative statements. For example:

They are lucky.
They are lucky, aren't they?

You know what I mean.

You know what I mean, don't you?

We will tell him the truth.
We will tell him the truth, won't we?

She could try harder.
She could try harder, couldn't she?

1. You are cold.
2. They passed the test.
3. I can do this well.
4. You live near the school.
5. He went downtown.
6. We should call them.
7. She likes toffee.
8. They could help us.
9. I won the race.
10. You were reading.
11. He rides a bicycle.
12. We would need more time.

13. Add affirmative tag questions to the following negative statements. For example:

She isn't well.
She isn't well, is she?

You don't eat fish.
You don't eat fish, do you?

He hadn't found it.
He hadn't found it, had he?

They won't mind.
They won't mind, will they?

1. They won't reach their destination before five o'clock.

2. He doesn't want to come with us.

3. She hasn't eaten breakfast yet.

4. They aren't very clever.

5. I couldn't have persuaded you.

6. You won't forget to come.

7. We weren't expecting company.

8. They wouldn't like that.

14. Write affirmative short to the following questions. For example:

Is he thirsty?

Yes, he is.

Haven't they read the book?

Yes, they have.

Can they finish the work by themselves?

Yes, they can.

Should she leave now?

Yes, she should.

1. Do we need any butter?

2. May they send for you?

3. Is she sure she is right?

4. Does he enjoy studying?

5. Had they been meaning to call us?

6. Couldn't he send us the information?

7. Would she like to listen to the radio?

8. Had he been wanting to travel?

15. Write negative short to the following questions. For example:

Wasn't he thirsty?

No, he wasn't.

Were they watching television?

No, they weren't.

Should we turn left here?
No, we shouldn't.

Will they want some coffee?
No, they won't.

1. Isn't she driving her own car?
2. Will he be visiting Denmark?
3. Would she mind?
4. Could they understand everything?
5. Will she have to get up early?
6. Should he warn them?
7. Didn't we sell all the chocolate bars?
8. Couldn't they find any evidence?

16. Add the short form construction using the words and so to each of the following affirmative statements. Use the subjects shown in brackets. For example:

He is lucky. (I)
He is lucky, and so am I.

She likes chocolate. (you)
She likes chocolate, and so do you.

They can swim well. (we)
They can swim well, and so can we.

1. We are thirsty. (they)
2. You have been helpful. (she)
3. I swam to the island. (he)
4. He was riding a horse. (you)
5. They can understand Dutch. (we)
6. She enjoyed the trip. (I)
7. You should study hard. (they)

8. He reads a great deal. (she)

17. Add the short form construction using the words and neither to each of the following negative statements. Use the subjects shown in brackets. For example:

He is not angry. (we)
He is not angry, and neither are we.

They didn't visit you. (I)
They didn't visit you, and neither did I.

I couldn't understand it. (she)
I couldn't understand it, and neither could she.

1. You haven't finished supper. (she)
2. He couldn't tell the time. (they)
3. She is not planning to go. (we)
4. We didn't wait long. (he)
5. He has not been feeling well. (I)
6. She cannot run fast. (they)
7. We do not own a canary. (he)
8. You won't be needing an umbrella. (we)

Answers

to Exercise 1:

1. Must I leave at four o'clock? 2. Might he be leaving for work now? 3. Can we solve the puzzle? 4. Should you have called him? 5. Could they have been waiting for the bus? 6. Shall I go out now? 7. Will you have finished the book? 8. Should we be making the arrangements? 9. Would she like to know the answer? 10. Can they explain what happened?

to Exercise 2:

1. You must not come with us. 2. It may not be sunny tomorrow. 3. She could not have won the race. 4. We might not be right. 5. You would not have liked that movie. 6. They cannot swim very well. 7. She might not

be finishing school now. 8. He should not have been walking to work. 9. I shall not be happy to see him. 10. You will not have been working all night.

to Exercise 3:

1. Should you not be wearing a warm hat? 2. Could he not have decided to stay at home? 3. Might they not have forgotten the message? 4. Will she not see you again next week? 5. Would they not enjoy riding on the ferry? 6. May he not decide to go camping? 7. Could they not have been playing football yesterday? 8. Shall we not visit our friends? 9. Must she not have wanted to join us? 10. Should he not be getting more sleep?

to Exercise 4:

1. She said he might go. 2. I thought we could finish on time. 3. They knew we would help them. 4. He said he must leave. 5. We believed she would be there. 6. Did you hope they would reply soon? 7. Did he not realize we might meet him there? 8. You thought we could reach our destination by nightfall. 9. I supposed he must be at home. 10. I predicted I should succeed.

to Exercise 5:

1. He thinks he may arrive early. 2. She feels she must make a phone call. 3. I maintain they will not have any difficulty. 4. They realize they cannot do all the work in one day. 5. We know we shall not be able to return home for Christmas. 6. They hope they can find their way. 7. He imagines he will be able to convince us. 8. She suspects they must be living nearby. 9. I hope you will enjoy the play. 10. We think you may know him.

to Exercise 6:

1. could call 2. could spend 3. could visit 4. could go 5. could find 6. could become 7. could describe

to Exercise 7:

1. could help 2. could accompany 3. could depart 4. could learn 5. could show 6. could send 7. could find

to Exercise 8:

1. could have seen 2. could have asked 3. could have explained 4. could have made 5. could, have lost 6. Could, have known 7. could, have been 8. could have convinced 9. could have guessed 10. could have contacted

to Exercise 9:

1. S 2. Q 3. V 4. S 5. V 6. Q 7. V 8. Q 9. S 10. S 11. Q 12. V

to Exercise 10:

1. may or might 2. must 3. may or might 4. must 5. may or might 6. must 7. may or might 8. must 9. may or might 10. may or might

to Exercise 11:

1. She will be able to describe it to you. 2. You will have to lock the doors when you leave. 3. He will be able to follow the instructions. 4. Will they be allowed to stay overnight? 5. We will have to remember to buy groceries. 6. She will be able to finish the work on time. 7. Will he have to take his glasses with him? 8. Will they be able to buy the tickets in advance? 9. She will have to learn to be more careful. 10. You will be allowed to choose your own seat.

to Exercise 12:

1. You are cold, aren't you? 2. They passed the test, didn't they? 3. I can do this well, can't I? 4. You live near the school, don't you? 5. He went downtown, didn't he? 6. We should call them, shouldn't we? 7. She likes toffee, doesn't she? 8. They could help us, couldn't they? 9. I won the race, didn't I? 10. You were reading, weren't you? 11. He rides a bicycle, doesn't he? 12. We would need more time, wouldn't we?

to Exercise 13:

1. They won't reach their destination before five o'clock, will they? 2. He doesn't want to come with us, does he? 3. She hasn't eaten breakfast yet, has she? 4. They aren't very clever, are they? 5. I couldn't have persuaded you, could I? 6. You won't forget to come, will you? 7. We weren't expecting company, were we? 8. They wouldn't like that, would they?

to Exercise 14:

1. Yes, we do. 2. Yes, they may. 3. Yes, she is. 4. Yes, he does. 5. Yes, they had. 6. Yes, he could. 7. Yes, she would. 8. Yes, he had.

to Exercise 15:
1. No, she isn't. 2. No, he won't. 3. No, she wouldn't. 4. No, they couldn't. 5. No, she won't. 6. No, he shouldn't. 7. No, we didn't. 8. No, they couldn't.

to Exercise 16:
1. We are thirsty, and so are they. 2. You have been helpful, and so has she. 3. I swam to the island, and so did he. 4. He was riding a horse, and so were you. 5. They can understand Dutch, and so can we. 6. She enjoyed the trip, and so did I. 7. You should study hard, and so should they. 8. He reads a great deal, and so does she.

to Exercise 17:
1. You haven't finished supper, and neither has she. 2. He couldn't tell the time, and neither could they. 3. She is not planning to go, and neither are we. 4. We didn't wait long, and neither did he. 5. He has not been feeling well, and neither have I. 6. She cannot run fast, and neither can they. 7. We do not own a canary, and neither does he. 8. You won't be needing an umbrella, and neither will we.

10. Subjectives

1. Fill in the blanks with the Simple Present Subjunctive of the verbs shown in brackets. For example:
    They insisted that she ______ at once. (to come)
    They insisted that she come at once.

    The proposal that she _______ us has merit. (to meet)
    The proposal that she meet us has merit.

1. He suggested that I _________ ready by eight o'clock. (to be)
2. We request that she _________ the window. (to open)
3. They demanded that he _________ the room. (to leave)
4. I will ask that she _____________ me. (to accompany)
5. They recommended that he _________ to Bermuda. (to fly)
6. The request that we ______ ready to leave at six is a nuisance. (to be)
7. The recommendation that she ______ a holiday was carried out. (to take)
8. It is necessary that you _________ able to come with us. (to be)
9. They asked that we _________ standing. (to remain)
10. The requirement that he _________ work will be hard to meet. (to find)
11. It is important that he _________ everything he can. (to learn)
12. The demand that she _________ the report has been carried out. (to complete)

2. Complete each of the following sentences with the Past Perfect Subjunctive of the verb shown in brackets. For example:
    They wished they ___ not ____. (to come)
    They wished they had not come.

    I wish I ________ ready on time. (to be)
    I wish I had been ready on time.

    Will she wish she _________ her bicycle? (to ride)
    Will she wish she had ridden her bicycle?

1. I wish I ______ not ___________ the . (to lose)

2. They wished they _______ not _____________ the appointment. (to forget)

3. He will wish he ___________________ us the book. (to show)

4. Will they wish we __________________ them some food? (to give)

5. We wish it _______________ yesterday. (to snow)

6. She wished she _______ not _________ the window. (to open)

7. I wished I _______________ the news. (to hear)

8. You wish you _______________ what to do. (to know)

3. Complete each of the following sentences with the Simple Past Subjunctive of the verb shown in brackets. For example:

He wished he ____ able to do it. (to be)
He wished he were able to do it.

I wish I _______ with you. (to agree)
I wish I agreed with you.

They will wish they ______ time to come. (to have)
They will wish they had time to come.

1. I wish it _________ possible to finish the work tonight. (to be)

2. Will he wish he _______ ready? (to be)

3. She wished she _________ how to sing. (to know)

4. We wish they ____________ to come with us. (to want)

5. You wished you ___________ better. (to feel)

6. They will wish it _________ warmer. (to be)

7. Does he wish he ____________ younger? (to be)

8. I wish I _________ the subject more interesting. (to find)

4. Complete the following sentences, using the indicated verbs in the Simple conjugation with would. For example:

They wished the sun ___________. (to shine)
They wished the sun would shine.

Does she wish it _________? (to snow)
Does she wish it would snow?

You will wish the bell _________. (to ring)
You will wish the bell would ring.

1. They wished she _________________ the arrangements. (to make)
2. He will wish you _________________ him. (to help)
3. She wishes the mail _____________. (to come)
4. We wished they _______________. (to hurry)
5. You will wish the door _______________. (to open)
6. They wish we _______________ for them. (to wait)
7. I wish you _______________ to me. (to write)
8. Will she wish you _______________ her? (to join)

5. Paying attention to the underlined adverbs indicating time, complete each of the following sentences with the correct form of the verb shown in brackets. Use the Past Perfect Subjunctive, the Simple Past Subjunctive, or the Simple conjugation with would, depending on whether the time of the action referred to in the subordinate clause is earlier than, the same as, or later than, the time of making the wish. For example:

 We wished they _________ us earlier. (to call)
 We wished they had called us earlier.

 She wishes she _____ in Rome now.
 She wishes she were in Rome now.

 I wish you __________ with us tomorrow. (to come)
 I wish you would come with us tomorrow.

1. I wish he ___________ here now. (to be)
2. I wish that you ______________ here yesterday. (to be)
3. We wish you ________________ tomorrow. (to come)
4. You will wish you ________________ earlier. (to leave)
5. They wished he ________________ with them the next day. (to come)
6. We wish you ________________ yesterday. (to arrive)
7. I wish that he ________________ us next year. (to visit)
8. She wishes that she __________ at home now. (to be)
9. You wish that he ______________ you last week. (to help)
10. He will always wish he ___________ rich. (to be)
11. The boy wished that he ___________ the competition the next day. (to win)
12. She will wish she _____________ the arrangements earlier. (to make)
13. I wish the weather ____________ warmer now. (to be)

14. We always wished we ______________ fluent in other languages. (to be)
15. They wish he ________________ them next week. (to telephone)

6. For each of the following sentences, rewrite the subordinate clause, using the form in which the word if is omitted. For example:

   If I were in your position, I would pay close attention.
   Were I in your position, I would pay close attention.

   If it had been raining, we would have used our umbrellas.
   Had it been raining, we would have used our umbrellas.

1. If he were here, he would lend us his car.
2. If I had remembered their address, I would have sent them a card.
3. If we were not waiting for a telephone call, we would go downtown.
4. If they had recognized her, they would have spoken to her.
5. If I had been intending to go shopping, I would have let you know.
6. If you had seen the movie, you would have liked it.
7. If it were not snowing, we would go out.
8. If he had been shoveling the walk, we would have seen him.

7. Complete the following sentences, using the indicated verbs in the Simple conjugation with would. For example:

   We __________ if we were ready. (to come)
   We would come if we were ready.

   ______ you ______ more if you had time? (to travel)
   Would you travel more if you had time?

   If they saw us, they ______ not __________ us. (to recognize)
   If they saw us, they would not recognize us.

   ______ you not ____ glad if you were rich? (to be)
   Would you not be glad if you were rich?

1. If we were hitchhiking, ________ you ________ to pick us up? (to stop)
2. If we waited for him, we ________ not ________ on time. (to be)
3. ________ he ________ us know if we made a mistake? (to let)

4. I ________ not _______ to have a party if you were not there. (to want)

5. If you knew more about her, you _________________ your opinion. (to change)

6. ________ you ________ pizza if you did not like it? (to order)

7. ________ they not ________ to come if we asked them? (to agree)

8. We ________ not ________ a car unless we were insured. (to drive)

8. Complete the following sentences, using the indicated verbs in the Perfect conjugation with would. For example:

If it had rained, I ________________ at home. (to stay)
If it had rained, I would have stayed at home.

______ you _________ with us if we had asked you? (to come)
Would you have come with us if we had asked you?

If he had hurried, he _____ not ___________ the bus. (to miss)
If he had hurried, he would not have missed the bus.

______ she not __________ if she had seen us? (to wave)
Would she not have waved if she had seen us?

1. If he had arrived late, ________ we ______________ without him? (to begin)

2. If they had felt thirsty, ________ they not ____________ the lemonade? (to drink)

3. If we had been here, we _______ not ____________ the fireworks. (to miss)

4. If his office had called, _______ he not ______________ to work? (to return)

5. She _______ not ____________ early if she had not had a good reason. (to leave)

6. If they had searched more carefully, they _____________________ the watch sooner. (to find)

7. If you had visited Rome, ________ you ___________ to the opera? (to go)

8. She _____________________ down if she had been tired. (to lie)

9. The following statements contain false or improbable conditions. Paying attention to the underlined adverbs indicating time, complete the

following sentences, using the indicated verbs in the appropriate conjugations with would. use the Simple conjugation for actions pertaining to the present or the future, and use the Perfect conjugation for actions pertaining to the past. For example:

If you came with us now, you _________ everything. (to see)
If you came with us now, you would see everything.

_____ he _________ us yesterday if we had slept in? (to wake)
Would he have woken us yesterday if we had slept in?

1. If he were here now he _______ not _________ to help us. (to hesitate)
2. I _________________ the book last week if I had known you wanted it. (to finish)
3. _______ you _____________ to him last night if you had seen him? (to speak)
4. If they were old enough, they ________________ the contest next week. (to enter)
5. _______ she not ___________ a vacation now if she had more time? (to take)
6. If he had sent a message, we _________________ it two days ago. (to receive)
7. I _________________ it if you came with me now. (to appreciate)
8. _______ she not _______ grateful if we offered to help her tomorrow? (to be)
9. _______ he ____________ yesterday if he had entered the race? (to win)
10. _______ they not _______________ more books last month if they had noticed the stock was low? (to order)
11. _______ she not __________ us now if she knew where we lived? (to visit)
12. ________ you ________________ cucumbers yesterday if they had been on sale? (to buy)

10. For each of the following sentences, complete the subordinate clause with the Simple Past Subjunctive of the verb shown in brackets. For example:

If he _____ in town, he would call us. (to be)
If he were in town, he would call us.

Would you go to the party if you _______ an invitation? (to receive)

Would you go to the party if you received an invitation?

If he ___ not ____ his work, he would find another job. (to like)
If he did not like his work, he would find another job.

1. If he _________ rich, he would travel. (to be)
2. _________ I not anxious to meet him, I would stay at home. (to be)
3. He would have more free time if he ______ not _________ so hard. (to work)
4. If I _________ a car, I would visit Cape Breton. (to have)
5. We would take the bus if it _________ to snow. (to begin)
6. If you _________ him, you would surely recognize him. (to see)
7. I would not confide in him if I _______ not _________ him. (to trust)
8. If we _______ not _________ time, we would let you know. (to have)
9. If he _____________ an expedition, I would certainly join it. (to organize)
10. I would not worry about it if I _________ you. (to be)

11. For each of the following sentences, complete the subordinate clause with the Past Perfect Subjunctive of the verb shown in brackets. For example:
If I _________ him to do it, he would have obeyed me. (to order)
If I had ordered him to do it, he would have obeyed me.

Had it not ______ yesterday, we would have raked the leaves. (to snow)
Had it not snowed yesterday, we would have raked the leaves.

1. I would not have got lost if I _______________ the map. (to study)
2. _______ he _________ at home, we would have visited him. (to be)
3. We would have invited him if we _______________ he would come. (to think)
4. He would have applied for the job if he _______________ the advertisement. (to see)
5. We would not have ordered tea, ______ we _________ how late it was. (to know)
6. ______ it not _________, they would have held the party in the park. (to rain)
7. We would have agreed with you if we _______________ what you meant. (to understand)

8. If you ______________ salt on the steps, they would not have been so slippery. (to put)

9. ______ he ____________ to us, we would have known when to expect him. (to write)

10. If he ________________ to take the course, he would have had to work hard. (to choose)

12. The following statements contain false or improbable conditions. Paying attention to the underlined adverbs indicating time, complete the subordinate clauses with the correct forms of the verbs shown in brackets. Use the Simple Past Subjunctive for actions pertaining to the present or the future, and use the Past Perfect Subjunctive for actions pertaining to the past. For example:

If she ____ here now, she would be admiring the rose bushes. (to be)
If she were here now, she would be admiring the rose bushes.

____ he ______ here last week, we would have met him. (to stay)
Had he stayed here last week, we would have met him.

1. If he _________ here now, we would ask his opinion. (to be)

2. We would have forgotten our tickets last night, if she ____not ________ us. (to remind)

3. _____ I ________ earlier, I would have arrived on time yesterday. (to leave)

4. Would you visit Spain next summer, if you _________ enough money? (to have)

5. If it ________________ yesterday, we would not need to water the lawn. (to rain)

6. If he _________ you last Wednesday, he would have asked your advice. (to see)

7. If they ___________ to leave now, they would need special permission. (to want)

8. ______ they _________ of the concert yesterday, they would have arranged to go. (to know)

9. Would you not have stayed longer last week, if you ___________ able to? (to be)

10. If they ____________ the letter tomorrow, they would receive an answer in two weeks. (to write)

11. If he _____________ the book now, he would enjoy it. (to read)

12. If we _____________ more attention yesterday, we would know what time to be there. (to pay)

13. Change each of the following sentences from a statement containing a probable condition to a statement containing a false or improbable condition. Following the model of the examples, change the underlined verb in the subordinate clause from the Simple Present Indicative to the Simple Past Subjunctive; and change the underlined verb in the main clause from the Simple Future to the Simple conjugation with would. For example:

If she is angry, she will scold us.
If she were angry, she would scold us.

If he wins, we will congratulate him.
If he won, we would congratulate him.

They will join us, if we send them a message.
They would join us, if we sent them a message.

1. If they want to see you, they will come to the party.
2. If he is curious, he will ask what we are doing.
3. She will help us, if she has time.
4. If they work hard, they will succeed.
5. If I find the culprits, I will teach them a lesson.
6. If she recognizes us, she will wave.
7. They will treat you well, if you are honest with them.
8. If she likes you, she will tell you.
9. If he is ready, we will invite him to come.
10. If they see me, they will want to speak to me.

14. Complete the following sentences by filling in the blanks with the Imperative form of the verbs shown in brackets. For example:

_____ the door. (to open)
Open the door.

Don't ______ to come. (to forget)
Don't forget to come.

1. Don't __________ out late. (to stay)
2. Please _________ ready on time. (to be)
3. Don't __________ about that. (to worry)
4. _________ your own business! (to mind)

5. ___________ careful not to trip. (to be)
6. Do not _____________ everything you hear. (to believe)
7. Always ___________ both ways before crossing the street. (to look)
8. You _________ here while I go into the store. (to wait)
9. __________ me! (to excuse)
10. _________ me a postcard if you have time. (to send)

Answers
 to Exercise 1:
1. be 2. open 3. leave 4. accompany 5. fly 6. be 7. take 8. be 9. remain
10. find 11. learn 12. complete

 to Exercise 2:
1. had, lost 2. had, forgotten 3. had shown 4. had given 5. had snowed 6.
had, opened 7. had heard 8. had known

 to Exercise 3:
1. were 2. were 3. knew 4. wanted 5. felt 6. were 7. were 8. found

 to Exercise 4:
1. would make 2. would help 3. would come 4. would hurry 5. would
open 6. would wait 7. would write 8. would join

 to Exercise 5:
1. were 2. had been 3. would come 4. had left 5. would come 6. had
arrived 7. would visit 8. were 9. had helped 10. were 11. would win 12.
had made 13. were 14. were 15. would telephone

 to Exercise 6:
1. Were he here, he would lend us his car. 2. Had I remembered their
address, I would have sent them a card. 3. Were we not waiting for a
telephone call, we would go downtown. 4. Had they recognized her, they
would have spoken to her. 5. Had I been intending to go shopping, I
would have let you know. 6. Had you seen the movie, you would have
liked it. 7. Were it not snowing, we would go out. 8. Had he been
shoveling the walk, we would have seen him.

 to Exercise 7:
1. would, stop 2. would, be 3. Would, let 4. would, want 5. would change
6. Would, order 7. Would, agree 8. would, drive

to Exercise 8:
1. would, have begun 2. would, have drunk 3. would, have missed 4. would, have returned 5. would, have left 6. would have found 7. would, have gone 8. would have lain

to Exercise 9:
1. would, hesitate 2. would have finished 3. Would, have spoken 4. would enter 5. Would, take 6. would have received 7. would appreciate 8. Would, be 9. Would, have won 10. Would, have ordered 11. Would, visit 12. Would, have bought

to Exercise 10:
1. were 2. Were 3. did, work 4. had 5. began 6. saw 7. did, trust 8. did, have 9. organized 10. were

to Exercise 11:
1. had studied 2. Had, been 3. had thought 4. had seen 5. had, known 6. Had, rained 7. had understood 8. had put 9. Had, written 10. had chosen

to Exercise 12:
1. were 2. had, reminded 3. Had, left 4. had 5. had rained 6. had seen 7. wanted 8. Had, known 9. had been 10. wrote 11. read 12. had paid

to Exercise 13:
1. If they wanted to see you, they would come to the party. 2. If he were curious, he would ask what we are doing. 3. She would help us, if she had time. 4. If they worked hard, they would succeed. 5. If I found the culprits, I would teach them a lesson. 6. If she recognized us, she would wave. 7. They would treat you well, if you were honest with them. 8. If she liked you, she would tell you. 9. If he were ready, we would invite him to come. 10. If they saw me, they would want to speak to me.

to Exercise 14:
1. stay 2. be 3. worry 4. Mind 5. Be 6. believe 7. look 8. wait 9. Excuse 10. Send

***

Question Bank

Set 1

1. Food prices have been … steadily for at least ten years.
a) rising
b) lifting
c) raising
2. I'll have to study hard, … I can pass the exam.
a) so that
b) such
c) in order
3. You … to eat if you are not hungry.
a) needn't
b) haven't
c) don't have
4. We'll dance and … we'll have lunch.
a) straight away
b) so
c) then
5. She has to go to Germany for the next … of the training.
a) step
b) stage
c) point
6. When the meeting had finished, we went … the plan once again.
a) up
b) down
c) over
7. I locked the animals in the cage to … them from getting away.
a) avoid
b) hinder
c) prevent
8. You're … your time trying to persuade her.
a) wasting
b) losing
c) missing

9. Our last cook was better than our … one.
a) latter
b) instant
c) current
10. I am grateful to Mary for being so patient … us.
a) for
b) with
c) at
11. Have you exchanged that lovely car … this?
a) with
b) by
c) for
12. The weather was … the poor harvest.

a) condemned for

b) found fault with for

c) blamed for

13. Olivia is teaching three classes and she is examining at a literature exam tomorrow. …, she is chairing a meeting at the Bright Owl Club.

a) On top of it

b) At top

c) On the top of it

14. I don't see any … in arriving early at the show.

a) cause

b) point

c) reason

15. Your application for a vise was turned … by the consulate.

a) aside

b) over

c) down

16. Shopping malls account for 70 percent of the retail business in this country because they are controlled environments which … concerns about the weather.

a) justify

b) foster

c) eliminate

17. It is … impossible to tell the twins apart.

a) virtually

b) closely

c) extremely

18. The man claimed that he was the … heir to the throne.

a) due

b) correct

c) rightful

19. The rather humid climate in no way … from the beauty of these places.

a) protracts

b) detracts

c) attracts

20. … no need to buy traveller's cheques.

a) It's

b) It has

c) There's

21. Is there … bread for all the sandwiches?

a) enough

b) plenty

c) equal

22. Teaching is not a/an … which pays very well.

a) work

b) post

c) occupation

23. This letter didn't come through the post. It was delivered personally, … hand.

a) from

b) by

c) with

24. I … do that if I were you.

a) shan't

b) won't

c) wouldn't

25. There was nothing to … her with the burglary until the police found two gold ring in her car.

a) link

b) place

c) join

26. The manufacturers are advertising a new … of perfume.

a) mark

b) pack

c) brand

27. … my stay in hospital, I lost three kilos.

a) During

b) On

c) In

28. I'm sorry to hear that they have … . They were good friends.

a) dropped out

b) fallen out

c) dropped against

29. Shall I use this … to fry the eggs?

a) dish

b) tin

c) pan

30. She … being given a receipt for the bill she had paid.

a) insisted on

b) demanded

c) asked to

31. These cars historically had two doors but the latest … has four.

a) brand

b) mark

c) model

32. That girl is far ahead … everyone else in the class.

a) of

b) with

c) from

33. She is also interested … art.

a) with

b) in

c) about

34. It's impossible to prevent the boys from quarreling … each other.

a) for

b) with

c) by

35. I'm thinking … looking for a new job in another city.

a) on

b) at

c) of

36. Steve prefers football … tennis.

a) to

b) over

c) than

37. The experience in a psychiatric ward … for the rest of his life.

a) had an influence on him

b) had influence on him

c) had an influence at him

38. If I had known the way to her house, I … her last Monday afternoon.
a) have been visiting
b) had been visiting
c) would have visited

39. He ... that he had been involved in the decision.
a) refused
b) declined
c) denied

40. As brown as … . This phrase means having a tanned skin after sunbathing.
a) dust
b) a berry
c) chocolate

41. It's an awful … your friend couldn't come.
a) shame
b) sorrow
c) shock

42. There is a problem at our TV station. Please do not … your set.
a) repair

b) change
c) adjust

43. Be careful! The cat may … you.
a) kick
b) scratch
c) tear

44. They agreed to … the question of payment.
a) discuss
b) control
c) increase

45. Owing to the bad weather, the garden party was … .
a) shouted off
b) spoken against
c) called off

46. I am sorry I opened your bag but I … it for mine.
a) confused
b) imagined
c) mistook

47. The … of these volunteers for hard work is remarkable.
a) ability
b) efficiency
c) capacity

48. I like this country, but I wish it … rain quite so much.
a) won't
b) didn't
c) hasn't

49. She was so tired that she … asleep in the chair.
a) fell
b) went
c) became

50. Mike has just taken an examination … chemistry.
a) on
b) in
c) for

51. They shouldn't have … the incident. It wasn't my fault.
a) accused me of
b) blamed me for
c) blamed me
52. They won't lend you the money without some … that you will pay it back.
a) profit
b) charge
c) guarantee
53. When you come tomorrow why not … your brother with you?
a) carry
b) bring
c) fetch
54. After she had broken her leg, Marry could only go up and down stairs … .
a) with difficulty
b) in difficulties
c) hardly
55. Who does this laptop belong … ?
a) for
b) with
c) to
56. All her handbags … of leather.
a) being made
b) are made
c) had been made

57. John is the perfect person to take on this difficult job. He's a really hard-… person and won't stand for any nonsense.
a) ship
b) nosed
c) bargain
58. What does a sabbatical year mean?
a) a miserable year
b) a year in which previously made plans are bound to
c) a year in which one is released from one's normal duties

59. It always … me as odd that she should go to work so late in the day.
a) hit
b) smacked
c) struck
60. I walked away as calmly as I could … they thought I was the thief.
a) in case
b) or else
c) to avoid
61. If it's raining tomorrow, we shall have to … the match till Sunday.
a) cancel
b) put off
c) put away
62. Call in and see our … of spring fashions today.

a) reputation
b) election
c) selection
63. We have no … in our files of your recent letters to the company.
a) record
b) account
c) list
64. When her aunt dies, she … a lot of money.
a) earned
b) inherited
c) paid
65. Give him a telephone number to ring … he gets lost.
a) whether
b) unless
c) in case
66. Her parents never allowed her … .
a) smoking
b) a smoking
c) to smoke
67. Bill is only interested … making money.
a) in

b) about
c) on
68. The boy was very upset by the … of his English examination.
a) failure
b) result
c) effect

69. Their actions caused the rate of inflation to … sharply.
a) lift
b) raise
c) rise
70. They were good friends. I was surprised when they … .
a) fell out
b) fell off
c) fell down
71. I had to leave early … I didn't feel very well.
a) too
b) because
c) also
72. After closing the envelope, the assistant manager … the stamps on firmly.
a) licked
b) stuck
c) struck
73. Don't be so sure … yourself! You might be wrong.
a) on
b) from
c) of
74. This book will prove useful … you.
a) for
b) to
c) on
75. You should not be so sensitive … criticism.
a) to
b) at
c) on

76. I am not familiar … his
novels.
a) with
b) about
c) for
77. You should study the
college … for full particulars of
enrolment.
a) prospect
b) syllabus
c) prospectus
78. A novel is a form of …
which may include many facts.
a) short story
b) legend
c) fiction
79. The relationship that matters
most in the life of a … is the
one between
him and his constituency party,
they say.
a) judge
b) politician
c) captain
80. The case of the missing
millionaire has become the …
of considerable
interest in the press.
a) focus
b) middle
c) target
81. These people are thought …
less friendly than people from
our country.
a) been
b) being

c) to be
82. Would you give this report
to Mr. Smith? Sorry, I can't. He
doesn't … .
a) any more work here
b) work any more here
c) work here any longer
83. After hitting her arm, she
had a large black … .
a) bruise
b) cut
c) swelling

84. This is not the right … to
ask for my help; I am away on
business.
a) situation
b) moment
c) opportunity
85. I hadn't seen him for years,
but when I saw him in the street,
I … him at
once.
a) reminded
b) realized
c) remembered
86. The dog was so frightened
that it ran … the bed to hide.
a) along
b) beside
c) under
87. John was unable to … my
party as he was ill.
a) visit
b) attend
c) be present

88. Jane bought red shoes to …
her red dress.
a) match
b) pair
c) mate
89. We'll have to … the
meeting until next month.
a) put down
b) put off
c) put round
90. I am not sure … the black
coat is.
a) whom
b) who
c) whose
91. I don't think he'll beat the
opponent. He's out of … .
a) fitness
b) practice
c) play
92. She is a very … person, but
she has no sense of humour.
a) pleasant

b) amusing
c) enjoyable
93. The university arranges a …
to Madrid every year.
a) travel
b) rout
c) trip
94. Beware … these people.
a) from
b) of
c) at
95. If you fail … this attempt,
don't count on me for help.

a) on
b) at
c) in
96. I separated them … each
other because they were
fighting.
a) of
b) from
c) against
97. I have to leave before six
and so … .
a) do you
b) leave you
c) you do
98. There were no lifeboats on
the little ship because it was …
to be
unsinkable.
a) claimed
b) told
c) believed
99. This church was … by a
famous architect.
a) outlined
b) designed
c) produced
100. Mary is plain, but her sister
is very … .
a) attractive
b) complex
c) sympathetic

101. Her boyfriend treated her
badly. I'm surprised she … it
for so long.
a) put off
b) put through

c) put up with

102. The manager … me to
open a deposit account.
a) warned
b) approved
c) advised

103. This organization tries to
send food to countries where
people are
suffering … malnutrition.
a) from
b) for
c) by

104. If they are to understand
the notice, the instructions must
be … clearer.
a) wrote
b) made
c) done

105. … you like what I want to
do or not, you won't make me
change my
mind regarding this situation.
a) If
b) When
c) Whether

106. Doctors usually have to
study for at least eight years
before becoming
fully … .
a) tested
b) proved
c) qualified

107. The weather was pleasant
with … a gentle wind to cool us
down.
a) just

b) almost
c) nearly

108. I wish you wouldn't …
your clothes all over the room.
a) sprawl
b) scatter
c) straggle

109. … she had no money for a
bus, Olive had to walk all the
way home.
a) As
b) For
c) Thus

110. I didn't want to make up
my mind until I had heard her
… of the story.
a) angle
b) edge
c) side

111. It's strange that Jane is as
… as her mother is beautiful.
a) dull
b) plain
c) raw

112. Since the accident he has
been walking with a … .
a) slope
b) lame
c) limp

113. I flew to the island, then …
a car for five days and visited
most places.
a) charged
b) bought
c) hired

114. In Russia, surgeons have given a man a/an … heart.
a) artificial
b) unreal
c) false

115. The examiners had to … most of the candidates.
a) fire
b) fail
c) fall

116. Our company made a record … last year.
a) benefit
b) wage
c) profit

117. They must economize … fuel.
a) on

b) in
c) with

118. When I understood what she was saying, everything … .
a) fell into the place
b) fell into place
c) fell off the place

119. I had to give a full … of my car when I reported it stolen.
a) detail
b) account
c) description

120. His version of the facts doesn't … with the version I heard from Jane.
a) accord
b) argue
c) amount

121. They have … to accommodate us and the children too.
a) such a small house
b) too small a house
c) a too small house

122. After they had … the carpet, the employees went back to the office.
a) laid
b) lain
c) lied

123. It will … be Christmas again.
a) fast
b) next
c) soon

124. Be careful not to … your coffee on this rug.
a) drip
b) spill
c) filter

125. Mary had to leave her family … when she went abroad to work.
a) at all costs
b) out
c) behind

126. Metal … at high temperatures.
a) grows
b) expands
c) enlarges

127. Because of the poor harvest, cereals prices have … in the last three

months.
a) gone up
b) jumped up
c) sprung up
128. I'm … worried about
Mary; she always seems to be
exhausted.
a) as
b) such
c) so
129. I have difficulty … without
glasses.
a) read
b) of reading
c) in reading
130. He arrived rather late. The
party was already … .
a) in full swing
b) at full tilt
c) in full bloom
131. My neighbour plays his
records … in his flat at night
and nobody can
get enough sleep.
a) at full tilt
b) at full blast
c) in full cry
132. It's unwise to … in a
quarrel between husbands.
a) involve
b) poke
c) interfere
133. I will … the project with
other members and see what
they think about
it.
a) discuss

b) talk
c) explain

134. The poor farmer was very
angry … the dogs chasing his
sheep.
a) about
b) because
c) with
135. I think she's quite honest
… her intentions.
a) about
b) with
c) in
136. I will be waiting … them at
the entrance door.
a) on
b) for
c) at
137. It's no use complaining …
the cold during winter.
a) of
b) from
c) on
138. Manufacturers are now …
of the latest credit restrictions.
a) smelling the rat
b) feeling the pinch
c) cooking the books
139. This music type is an
American art form which is now
… in Eurrope
through the efforts of
expatriates.
a) foundering
b) waning
c) flourishing

140. She was … disappointed when she learned that she hadn't got the job
she dreamt of.
a) fully
b) highly
c) bitterly

141. They have … the castle and it is now a luxury hotel.
a) undone
b) remade
c) transformed

142. I … so much last night: I feel terrible.
a) shouldn't have eaten
b) mustn't have eaten
c) didn't have to eat

143. The man stole one of the officers' uniforms and managed to escape by
passing himself … as a guard.
a) out
b) off
c) through

144. … we set off in the next minutes, we'll be there on time.
a) In case
b) So long
c) Provided

145. If he drinks any more beer, I don't think he'll be … to football this
afternoon.
a) skilled
b) capable
c) fit

146. My manager's … of my work doesn't matter to me at all.
a) opinion
b) belief
c) meaning

147. The recent … domestic violence is worrying the police.
a) increase in
b) increase of
c) increase about

148. There's … to hurry.
a) no purpose
b) no need
c) impossible

149. The officers … the kidnapper from escaping by blocking all exits.
a) allowed
b) avoided
c) prevented

150. This meat isn't suitable … .
a) the grill
b) for grilling
c) being grilled

151. A bridge is already … over the river.
a) being built
b) erecting
c) been erected

152. The painting is …; the thief will be disappointed.
a) invalid
b) priceless
c) worthless

153. Even though he is thirty-three, he lives … his mother's salary.
a) from
b) at
c) on

154. It should be obvious … you that this problem will be solved.
a) for
b) to
c) at

155. Mike often forgets to do what he has been told and is scolded for being … .
a) rebellious
b) malicious
c) disobedient

156. The house is quite warm. The oil heater gives … .
a) out a good heat
b) off a good heat
c) out good heat

157. In the middle of my trip I stopped … a rest on the river bank.
a) have
b) to have
c) having

158. After ruling that the article had unjustly … the reputation of the businessman, the judge ordered the magazine to … its libelous statements in print.
a) praised…publicize
b) injured…retract
c) sullied…communicate

159. When she heard the news she went completely … .
a) fuse
b) thunder
c) spare

160. I won't … those children making a noise in my apartment!
a) have
b) allow
c) let

161. It's great that your father managed to … that man. Somehow he had deceived many people.
a) see to
b) see through
c) see out

162. My car is much older … than yours.
a) form
b) manufacture
c) model

163. I … in bed all night thinking about it.
a) laid
b) led
c) lay

164. According to the medical doctor, there's absolutely nothing the … with you.
a) wrong

b) matter

c) problem

165. I looked everywhere but I couldn't find … at all.

a) anyone

b) no one

c) someone

166. It was … a simple question that everyone answered it.

a) much

b) such

c) too

167. I like my eggs soft …, not hard.

a) cooked

b) steamed

c) boiled

168. I was utterly amazed when the train arrived exactly … time.

a) on

b) by

c) in

169. I'd like to take this … of wishing you all the best.

a) chance

b) opportunity

c) occasion

170. Learners of English may fail to .. between unfamiliar sounds.

a) separate

b) differ

c) distinguish

171. … her opinion, English cheese is better than French cheese.

a) To

b) By

c) In

172. Their parents would not ... them to go there for the weekend.

a) agree

b) permit

c) consent

173. Every Sunday the old man's dog goes to the shop to … him a newspaper.

a) carry

b) fetch

c) take

174. It's late! It's time we … .

a) are gone

b) are going

c) were gone

175. I drove around the area for half an hour but I couldn't find a car … .

a) park

b) plan

c) garage

176. The smell was so bad that it … me off my food.

a) took

b) put

c) got

177. Although she hasn't said anything she … to be upset about it.

a) seems

b) acts

c) behaves

178. It's strange: his sister is blonde, … he is very dark.

a) therefore

b) however

c) whereas

179. I very much … that you will come to dinner next Monday.

a) hope

b) want

c) wish

180. Crops are sometimes completely destroyed by … of locusts.

a) bands

b) swarms

c) flocks

181. There's something wrong with my watch: it has … five minutes in the last hour.

a) gained

b) won

c) advanced

182. Keep in mind that if you are … to customers, they'll walk out of the shop.

a) brush

b) rough

c) rude

183. The air in the house felt cold and … after some days of bad weather.

a) wet

b) damp

c) moist

184. Do you want to wait for a table at this restaurant or shall we go … else?

a) anywhere

b) everywhere

c) somewhere

185. Children who use escalators should always be accompanied … an adult.

a) with

b) by

c) beside

186. I took someone else's coat by … .

a) fortune

b) error

c) mistake

187. How long does it … to get home in the morning?

a) take you

b) need you

c) demand

188. It's becoming more and more … that the Government has lost its confidence.

a) apparent

b) expected

c) anticipated

189. You need a special … to go into this building.

a) agreement

b) allowance

c) permit

190. I don't like her, so I have no intention … speaking to her.

a) about

b) of

c) with

191. I had to drive carefully because the road was icy in several … .

a) places

b) blocks

c) pieces

192. Don't invite him; I can't stand his bad … .

a) mood

b) mind

c) temper

193. Not only … the movie, but she had also read the book.

a) she did see

b) she saw

c) had she seen

194. I had a meeting at work which went … much longer than I expected.

a) in

b) on

c) by

195. Tom … me to take a lawyer to court with me.

a) suggested

b) insisted

c) advised

196. Poor woman! She has so much to cope … .

a) with

b) in

c) by

197. Tim has always gone … strange hobbies like inventing secret codes.

a) by

b) into

c) in for

198. As he is an expert, his opinions would be worth … .

a) to have

b) having

c) of having

199. Nowhere … this room.

a) is as cold as in

b) is it as cold as

c) it is as cold as in

200. There's just something about him that really puts my … up.

a) handle

b) teeth

c) back

201. The explorer walked all the way along the river, from its mouth to its … .

a) cause

b) source

c) well

202. She soon received promotion, for her superiors realised that she was a woman of considerable … .

a) ability

b) future

c) possibility

203. It is … knowledge that they quarrel violently several times a month.

a) complete

b) normal

c) common

204. After his mother died, he was … up by his grandparents.

a) taken

b) brought

c) grown

205. You should do something worthwhile with your time instead of … it!

a) spending

b) using

c) wasting

206. The police have issued … to local citizens to be on the lookout for thieves.

a) warnings

b) advice

c) information

207. If you require any more … about the event, please telephone us.

a) news

b) fact

c) information

208. Wait … you get at the office before you unpack this.

a) when

b) until

c) after

209. The students … names appear on the list all failed the exam.

a) whose

b) which

c) their

210. When the police appealed for witnesses, many people came … .

a) across

b) on

c) forward

211. Can you give me a rough … of how much it will cost?

a) esteem

b) value

c) estimate

212. I do play billiards, but I … tennis.

a) prefer

b) like

c) would rather

213. The consultant gave me … useful information.

a) one

b) some

c) the

214. One of the … has fallen off the clock.

a) hands

b) pointers

c) arms

215. How old do you have to be … you can drive a car in your country?

a) when

b) since

c) before

216. I'll let you have the book back next Friday without … .

a) miss

b) fail

c) doubt

217. … I ask him for money he owes me, he says he will bring it in a few weeks.

a) However

b) Whatever

c) Whenever

218. I … to inform you that we cannot exchange articles.

a) resent

b) regret

c) sense

219. I am responsible … what has happened.

a) with

b) for

c) by

220. They have to arrange for the … of their furniture accessories.

a) sole

b) sale

c) seal

221. The boy wouldn't go into the sea … his parents went too.

a) unless

b) except

c) but

222. The … part of the week is always busy for Steven.

a) start

b) near

c) early

223. I … to take my neighbour to court if he didn't stop making so much noise.

a) offered

b) suggested

c) threatened

224. It wasn't his … that he was late.

a) blame

b) fault

c) error

225. She sat there with her arms … doing nothing.

a) turned

b) folded

c) twisted

226. Our neighbours … their hedge cut once a year.

a) have

b) do

c) make

227. I could tell she was pleased … the expression on his face.

a) at

b) by

c) for

228. Steve calls himself Steve Milton, but his … surname is Smith.

a) natural

b) current

c) real

229. If you keep trying you might … to do it.
a) succeed
b) manage
c) understand

230. Their child was born in the ambulance … to the hospital.
a) on the way
b) by the way
c) a long way

231. The meeting is now … .
a) on end
b) at the end
c) at an end

232. She promised to write … I never heard from her again.
a) except
b) but
c) because

233. I … to Tim for my bad behaviour.
a) coped
b) excused
c) apologised

234. Ever … she was in school she has wanted to become a medical doctor.
a) since
b) always
c) after

235. The bottle was on the top shelf, out of … .
a) achievement
b) arrival
c) reach

236. Laptops are supposed to … time, but I'm not so sure they do!
a) spare
b) save
c) waste

237. I didn't mean to do it; it was … accident.
a) in
b) on
c) by

238. His speech was …, eliciting thunderous applause.
a) tedious
b) cowardly
c) well-received

239. What does "a wild goose chase" mean?
a) a wild night on the town
b) a search for something that cannot be found
c) a dangerous race in the streets between cars

240. You should have avoided risking …, General!
a) the lives of your soldiers
b) your soldiers' life
c) the life of your soldiers'

241. … goes the train; now we will have to walk!
a) On time
b) There
c) At once

242. Jane is important to him. He wouldn't get … without her.
a) by
b) over

c) round

243. They live in the house ...
the blue door.
a) which
b) where
c) with

244. I phoned the bank to ...
how much money I had to pay.
a) control
b) check
c) test

245. His parents give him
anything he wants and as a
result he's very ... .
a) ruined
b) spoilt
c) damaged

246. ... I am studying at the best
university and I hope to get a
job soon.
a) In a moment
b) At present
c) At this instant

247. He is a fast typist but his
letters are full of spelling ... .
a) mistakes
b) wrongs
c) faults

248. The officers have asked
that ... who saw the accident
should inform
them.
a) one
b) someone
c) anyone

249. If the greengrocer has some
tomatoes ... buy some?
a) you will
b) would you
c) shall you

Set 2

250. I will offer a small ... to
anyone who finds my missing
cat.
a) reward
b) receipt
c) repayment

251. The party has ... to win the
elections.
a) achieved
b) managed
c) attained

252. You ... do the washing-up:
we can do it later.
a) wouldn't
b) daren't
c) needn't

253. They demand higher wages
because prices are ... .
a) growing
b) exceeding
c) rising

254. You should be careful
when you wash this ... blouse.
a) weak
b) feeble
c) sensitive

255. My parents always fall … in front of the TV.
a) asleep
b) sleepy
c) sleeping

256. You can never rely … her to be punctual.
a) of
b) with
c) on

257. Are you interested … rock music?
a) on

b) in
c) of

258. You should reply … his letter.
a) on
b) for
c) to

259. I will certainly act … your advice.
a) with
b) at
c) on

260. as sound as … . This phrase means healthy, in good condition.
a) steel
b) a monkey
c) a bell

261. Buy the … of soap which is now on sale.
a) model
b) brand
c) mark

262. My uncle took … jogging when he retired.
a) up
b) on
c) over

263. There has been a rather worrying … five per cent in our profits last year.
a) drop in
b) fall in
c) drop of

264. … you hurry, you won't catch the train.
a) Unless
b) Except
c) As

265. The customer … his money back.
a) asked
b) demanded
c) requested

266. I … him to go to the Lost Property office.
a) noticed
b) announced
c) advised

267. I couldn't resist having another slice of pizza even … I was supposed to be on diet.
a) though
b) however
c) although

268. These old buildings are going to be … soon.

a) laid out
b) run down
c) pulled down

269. … as I like ice-cream, I can't eat any more now.
a) Much
b) Even
c) So

270. You may borrow ten books, provided you show them to … is at the desk.
a) who
b) whoever
c) whom

271. Is he playing computer games? He's … to be washing the car.
a) hoped
b) supposed
c) expected

272. Mary was angry with me for breaking the windows, but it happened … accident.
a) by
b) in
c) on

273. The room was crowded with over fifty people … into it.
a) pushed
b) packed
c) stuck

274. Beware of the friends who appear to be enthusiastic … your success.

a) of
b) with
c) about

275. They want to watch the latest movie … TV.
a) in
b) at
c) on

276. … to leave early is rarely granted.
a) Permission
b) Leave
c) Allowance

277. …, my colleagues didn't laugh at me.
a) For my surprise
b) To my surprise
c) As to surprise me

278. If you had gone there, you … my sister.
a) would have met
b) would meet
c) had met

279. She never goes in lifts because she is terrified of … spaces.
a) constricted
b) compressed
c) contained

280. It never … to me that she would be there.
a) recurred
b) occurred
c) contemplated

281. The assistant was … helpful, but Mike felt she could have given him

more information.

a) exactly

b) totally

c) quite

282. The meal was excellent; the steak was particularly … .

a) flavoured

b) tasteful

c) delicious

283. Are there any seats left for this evening's …?

a) opera

b) act

c) performance

284. Having … the table, she called the family for supper.

a) laid

b) spread

c) ordered

285. As I have been ill, I have had no … to discuss the business plan.

a) suitability

b) possibility

c) opportunity

286. Tom … to turn up for the football match.

a) omitted

b) failed

c) stopped

287. The manager's presence was helpful, but he could … us more money.

a) give

b) gave

c) have given

288. There are five lawyers in my town and I have consulted … of them in turn.

a) every

b) each

c) any

289. The final course was so difficult that I didn't … any progress at all.

a) do

b) create

c) make

290. I'm tired of looking at ancient … .

a) ruins

b) foundations

c) remnants

291. My bike is gone: it must … .

a) have been stolen

b) have stolen

c) be stolen

292. There's a … to her patience.

a) top

b) limit

c) bottom

293. I … hands with the guests.

a) gave

b) nodded

c) shook

294. We had a great … of trouble getting through customs.

a) level

b) lot

c) deal

295. Rose trees need to be … regularly.

a) cut

b) clipped

c) pruned

296. What made you think … such a thing?

a) of

b) on

c) at

297. I would go to the pool if the weather … good.

a) is

b) were

c) has been

298. I rang you up while he … his report.

a) was finishing

b) has been finishing

c) had finished

299. The bus … is 50 cents.

a) cost

b) fare

c) charge

300. Before the invention of refrigeration, the … of meat was a problem.

a) preservation

b) keeping

c) maintenance

301. Could I have another one? Oh, there doesn't seem to be …
.

a) any left

b) some left

c) left any

302. I will go on working on the farm … I can.

a) through

b) during

c) as long as

303. I'll ask Ms. Thompson to … to you as soon as she returns.

a) ring

b) contact

c) speak

304. This new model works by letting light through a small … at the front.

a) leak

b) hole

c) break

305. You will have to … your holiday if you are too ill.

a) cut down

b) call off

c) put aside

306. If you go to the market you might find a … .

a) chance

b) bargain

c) trade

307. The train was … by three hours because of bad weather.

a) postponed

b) put off

c) delayed

308. My guests didn't leave until 3 a.m.; they … have enjoyed themselves.

a) can't

b) must

c) might

309. She was sitting just ...
Steve and John.

a) beside

b) off

c) besides

310. Mary remembered the
correct address only ... she had
posted the
letter.

a) since

b) following

c) after

311. I have never ... any
experience of living in a small
village.

a) wished

b) made

c) had

312. I'm very ... of cash at the
moment.

a) down

b) empty

c) short

313. The ... were told to fasten
their seat belts.

a) passengers

b) flyers

c) customers

314. There are ... trains running
today.

a) scarcer

b) fewer

c) little

315. Mary isn't ... well with the
new manager.

a) going on

b) taking on

c) getting on

316. Has this idea ever occurred
… you?

a) at

b) to

c) on

317. I'm … with your stupid
ideas.

a) get rid

b) fed over

c) fed up

318. If they had been able … it
for you, they would have helped
you.

a) to do

b) doing

c) is doing

319. The officers carried out a
… search for the missing
diplomat.

a) through

b) thoughtful

c) thorough

320. Fitting together the
fragments was a … task.

a) minute

b) minuscule

c) painstaking

321. It will … rain later so we
should go now.

a) probably

b) likely

c) usually

322. I would have cleaned this mess if I … you were coming.
a) would have known
b) had known
c) have known

323. We have … to meet at the station at 8 o'clock.
a) confirmed
b) combined
c) arranged

324. There is always … traffic in the city centre.
a) full
b) strong
c) heavy

325. He's … to drink too much at parties.
a) adequate
b) apt
c) common

326. We must get there … or other.
a) somehow
b) anyhow
c) anywhere

327. She was left to make all the … for the meeting.
a) procedures
b) provisions
c) arrangements

328. The new girl … type at 45 words per minute.
a) need
b) can
c) dare

329. I'll wait over there until … ready.
a) you are
b) you will be
c) you were

330. You must move your car; … I have to give you a ticket.
a) whether
b) therefore
c) otherwise

331. A manager of a large company is given a big … .
a) money
b) pay
c) salary

332. Heavy goods delivery vehicles may not carry … of more than fifteen tons.
a) masses
b) sizes
c) loads

333. After they went on strike there was a … of water.
a) shortage
b) drain
c) loss

334. She's entitled to a pension, but she won't dream … retiring yet.
a) on
b) of
c) to

335. Mix the contents … a little water.
a) of

b) with

c) at

336. You can try ... if you really need to improve your language skills.

a) listening to BBC

b) listening at BBC

c) to listening to BBC

337. His ... of Alexander the Great was acclaimed as one of the best.

a) entertainment

b) portrayal

c) spectacle

338. The army ... defeat at the hands of such powerful enemies.

a) bore

b) supported

c) suffered

339. Their accounts were phony. They had been cooking the ... for years.

a) books

b) spinner

c) trade

340. Practical ... is desirable for candidates.

a) exploit

b) initiative

c) experience

341. The director opened the letter without ... to read the address on the envelope.

a) worrying

b) bothering

c) caring

342. Hurry! She's already here. I didn't think she ... till tomorrow.

a) was coming

b) is coming

c) is to come

343. If you have any ... concerning this report please phone us.

a) requests

b) wishes

c) queries

344. Could you ... exactly what you saw?

a) inform

b) describe

c) point

345. He has brought you a ... of flowers.

a) branch

b) bunch

c) bush

346. The child seems to be incapable ... keeping his room tidy.

a) at

b) with

c) of

347. In the summer I often sleep in the ... air on the terrace.

a) clean

b) clear

c) open

348. This dress ... you perfectly.

a) likes
b) suits
c) matches
349. I bought the phone because the colours ... the colours of the car.
a) match
b) fit
c) suit
350. To promote her so quickly you must have a high ... of her ability.
a) view

b) idea
c) opinion
351. We ... as well go without him.
a) can
b) may
c) just
352. She ... out of the window for a moment and then went on writing.
a) glanced
b) glimpsed
c) regarded
353. You should keep receipts from shops as proof ... purchase.
a) to
b) for
c) of
354. Don't mention it ... my girlfriend, but I paid $80 for this perfume.
a) to

b) at
c) with
355. The child knocked ... the door.
a) on
b) for
c) at
356. You must have ... the examination before Friday.
a) passing
b) entered for
c) sit for
357. They ... for you for more than one hour now.
a) have waited
b) have been waiting
c) wait
358. I would have come home earlier if you ... me.
a) had told
b) have told
c) told

359. Petrol is so expensive ... they use public transport.
a) then
b) thus
c) that
360. There has been some ... in their bilateral relations.
a) destitution
b) deterioration
c) depreciation
361. They take too much ... of his kindness.
a) profit
b) use

c) advantage

362. I can easily … you up for the night.

a) put

b) take

c) keep

363. My car is very old, but I can't … to buy a new one.

a) achieve

b) reach

c) afford

364. Two passengers were killed and the other was … injured.

a) hardly

b) severely

c) unusually

365. After ten years the bedroom wallpaper had considerably … .

a) faded

b) mixed

c) lighted

366. My attempt to pass the final exam was … .

a) unmerciful

b) unhelpful

c) unsuccessful

367. She … at the Latin College for French.

a) enlisted

b) inscribed

c) enrolled

368. I admit I suffer from a … of patience with old people.

a) lack

b) limit

c) shortage

369. The building is in good … though it needs to be painted.

a) state

b) condition

c) position

370. I can't be sure I'll be there in time. I … be late.

a) should

b) must

c) may

371. His suit didn't … him properly.

a) meet

b) fit

c) frame

372. She may be quick … understanding, but she's not capable of doing it.

a) at

b) in

c) for

373. We have some important business to attend … .

a) with

b) at

c) to

374. Steve, you should not boast … your success.

a) of

b) with

c) from

375. I'm sorry, I haven't got … change.

a) all

b) any

c) lots

376. An oppressive ..., and not
the festive mood characterized
the mood of
the gathering.
a) senility
b) inanity
c) solemnity
377. I think it's ... your luck to
drive without a license.
a) risking
b) tempting
c) pushing
378. If you looked back far
enough, you would see that you
are ... related
to Karl Marx.
a) distantly
b) slightly
c) previously
379. I can't understand it; your
handwriting is ... .
a) illegible
b) illicit
c) illusive
380. Hello! You ... be the new
employee.
a) could
b) should
c) must
381. Last year the cereals
harvest was disappointing, but
this year it looks
as if we shall have a better ... .
a) crop
b) amount

c) product
382. She was in ... of a large
number of men.
a) direction
b) leadership
c) charge
383. Tom was born during the
last war, which would ... him
about 50 now.
a) give
b) make
c) calculate

384. The actor never married,
choosing to remain ... all his
life.
a) separate
b) single
c) individual
385. The consultant showed me
... the washing machine.
a) the working of
b) to work
c) how to use
386. The driver failed to signal
his ... to turn left.
a) idea
b) purpose
c) intention
387. I wish you wouldn't call
her ... that name.
a) by
b) with
c) under
388. I had ... reached the park
when I saw everyone leaving.
a) quite

b) almost

c) rather

389. She tried to … to see him at least once a week.

a) call up

b) come on

c) drop in

390. No, Kate isn't stupid. …, she's rather clever.

a) Now

b) Currently

c) Actually

391. The Minister resigned as a/an … of the incident.

a) effect

b) result

c) cause

392. The names of the winners will be … in the next magazine issue.

a) told

b) informed

c) announced

393. When the clock … twelve, I left.

a) struck

b) beat

c) shot

394. The store is only open … weekday mornings now.

a) for

b) in

c) on

395. They think he is very good … drawing.

a) at

b) for

c) in

396. Every day thousands of … fly the Atlantic for negotiations.

a) dealers

b) merchants

c) businessmen

397. Prices continued to rise … the ruling party became unpopular.

a) on condition that

b) with the result that

c) on the chance that

398. I would help the old lady in her shopping if she … me.

a) will ask

b) ask

c) asked

399. … for a trip last Friday?

a) Did you go

b) Will you go

c) Have you gone

400. The child was taught that it was … to interrupt.

a) coarse

b) rude

c) crude

401. She was … better than her brother at chess.

a) miles

b) feet

c) inches

402. I often speak to her on my … to work.

a) travel

b) way

c) road

403. The noise prevented me from … to sleep.

a) starting

b) going

c) beginning

404. This horse is famous for … the National race two times.

a) gaining

b) conquering

c) winning

405. Before starting a new chapter, I'd like to … what we discussed yesterday.

a) run up

b) run along

c) run through

406. I think it's time we … on our way.

a) are

b) were

c) will be

407. Would you … taking care of the cat for two hours?

a) mind

b) matter

c) agree

408. The world record for this event is almost impossible to … .

a) beat

b) meet

c) compare

409. We've been … with this business partner for many years.

a) competing

b) shopping

c) dealing

410. She applied for training as a pilot, but they turned her … .

a) down

b) over

c) back

411. The child wasn't accustomed … by coach.

a) travel

b) to travel

c) to travelling

412. She has left her phone at home. She's always so … .

a) forgetful

b) forgotten

c) forgetting

413. Newly-… coins always look clean.

a) moulded

b) minted

c) printed

414. I had to go to the library to … some books.

a) give

b) return

c) buy

415. It was such a hot day … the surface of the material was damaged.

a) as

b) so

c) that

416. She always … out in a crowd because of her style.

a) stood

b) found
c) looked
417. Please apply … the secretary for this type of information.
a) for
b) at
c) to

418. Though the concert had been enjoyable, it was overly …
.
a) sublime
b) protracted
c) extensive
419. A skillful …, John adopted a posture of patience and …
toward the
protestors.
a) academician/understanding
b) pundit/tolerance
c) negotiator/compromise
420. Could you give me a rough … of the costs?
a) estimate
b) value
c) correlation
421. There is a … of $2,000 for information leading to the thief.
a) gift
b) reward
c) prize
422. The manager didn't pay for the meal himself – he put it on
his
company's … account.
a) expense

b) price
c) value
423. I knew her … we were young.
a) until
b) as
c) when
424. I … them run away from the bank.
a) allowed
b) saw
c) felt
425. I only have … days left in Spain.
a) little
b) a few
c) a little

426. She pretended that she agreed with me to avoid … my feelings.
a) hurting
b) to hurt
c) hurt
427. Many fires could be … if new safety standards were introduced.
a) protected
b) excluded
c) prevented
428. My watch stopped so I had no way of knowing the right … .
a) moment
b) time
c) hour

429. He came … an unknown poem while he was searching for something else.
a) round
b) across
c) off

430. I couldn't beat him at chess; I'm just not in his … .
a) class
b) type
c) set

431. Too much exercise can be harmful but walking is good … you.
a) by
b) with
c) for

432. I find it difficult to talk to her because we have so … in common.
a) few
b) less
c) little

433. His attitude … his parents is very disrespectful.
a) as far as
b) towards
c) as for

434. Surely Anna is not going to drive, … she?
a) does

b) will
c) is

435. You … pay for this. It's free.

a) shouldn't
b) mustn't
c) don't have to

436. A child learns a language best … .
a) when being brought up to it
b) by being brought up to it
c) while being brought into it

437. Urgent discussions will continue … .
a) behind the scenes
b) behind the curtain
c) behind the bars

438. Our house is nothing out of the … .
a) normal
b) usual
c) ordinary

439. "A ladies' man" means:
a) a man most women fall for
b) a man who dresses up like a woman
c) a man who enjoys the company of women

440. The manager warned Kate that the laziness and … could result in her dismissal.
a) procrastination
b) ambition
c) fortitude

441. The butcher cut some steak and … it up.
a) closed
b) wrapped
c) wound

442. The man … to take a
breath test after the incident.
a) denied
b) objected
c) refused

443. I do my best to practise
every day … it is difficult
sometimes.
a) although
b) also
c) even

444. His arm was so … injured
that he couldn't play anymore.
a) deeply
b) badly
c) hardly

445. His home is a … between a
palace and a hotel.
a) union
b) link
c) cross

446. The woman … case was
described in the article never
fully recovered.
a) what
b) whom
c) whose

447. I … put my money there if
I didn't consider it was safe.
a) didn't
b) wouldn't
c) hadn't

448. Driving in this city is
supposed to be confusing but I
didn't find it at …
difficult.

a) all
b) once
c) least

449. I enjoy … but don't like
jogging.
a) to swim
b) in swim
c) swimming

450. Would you … the kettle on
for some coffee?
a) set
b) put
c) have

451. I suggest … the "meal of
the day" rather than fish.
a) to have

b) we have
c) for us having

452. Her father won't … to my
marrying Olivia.
a) agree
b) allow
c) approve

453. It was way to hot. I
couldn't … it any longer.
a) carry
b) hold
c) stand

454. They had always liked the
sea … they moved to the Coast.
a) so
b) since
c) such

455. Just keep .. on him, will
you?
a) a look

b) an eye

c) a care

456. By the time you receive this message, I … for China.

a) will leave

b) have left

c) will have left

457. You can depend … me.

a) in

b) of

c) on

458. I invested a lot of money … residential buildings.

a) in

b) for

c) at

459. She is trying to lose weight by … sweets.

a) cutting down at

b) stopping down at

c) cutting down on

460. The terrorist tried to persuade the hostage that he was neither … nor … . He was just interested in calling attention to his cause.

a) impeccable/sincere

b) antagonistic/vindictive

c) recalcitrant/clandestine

461. The professor was surprised that her English was so … .

a) liquid

b) definite

c) fluent

462. I went to … some pictures by a renowned painter.

a) watch

b) look at

c) see to

463. If it … fine, she shall go out.

a) was

b) were

c) is

464. The idea of a balanced diet is difficult to … in this group.

a) put across

b) take in

c) make over

465. There was a small room into … we all gathered.

a) where

b) that

c) which

466. You … go to dentist's.

a) rather

b) ought to

c) better

467. His speech was interesting at first, but it was … long.

a) so much

b) far too

c) too much

468. The soldier has been on … for twenty-four hours without a break.

a) work

b) job

c) duty

469. When she braked on the icy road, the car … .
a) slid
b) slipped
c) skidded

470. This is the … building in the city.
a) oldest
b) elder
c) elderly

471. You must put your name on this side and then sign on the … side.
a) other
b) under
c) back

472. I will always … our wonderful holidays.
a) reflect
b) remind
c) remember

473. The Prime Minister … his intention to retire.
a) told
b) announced
c) informed

474. As the child walked through the fields, he heard sheep … .
a) braying
b) bleating
c) crying

475. I'm afraid I can't comment … your project yet.
a) about
b) with
c) on

476. Steve was employed … a factory in 2010.
a) in
b) to
c) by

477. It was such a good weather that I decided to go … .
a) fish
b) fishing
c) to fishing

478. I think she … you my regards when you met two days ago.
a) gave
b) has given
c) give

479. Not … did she refuse to speak to me, but she also blamed me for failing.
a) even
b) at all
c) only

480. "To come through flying colours" means:
a) to succeed in one's study
b) to accomplish something with great success
c) to be understood loud and clear

481. I hope she is … to buy some milk.
a) proposed
b) suggested
c) remembered

482. If I were you, I … that gaming PC.
a) would buy
b) will buy
c) am buying
483. The vet decided that he had to operate … the dog.
a) with
b) on
c) at
484. I … like to apologize.
a) could
b) must
c) would
485. Many accidents in the home could be … by taking simple safety measures.

a) protected
b) avoided
c) preserved
486. Try to remember … bring your debit card.
a) me to
b) yourself to
c) to
487. The bride looked … in her dress.
a) beauty
b) lovely
c) handsome
488. We didn't leave for the station until the very … moment.
a) late
b) least

c) last
489. When are you going to give back that book you … me?
a) owe
b) debt
c) lend
490. The poor man was … by a gang last month.
a) murdered
b) destroyed
c) slaughter
491. Each … of the family had to do the washing up.
a) person
b) member
c) individual
492. The woman performs beautifully … the piano.
a) in
b) from
c) on
493. The boy comes … drawing lessons four times a week.
a) to
b) for
c) at

494. She … a coloured thread round her finger so as not to forget about the meeting.
a) rang
b) wound
c) curved
495. You have a new baby?! …!
a) What wonderful news
b) What a wonderful news

c) How wonderful news

496. If my diploma … last week, I would have been able to come sooner.

a) are found

b) were found

c) had been found

497. Old people do not take kindly to having their daily … upset.

a) routine

b) habit

c) custom

498. You were warned never … with those members.

a) to assign

b) to assume

c) to associate

499. If your company wants to attract workers it must … the wages.

a) spread

b) raise

c) rise

500. This computer package is totally … for our need.

a) unsuitable

b) undeniable

c) unspeakable

501. Some people think it is … to use little-known words.

a) clever

b) skilled

c) sensitive

502. He decided to … from the committee.

a) cancel

b) resign

c) prevent

503. Be here at nine o'clock without … .

a) fault

b) late

c) fail

504. The children were … by the cartoons.

a) fascinated

b) fascinating

c) fascination

505. The murderer … escape from the prison.

a) could

b) managed to

c) succeeded in

506. A witness … now been found.

a) was

b) had

c) has

507. She couldn't tell the truth. She had to … a story.

a) invent

b) manage

c) combine

508. She woke up crying because she had … a nightmare.

a) seen

b) dreamt

c) had

509. I hope to get an answer to my final letter by … of post.

a) round

b) return

c) back
510. Didn't it ever … to you
that you would be caught?
a) occur
b) enter
c) strike

511. I started early … to avoid
the worst of the traffic.
a) so that
b) in so far
c) in order
512. The children threw
snowballs at … on their way.
a) themselves
b) each other
c) their own
513. Don't be so sure …
yourself.
a) of
b) with
c) on
514. My grandmother buys eggs
… the dozen.
a) to
b) for
c) by
515. She's entitled … a pension,
but she doesn't want to retire.
a) to
b) on
c) in
516. Before you run … other
people, you should consider
your own faults.
a) over
b) up

c) down
517. The child won't go to sleep
… we leave a light on.
a) except
b) unless
c) but
518. The effectiveness of his
work relies … the use of
advanced
technologies.
a) on
b) by
c) of
519. The minority are suing the
government for the return of
their … lands.
a) antique

b) ancestral
c) inherited
520. Some species are on the …
of becoming extinct.
a) edge
b) side
c) verge
521. One … of my job is that it
is near where I live.
a) advantage
b) pleasure
c) preference
522. The little child loved … the
old castle.
a) hunting
b) detecting
c) exploring

523. This is a photo of the university I … when I lived in Hamburg.
a) used
b) attended
c) joined

524. It's the first time … here.
a) I have been
b) I was
c) I am coming

525. Many accidents in this town are caused by … driving.
a) harmful
b) careful
c) careless

526. I was delighted when I … to sell my car so quickly.
a) managed
b) could
c) risked

527. It sounds … the situation isn't about to improve.
a) how
b) as if
c) so that

528. This patient … quickly after his illness.
a) recovered
b) covered
c) discovered

529. Caring for her cousin is a … burden for her.
a) sour
b) bitter
c) heavy

530. The manager made a wonderful … .
a) message
b) talk
c) speech

531. There is a fault at our latest TV station. Please don't … your TV set.
a) repair
b) adjust
c) switch

532. The man … going by plane instead of car.
a) suggested
b) agreed
c) convinced

533. Please concentrate … your tasks!
a) with
b) to
c) on

534. Many men do not approve … blood-sports.
a) for
b) of
c) with

535. You must encourage Mary … her efforts.
a) in
b) at
c) with

536. The ball … two or three times before disappearing.
a) leapt
b) bounced
c) hopped

537. It's … helping that man.
He will die anyway.
a) good
b) no good
c) not good

538. Would you agree that a
man pays less attention … than
a woman does?
a) to dress
b) on dress
c) to the dress

539. Our institution can give
you the … number of refugees.
a) unclear
b) suggestive
c) approximate

540. As drunk as … . This
phrase refers to someone very
drunk.
a) a fish
b) a lord
c) a barrel

541. How … you manage to get
there so fast?
a) used
b) had
c) did

542. The touristic guide walked
so … that most of the people
could not
keep up with him.
a) fast
b) quick
c) rapid

543. Membership of the club, …
costs $12,000 a year, is only
open to
women.
a) what
b) that
c) which

544. The boy swore that he
would take … his family's
killer.
a) revenge in
b) revenge on
c) revenge at

545. … she wasn't feeling very
well, she went to visit her
parents as usual.
a) Still
b) Although
c) However

546. That guy has a dishonest
… in his character.
a) stripe
b) strip
c) streak

547. Having looked the place
…, the strange man went away.
a) down
b) out
c) over

548. I'm selling the building …
of the summer.
a) at the end
b) in the end
c) on the end

549. She was complaining … a
headache this morning.
a) at
b) from
c) of

Set 3

550. You need to hurry because the … train leaves in five minutes.
a) latter
b) last
c) latest

551. I am not used … spoken to in such a manner.
a) for being
b) to being
c) to be

552. There was a small house standing … hundreds of palm trees near the beach.
a) in
b) among
c) between

553. As the team were … at the end of the game, he lost the bet.
a) equal
b) fair
c) correct

554. These little stores are always … of people at Christmas time.
a) stuffed
b) busy
c) crowded

555. Their request … me completely by surprise.

a) left
b) made
c) took

556. I have … why the Browns went to live in that country.
a) puzzled
b) surprised
c) wondered

557. You have to be patient … him.
a) for
b) with
c) about

558. Most women never … with violent crimes.
a) get into contact
b) come into contact
c) get in touch

559. I don't think I … this game before.
a) have played
b) will play
c) would play

560. "A City man" refers to:
a) any man with a higher education
b) a man who works in a city, which is a financial power of an area
c) someone who is constantly showing off

561. Is there a bank where I can … these pounds for euros?
a) turn

b) alter
c) exchange

562. The officer said that he saw no … between the murders.
a) joint
b) connection
c) join
563. Drinking is a bad habit, which many people find difficult to … .
a) beat
b) cough
c) break
564. Would you … passing this magazine to him?
a) mind
b) agree
c) want
565. There's … to be frightened of the cat.
a) a fear
b) no need
c) no fear
566. Her boyfriend won't … her drive his car.
a) allow
b) leave
c) let
567. The competitors in the rally had to follow the … laid down by the sponsors.
a) direct
b) route
c) address
568. If only I …play the piano as well as you!
a) might
b) would
c) could
569. It's a great … that the exhibition was cancelled.
a) sorrow
b) sadness
c) pity

570. On our … to Madrid, the car broke down.
a) way
b) road
c) voyage
571. She has adopted two orphans … her own children.
a) except
b) besides
c) in place of
572. I cannot understand how you put … this residential area.
a) out
b) by
c) up with
573. You will have to take things … .
a) like you find them
b) as you find them
c) so as you find them
574. We … to the concert, but we didn't make it.
a) were to have gone
b) would go
c) were gone
575. No one … she was.
a) could be quicker than
b) can be as quick as
c) could be so quick as

576. This computer is cheap, but that one is … .
a) cheaper yet
b) more cheaper
c) even cheaper

577. If the line is busy, don't wait and … .
a) hang on
b) hang up
c) hang down

578. If they … to that event, they would certainly have decided to attend it.
a) will be invited

b) had been invited
c) were invited

579. If I saw Olive, I … her to my party.
a) invite
b) will invite
c) would invite

580. I was very … not to pass the message further.
a) cajoled
b) tempted
c) elicited

581. After the party the dog was allowed to finish off the … sandwiches.
a) left
b) leaving
c) remaining

582. I would much … a reply by the end of the week.
a) appreciate
b) require

c) value

583. When she heard the joke, she burst into loud … .
a) smiles
b) laughter
c) enjoyment

584. I couldn't get used to … to work so early.
a) go
b) going
c) be going

585. … amount of money can buy a true friend.
a) No
b) Never
c) None

586. They should be spending money on a house … than on a car.
a) other
b) better
c) rather

587. I was very … of myself for forgetting that.
a) disgraced
b) ashamed
c) shocked

588. Mary earns a great … of money.
a) quantity
b) level
c) deal

589. He is an expert … coronaviruses.
a) about
b) on

c) in

590. They look exactly the … .

a) alike

b) identical

c) same

591. There was no need to be uneasy … the results.

a) for

b) about

c) on

592. It's impossible to prevent the boys … quarrelling with each other.

a) to

b) in

c) from

593. This bike is inferior … the one I bought last year.

a) to

b) at

c) by

594. Tom plays … the school team.

a) by

b) in

c) on

595. The teacher despairs … ever teaching him anything.

a) of

b) in

c) on

596. Our family is fortunate in having sufficient supplies … the winter.

a) for

b) on

c) to

597. The old man was found guilty … many crimes.

a) from

b) for

c) of

598. … Sam, he can't go alone.

a) As if

b) As for

c) As far as

599. I know nothing about that battle. It was … .

a) behind the times

b) as the same time

c) before my time

600. Many jobs in this area can be directly … to tourism.

a) attributed

b) attracted

c) dedicated

601. When the director went to China on business his … took over all his duties.

a) officer

b) deputy

c) caretaker

602. She saw the plane crash when its engines … .

a) failed

b) struck

c) held

603. You are going to come to the meeting, …?

a) will you

b) do you

c) aren't you

604. You will not finish that project by tomorrow unless you … some help.
a) get
b) would get
c) will get

605. It's difficult to pay my bills when prices keep … .
a) rising
b) gaining
c) raising

606. After the death of her father, she was brought … by her uncle.
a) round
b) about
c) up

607. Why did the police suspect you? It doesn't make … to me.
a) right
b) sense
c) truth

608. When they heard that their children had crossed the road without
looking, they told them they … do it again.
a) mustn't
b) needn't
c) didn't need to

609. He went to Germany hoping to find a teaching … .
a) work
b) occupation
c) post

610. I can't … what they are doing; it's way too dark down there.
a) look into
b) make out
c) see through

611. This country has … good transport.
a) the
b) a
c) very

612. I'd like you to meet a very good friend of …, Dave.
a) me

b) my
c) mine

613. We travelled to Australia by the most … route.
a) direct
b) unique
c) easy

614. This film is based ... a novel.
a) of
b) on
c) in

615. I should be grateful … any advice you can give regarding this
situation.
a) for
b) about
c) with

616. I was shocked … her indifference!
a) on

b) with
c) at
617. The manager has just gone on her … leave. She gets three weeks'
holiday a year.
a) regular
b) annual
c) regular
618. He have … this minute left for the city centre.
a) ever
b) already
c) just
619. To my …, a pandemic is more dangerous than nuclear arms.
a) mind
b) view
c) disbelief
620. They are always … with each other about investments.
a) shouting

b) arguing
c) annoying
621. I took that faulty laptop back to the shop where I'd bought it and asked
the … if they would change it for me.
a) clerk
b) official
c) assistant
622. I … to the cinema last night. I'm so tired now.
a) had not to go

b) shouldn't have gone
c) haven't had to go
623. You will spend at least one year working in this company … you can
find out how things operate here.
a) so that
b) so as to
c) because
624. I can … with most things but I cannot stand lies.
a) put aside
b) put up
c) put off
625. I think she is … her time looking for a job here.
a) losing
b) wasting
c) missing
626. It is a very good idea to be … dressed when you have a business
meeting.
a) finely
b) smartly
c) boldly
627. I was pleased to see how … he looked after his recent COVID-19
illness.
a) well
b) pleasant
c) nice

628. Let's … across this field instead of going by the road.

a) set
b) come
c) cut
629. Tell me … about your
holiday in Spain.
a) every
b) much
c) all
630. It's fairly rude to interrupt
when someone is … .
a) talking
b) saying
c) discussing
631. I didn't enjoy the event.
No, and … .
a) neither we did
b) we didn't either
c) so didn't we
632. … of the week, I hope I
shall have lost another kilo.
a) By the end
b) At the end
c) To the end
633. I reasoned … her, but she
would not listen to me.
a) to
b) for
c) with
634. She is responding …
treatment and will be cured.
a) on
b) for
c) to
635. Nothing will prevent me …
succeeding.
a) on
b) from

c) in
636. Jennifer criticised
everything and even ran … his
friends.
a) up
b) down
c) into
637. Why did you have … his
last tutorial?
a) such difficulties to follow
b) such a difficulty to follow
c) such difficulty in following
638. I was sitting in a famous
café … afternoon when I saw
her.
a) one
b) in
c) the
639. The … question in this
case is whether she was there or
not.
a) crucial
b) valuable
c) supreme
640. He's the best employee
I've ever had. I couldn't … for a
better one.
a) abide
b) average
c) ask
641. You are not allowed … in
this room.
a) smoke
b) smoking
c) to smoke

642. I think you'd better …
before the manager returns.
a) be gone
b) be going
c) being gone

643. "I … you all", she said, as
she left.
a) am hating
b) can hate
c) hate

644. I'm sorry. It's all my …!
a) guilt
b) fault
c) wrong

645. I chose these because they
are my … shade of blue.
a) popular
b) favourite
c) fancy

646. I wonder … like to travel
by boat.
a) what it is
b) how it is
c) what is it

647. Two other … in their
report are worth mentioning.
a) effects
b) points
c) notices

648. Many soldiers were …
wounded in the war. They
needed a lot of help.
a) hardly
b) seriously
c) utterly

649. She's a luck person. She
always seems to fall on her … .
a) ankles
b) legs
c) feet

650. … experience of working
in a factory is required.
a) Previous
b) First
c) Initial

651. For a short time after the
car crash, I suffered from
constant … in my
back.
a) hurt
b) pain
c) ache

652. An enormous … of rubbish
had built up here.
a) pile
b) hill
c) tower

653. Children can be instructed
… swimming at a very early
age.
a) with

b) for
c) in

654. Marry will come … home
late. Don't wait for her.
a) to
b) into
c) back

655. I was instructed … driving
once upon a time.
a) in

b) about

c) at

656. How can you agree … such an idea?

a) with

b) at

c) by

657. It was … to meet you. That's what she said to me.

a) pleasure

b) a pleasure

c) some pleasure

658. Only by shouting loudly … a taxi.

a) she got

b) she's got

c) did she get

659. The lights … out and I was left in the darkness.

a) turned

b) went

c) gave

660. For this meal to be a real success, you … cook the meat for at least three hours.

a) need

b) ought

c) must

661. It is logical that when factories are … workers tend to lose their jobs.

a) automatic

b) automation

c) automated

662. They are not used … supper so late.

a) to having

b) of having

c) to have

663. Be careful; she has her eyes … you.

a) for

b) at

c) on

664. In spite of the anesthetic, I was fully … during the operation.

a) awake

b) sensitive

c) conscious

665. Today a man was … down the street by my dog.

a) chased

b) hunted

c) sped

666. I don't … to see her again until next month.

a) think

b) expect

c) wait

667. Some drivers, after …, annoy their fellows.

a) passing by

b) taking over

c) overtaking

668. I had … news of what she was doing in London.

a) several

b) little

c) few

669. Now that he is retired, he enjoys … more time watching documentaries.
a) spending
b) to take
c) taking

670. His debt now amounts … $10,000.
a) in
b) with
c) to

671. You demand too much of them; they are not really equal … the
project.
a) for
b) to
c) with

672. The student is still dependent … his parents.
a) on
b) from
c) with

673. Will you have … to tell your manager about it?
a) some nerves
b) some nerve
c) the nerve

674. Boys and girls … enjoyed the show.
a) both
b) either
c) alike

675. The reconstruction of the city is now … .
a) well under way
b) well in the way
c) through the way

676. The production goes well now, although there were some
… .
a) last straws
b) teething troubles
c) starting problems

677. If I could understand this alphabet, I … the article.
a) read
b) will read
c) would read

678. Please … and see me some time – you are welcome.
a) come to
b) come away
c) come around

679. I could … panic in her voice.
a) desist
b) detect
c) detest

680. Thousands of tourists use the … of footpaths across these hills.
a) network
b) grid
c) circuit

681. The professors … with coronavirus infection one after the other.
a) went down
b) went off
c) went under

682. He agreed to give me $100, … the $300 he had already lent me.
a) extra to
b) surplus to
c) in addition to

683. What do you usually … for delivering things?
a) demand
b) charge
c) cost

684. We chose some attractive … paper for the present.
a) covering
b) wrapping
c) packing

685. It was a beautiful cloth … from velvet.
a) worn
b) threaded
c) woven

686. We have … of time to catch the flight.
a) enough
b) plenty
c) great deal

687. She put the letters into the wrong envelopes … mistake.
a) on
b) with
c) by

688. Mike seems confident but you … never judge by appearances.
a) might
b) should

c) could

689. I couldn't go fishing because it began to … with rain.
a) flow
b) drench
c) pour

690. They … for the same job.
a) chose
b) referred
c) applied

691. The plane was … for over two hours because of fog.
a) delayed
b) landed
c) cancelled

692. She has to be careful which soap she uses, because her skin is … .
a) sensible
b) senseless
c) sensitive

693. The local authorities want people to set … their own businesses.
a) off
b) up
c) in

694. She is quite intelligent but she … common sense.
a) wants
b) fails
c) lacks

695. I wonder who drank all the wine. It … have been Mike because he was out all day.
a) can't

b) could

c) must

696. They are opposed …
giving people large pay rises.
a) for
b) to
c) against

697. I will show you the
document if I … it.
a) could find
b) will find
c) find

698. Being exhausted, he sent a
request asking that his
colleagues … their
meeting for one hour.
a) defray
b) defer
c) commence

699. The reporter gave a
dramatic … of his adventures.
a) tale
b) saga
c) account

700. Some people are camping
for the … of rare species
hunting.
a) extinction
b) abolition
c) annihilation

701. I am … in information
about this laptop.
a) interested
b) bored
c) concerned

702. They say we're likely to
have a … winter.
a) calm
b) smooth
c) mild

703. Do you think Sarah and
Tom marry …?
a) lastly
b) at last
c) in the end

704. You should … a lawyer
before you sign that contract.
a) check

b) consult
c) counsel

705. "You can take a horse to
water, but you can't … it
drink!"
a) make
b) compel
c) save

706. The old man is a little bit
… in his right ear.
a) disabled
b) deaf
c) dead

707. Some explorers did not
survive the terrible … across the
mountains.
a) journey
b) step
c) travel

708. Heavy snowfalls have …
all flights.
a) omitted
b) delayed

c) postponed

709. The rainstorms ... more than three days.

a) went

b) took

c) lasted

710. There will be a ... interval for snacks.

a) small

b) short

c) light

711. The play was very long, but there were three ... .

a) rests

b) intervals

c) gaps

712. The jewels were ... a lot of money.

a) cost

b) valued

c) worth

713. They had a plan to trick me, but I didn't fall ... it.

a) for

b) to

c) at

714. It is unreasonable to demand this ... Mary.

a) in

b) at

c) of

715. It took me a long time to get rid ... the infection.

a) of

b) against

c) from

716. They differ ... each other so much.

a) of

b) with

c) from

717. There is little ... in this company.

a) hanging around

b) to hang around

c) hung around

718. I would let her go, if I ... all about this mission.

a) know

b) have known

c) knew

719. They were ... for smuggling perfumes into the country.

a) judged

b) warned

c) arrested

720. They didn't believe his theory because it didn't seem at all ... .

a) feasible

b) plausible

c) creditable

721. ... you leave for the airport, you'll miss the flight.

a) Unless

b) However

c) When

722. I haven't met her, but I did once ... across her boyfriend.

a) look

b) go

c) come

723. She … her next appointment at the dentist's.
a) erased
b) cancelled
c) wiped

724. Because of the earthquake, the windows … in their frames.
a) rattled
b) slapped
c) shocked

725. I would … go by air than spend two days travelling by car.
a) prefer
b) better
c) rather

726. It's all over between them: she's walked … on him.
a) off
b) away
c) out

727. Our best player got infected and won't be … to play tomorrow.
a) adequate
b) fit
c) proper

728. Sarah spoke so fast I couldn't understand … she was talking about.
a) what
b) which
c) how

729. Mr. Smith is free … you now.
a) see
b) will see
c) to see

730. Everyone felt … for Mr. Brown when he lost his management position.
a) discontent
b) sorry
c) unhappy

731. What … will this decision have on the future of this company?
a) effect
b) result
c) answer

732. This year the trees were … two weeks earlier than usual.
a) in full cry
b) in full bloom
c) at full blast

733. During the last meeting everyone shared … his happiness.
a) in
b) against
c) at

734. The professional climber failed … his attempt.
a) with
b) at
c) in

735. I tried to reason … her, but she was rude to me.
a) on
b) with
c) for

736. Are you aware … the difficulties that lie ahead?
a) by
b) on
c) of

737. It's just an illusion. He's not different … anyone else.
a) for
b) from
c) on

738. Dave usually goes there … him.
a) with

b) to
c) at

739. Alexia worships the sun and … she spends her holidays in Greece.
a) yet
b) however
c) accordingly

740. I can't come. I'm tied … at the office.
a) in
b) up
c) down

741. Guests wore … they liked to the party.
a) everything
b) anything
c) nothing

742. The pilot drives so quickly that I am afraid that one day he will …
someone.
a) crash down

b) turn over
c) knock down

743. Don't worry. This dog is perfectly … .
a) harmless
b) harmful
c) tame

744. One of the main advantages … the new operating platform is that it is very simple to use.
a) for
b) of
c) on

745. You'd better set off twenty minutes early … there is traffic.
a) in case
b) so that
c) as if

746. When I saw Olivia's reaction, I regretted … told her.
a) to have

b) to having
c) having

747. The shirt I was wearing that day was dirty, but I don't think anyone …
.
a) watched
b) noticed
c) remarked

748. This is the oldest house … the village.
a) in
b) by
c) to

749. Jane was singing an old rock song, a favourite of … .
a) her
b) herself
c) hers

750. So … people came to the meeting that they had to cancel it.
a) a few
b) few
c) little

751. Scientists are still looking for a cure … COVID-19.
a) for
b) against
c) to

752. Put the salt in the water and let it … before adding anything else.
a) melt
b) dissolve
c) soften

753. It's too hot for you … this parcel.
a) digging
b) for digging
c) to dig

754. He told Steve … for borrowing his laptop without permission.
a) on
b) out
c) off

755. In this company, if you interfere … other people's affairs, you will regret it.
a) with
b) to
c) about

756. Are you at least partially aware of the difficulties that lie ahead … you?
a) for
b) of
c) to

757. I left my office after I … the report.
a) had written
b) have written
c) should have written

758. Her medical doctor made her … in bed for two weeks.
a) to stay
b) staying
c) stay

759. As quick as … . This phrase means very quick.
a) cats
b) fire
c) lightning

760. The officers haven't had time to complete the investigation, but they have concluded … that he committed suicide.
a) tentatively
b) tenuously
c) temporally

761. I'm going to buy a new car; I'm tired … this one.
a) of

b) in

c) with

762. … a personal computer can help you work much faster.

a) To have

b) In having

c) Having

763. I … be delighted to show you the way.

a) might

b) ought to

c) would

764. … the weather, the match went ahead.

a) Owing to

b) In spite of

c) However

765. Melania rang to make an early … at the hairdresser's.

a) order

b) appointment

c) date

766. Adrian was the … in his family.

a) lowest

b) littlest

c) shortest

767. Could you buy a cake please … they come this afternoon?

a) if only

b) in case

c) on account of

768. One … of old public transport is its unreliability.

a) disorder

b) dislike

c) disadvantage

769. Did you know that she is … a baby?

a) expecting

b) hoping

c) waiting

770. The main … to progress is not technical but political.

a) clash

b) obstacle

c) prevention

771. The best rooms in this hotel … the bay.

a) regard

b) overlook

c) view

772. All dogs … be kept on a lead in public.

a) must

b) ought

c) need

773. You should separate the eggs and then beat with a … .

a) whip

b) wick

c) whisk

774. The man was … to steal the laptop when he saw it on the table.

a) dragged

b) tempted

c) brought

775. My parents … me to learn English when I was a child.

a) let

b) heard

c) persuaded

776. I am accustomed … bad weather.

a) to

b) of

c) from

777. She was afraid … mentioning it to her husband.

a) in

b) at

c) of

778. I warned them … the danger.

a) at

b) of

c) in

779. Gold is feared … in price this week.

a) to go up

b) going up

c) to be going up

780. I will ask Jane to come if I … her.

a) saw

b) will see

c) see

781. In the jar there was a … which looked like jam.

a) material

b) solid

c) substance

782. Because his presentation was so confusing, … people understood it.

a) clever

b) few

c) less

783. I am … her to arrive at any moment.

a) expecting

b) waiting

c) hoping

784. You … worry about the bill – I've already paid it.

a) daren't

b) might not

c) needn't

785. I've made an appointment for 11 o'clock. Is that … for you?

a) fit

b) convenient

c) right

786. You look … you've seen a ghost!

a) so that

b) that

c) as if

787. You … blame yourself. It wasn't your fault.

a) daren't

b) won't

c) mustn't

788. I'm … that I didn't pass the examination.

a) deceived

b) despaired

c) disappointed

789. This magazine has … interesting article on space travel.

a) quite an
b) a partly
c) nearly an
790. Your sister is much taller
… you.
a) how
b) than
c) from
791. They always quarrel about
coffee; she likes it strong, but he
wants it …
.
a) small
b) feeble
c) weak
792. Getting divorced was a ...
decision for us.
a) firm
b) hard
c) large
793. Mr. Smith was … in a road
accident.
a) damaged
b) wronged
c) injured
794. I expected her at eight but
she finally … at midnight.
a) came to
b) turned up
c) came off
795. Buses into town run … ten
minutes or so.
a) each
b) all
c) every
796. Can you make … what she
has written there?

a) for
b) out
c) up for

797. I can't say what his name is
though it is … .
a) on the tip of my tongue
b) on top of my tongue
c) on my tongue's tip
798. Whether or not to abolish
corporal punishment is still …
in political
circles.
a) proposal of contention
b) a bone of contention
c) bone of agreement
799. I … a nice watch two days
ago.
a) was given
b) have been given
c) would give
800. As bold as … . This phrase
means cheeky, impudent.
a) bones
b) a bear
c) brass
801. He was an … writer
because he persuaded many
people.
a) ordinary
b) influential
c) accurate
802. I … seeing Mary tomorrow
so I will give her your message.
a) may be
b) shall be
c) could be

803. The temperature yesterday was about … for this season.
a) average
b) middle
c) moderate

804. Steven swims well and … does his sister.
a) also
b) even
c) so

805. The old man was very … for my help.
a) grateful

b) pleased
c) delighted

806. … it was raining she went out without a raincoat.
a) In spite
b) However
c) Although

807. Your progress will be … in three months' time.
a) valued
b) evaluated
c) counted

808. I don't know why she complains. She doesn't earn as … as I do.
a) less
b) few
c) little

809. The organization will not be … any new members.
a) taking up
b) taking off
c) taking on

810. She can make a delicious … out of almost anything.
a) food
b) meal
c) plate

811. From now on, everything will be … sailing, I hope.
a) plain
b) simple
c) pretty

812. She could hardly … such a generous offer.
a) turn for
b) turn off
c) turn down

813. Tom has made his money by developing a travel … .
a) shop
b) business
c) affair

814. Do you believe … all that nonsense? I honestly don't.
a) in
b) to
c) at

815. I'm not sure … the exact date.
a) with
b) of
c) for

816. She's not capable … bringing up this child.
a) of
b) on
c) for

817. Steven was born … .

a) without wedlock

b) out of a wedlock

c) out of wedlock

818. Although he has travelled extensively, he has never been … .

a) to the Antipodes

b) at Antipodes

c) to Antipodes

819. At that hour, the street was … as people were fast asleep in bed.

a) denuded

b) deserted

c) devastated

820. Artists struggle with the conflict between … their own talent and
knowledge that very few succeed.

a) faith in

b) neglect of

c) dissolution to

821. My house isn't difficult to find. It's … the high school.

a) against

b) beside

c) between

822. A lot of my friends have … smoking in the last year.

a) put off

b) given up

c) held back

823. Please tell me … there is anything special that you would like to eat.

a) which

b) so

c) if

824. I'm making you responsible for this report. Please see … it that it is finished on time.

a) for

b) into

c) to

825. Olivia suggested … to the cinema together.

a) that we should go

b) us to go

c) we are going

826. It will be mostly cloudy, with … of rain in the west.

a) bursts

b) outbreaks

c) times

827. I … of people who smoke.

a) dislike

b) distrust

c) disapprove

828. Jane bought a new … for the party.

a) dress

b) clothes

c) vest

829. When the organization got a new computer, we had to … a programming course.

a) do

b) make

c) study

830. This history lesson seemed to go … .

a) over and over

b) on and on

c) off and on

831. I know her by ..., but I don't what her name is.

a) sight

b) heart

c) chance

832. The bus burst into ... but the driver managed to escape.

a) heat

b) fire

c) flames

833. I know Jane is slow ... understanding, but please be patient.

a) to

b) at

c) on

834. I'll be absent ... class this week.

a) from

b) at

c) to

835. It gives me ... to introduce her.

a) great pleasure

b) a great pleasure

c) much pleasures

836. They ... in Germany for more than two years now.

a) were staying

b) are staying

c) have been staying

837. Look, I'm not drunk. I am as ... as a judge.

a) calm

b) sober

c) clear

838. The working atmosphere has gone downhill. You have a lot to ... for.

a) agree

b) abide

c) answer

839. That incident happened because of the ... of the employees.

a) infallible

b) negligence

c) diligence

840. "A sore point" means:

a) a very dangerous crossroads

b) a matter that irritates or hurts when it is brought up

c) a blister on a foot

841. She likes to sit there and ... what goes on below.

a) look

b) gaze

c) watch

842. Keep ... the good work!

a) with

b) on

c) up

843. ... he joined the army, Steve had never been abroad.

a) Until

b) Since

c) While

844. If you want to join our club, you must first … this application form.
a) do up
b) fill in
c) make up

845. I haven't got … furniture like theirs.
a) some
b) any
c) the

Set 4

846. The librarian went to search for the book in a place … rare ones were
kept.
a) where
b) there
c) that

847. A teacher must … children to be kind to each other.
a) let

b) force
c) encourage

848. You'll … a lot of time if you take the car.
a) spend
b) make
c) save

849. They took out a/an … to that newspaper.
a) inscription
b) subscription

c) conscription

850. The local authorities … increase taxes soon.
a) may
b) need
c) dare

851. The child hit the vase with his elbow and it … to the floor.
a) crashed
b) smashed
c) broke

852. I completely … with what has been said.
a) accept
b) agree
c) approve

853. She lost her homework and she … do it again.
a) ought
b) needs
c) has to

854. You are not … to smoke inside.
a) let
b) allowed
c) accepted

855. I believe … this town needs is a new shopping mall.
a) as
b) how
c) what

856. It's still not … that I am going to Madrid tomorrow.
a) certain
b) right
c) exact

857. Even though the old man was often cruel to his dog, it remained
faithful … him.
a) for
b) in
c) to

858. You should encourage your daughter … her efforts.
a) to
b) for
c) in

859. The artists … our town by … .
a) have taken/by surprise
b) have taken/by storm
c) have brought/by storm

860. There is an increasing … to make films portraying love.
a) trend
b) surge
c) tradition

861. I felt sorry … him when he lost his job.
a) with
b) to
c) for

862. It was difficult for me to … what the recommendations I should make.
a) decide
b) realize
c) settle

863. The gorgeous lady walked to the … of the pool and jumped in.
a) extent
b) border
c) side

864. I thought she would like me to buy her a … brown bag.
a) black
b) French
c) new

865. The officer … me the way.
a) said
b) told
c) directed

866. Her boyfriend was sent to prison for … a bank.
a) stealing
b) robbing
c) lending

867. I'm going to stay here … she phones me.
a) for
b) when
c) until

868. You can trust what Daniel says. He's a very … person.
a) trustful
b) profitable
c) reliable

869. Don't worry. I still have one or two … up my sleeve.
a) tricks
b) defenses
c) jokes

870. The Prime Minister got up to … a short speech.
a) tell
b) make
c) hold

871. Mike was an ... writer who persuaded many people.
a) influential
b) accurate
c) ordinary

872. If I hadn't done that, I think you ... .
a) could die
b) might have died
c) may have died

873. People who live in big cities ... to suffer from stress.
a) develop
b) tend
c) lean

874. She has provided ... every emergency.
a) to
b) with
c) for

875. There was a note attached ... the package.
a) to
b) with
c) on

876. They say Italian is a splendid language ... .
a) for singing in
b) to sing in
c) for sing in

877. I saw him ... the street.
a) crosses
b) to cross
c) cross

878. Although we have a large number of employees, each one receives ... attention when needed.
a) only
b) individual
c) single

879. We negotiated for hours but we weren't able to ... at an agreement.
a) agree
b) abide
c) arrive

880. The missing climber appeared at the mountain hut ... and kicking.
a) alive
b) hale
c) safe

881. Sarah had had a special ... with her aunt ever since her mother died.
a) sense
b) feeling
c) relationship

882. The little boy was so noisy that his mother told him not to be such a ...
.
a) trouble
b) nuisance
c) worry

883. I took ... football again at the beginning of this month.
a) up
b) with

c) by

884. Would you … the stamps on to the documents?
a) spit
b) suck
c) stick

885. The robber … everyone in the bank lie on the floor.
a) obliged
b) made
c) forced

886. There are … employees who always cause trouble.
a) these
b) that
c) some

887. I am late because my alarm clock … this morning. I'm sorry.
a) came on
b) went off
c) turned on

888. In spite of his protests, Steve … the athlete train two hours a day.
a) made
b) let
c) cause

889. The man was standing … of the diving board, showing off his muscles.
a) by the end
b) on the end
c) in the end

890. I mustn't stop … on this project for another two hours.

a) to work
b) working
c) to have work

891. Would you mind if I … the windows? It's hot in here.
a) did open
b) opened
c) were opening

892. The next time you see Jane, you … apologize.
a) ought to
b) need
c) dare to

893. If she's not back … midnight, I'm going to phone the police.
a) on
b) till
c) by

894. The man … his wife and children and left them to take care of themselves.
a) let
b) spoilt
c) abandoned

895. The customer … on complaining to the manager in person.
a) insisted
b) argued
c) demanded

896. They have a great … for that island because they spent their honeymoon there.
a) feeling

b) affection

c) connection

897. Like her, I hope …
something better.

a) to

b) in

c) for

898. I would go to Rome if I …
time to do it.

a) have

b) had

c) would have

899. I will play the piano but
I'm a little … .

a) out of practice

b) out of use

c) out of turn

900. In this area coal is mined
day … night.

a) into

b) after

c) and

901. I had to leave my family …
when I went abroad to work.

a) at a loss

b) behind

c) out

902. The author had qualified as
a medical doctor but later gave
up the …
of medicine.

a) practice

b) procedure

c) prescription

903. It was … . I had to talk
quickly to keep warm.

a) fresh

b) mild

c) cold

904. Her novel was more
exciting … any she has written.

a) than

b) as

c) to

905. I'm having a party on
Sunday. …?

a) Will you come

b) Don't you come

c) Need you come

906. The boy … his head,
wondering how he could solve
the equation.

a) shaved

b) screwed

c) scratched

907. She swatted some flies on
the windows and … the glass.

a) crashed

b) smashed

c) cut

908. She received a e-mail this
morning … her a place at
university.

a) inviting

b) offering

c) proposing

909. The Browns spent so much
money that they're … debt.

a) out of

b) with

c) in

910. … you open the windows, please?
a) Need
b) Will
c) May

911. Will you … what you said? It was rude!
a) take off
b) take up
c) take back

912. Stick this … on the parcel that says "fragile".
a) label
b) sign
c) advice

913. The manager … that the people he works with are very committed.
a) talks
b) says
c) tells

914. The girl learnt to ski on a slope that was not too … .
a) high
b) tall
c) steep

915. The trade … of the company if a bee.
a) mark
b) class
c) brand

916. You will not succeed … working harder on this project.
a) although
b) if
c) without

917. The old lady will never part … her precious possessions.
a) from
b) to
c) with

918. I am grateful … you.
a) to
b) for
c) by

919. They have to work hard for money while the fat … in the city make money doing very little.
a) pack
b) fish
c) cats

920. Youngsters need all the help and … when applying for jobs.
a) incentive
b) stimulation
c) encouragement

921. I'm sorry but I haven't got … change.
a) some
b) lots
c) any

922. Volkswagen is one of the most popular … of car in Germany.
a) makes
b) brands
c) marks

923. I must … shopping tomorrow.
a) to go

b) going

c) go

924. I can't see any … to this complicated problem.

a) result

b) solution

c) reason

925. Yesterday I came … a beautiful old car.

a) across

b) over

c) down

926. I can't find my book anywhere; it has simply … .

a) missed

b) lost

c) vanished

927. Scientists have discovered a close … between smoking and cancer.

a) action

b) connection

c) union

928. He came in quietly … not to wake the children.

a) so as

b) if so

c) as if

929. I decided to … a party to celebrate my promotion.

a) offer

b) give

c) make

930. I have no doubt … the innocence of the accused.

a) over

b) on

c) about

931. Everybody … me for the incident.

a) blamed

b) arrested

c) charged

932. Tomorrow the children are going to see the works … Van Gogh.

a) from

b) of

c) with

933. I consulted my lawyer … the matter and I shall continue.

a) for

b) to

c) on

934. She didn't enjoy … at her aunt's.

a) to stay

b) staying

c) stayed

935. There are … when I have to drive for long distances.

a) times

b) a long time

c) at times

936. … by the rejections of his articles, Daniel … to submit his works to other publishers.

a) Undaunted/continued

b) Elated/planned

c) Inspired/complied

937. When Mary heard the latest
bad news, she hit the … .
a) head
b) bend
c) roof
938. It has been suggested that
environment is the … factor in
the incidence
of drug addiction.
a) logical
b) conclusive
c) predominant
939. If the door bell … she
would rush to answer it.
a) rings
b) rang
c) has rung

940. The five friends all … for
the same job.
a) applied
b) referred
c) requested
941. My laptop is out of order,
which is a … .
a) hurt
b) harm
c) nuisance
942. We decided to go ahead
with the match … the bad
weather.
a) unless
b) in spite
c) despite
943. She kept the job … the
manager had threatened to sack
her.

a) although
b) even
c) unless
944. It takes most people seven
to ten days to … from COVID-
19.
a) cure
b) recover
c) prevent
945. The building has been left
empty for five years; it will be
expensive to
… the damage that has been
done.
a) fix
b) repair
c) mend
946. The children were … by
the noise in the forest.
a) afraid
b) feared
c) frightened
947. No, thanks. I'm trying to
… weight.
a) lose
b) rid
c) throw
948. Is there … at all I can do to
help you?
a) someone

b) anything
c) no one
949. I'll have to wait until the
mechanic … .
a) will come
b) is coming

c) comes

950. … you improve this project, you won't pass the exam.
a) When
b) Unless
c) If

951. We got up early this morning … pack the car for the journey.
a) in order to
b) so that
c) in case

952. I … that a shame!
a) calling
b) might call
c) call

953. When there are people about a deer … for the shelter of the forest.
a) takes
b) makes
c) seeks

954. I am anxious about the … of the negotiations.
a) output
b) outlook
c) outcome

955. We have been corresponding … each other for some years.
a) with
b) to
c) by

956. When questioned about the missing report, he firmly … that he had

ever seen it.
a) defied
b) refused
c) denied

957. Have you ever been introduced to …?
a) royalty
b) the royalty
c) royalties

958. Mary's rung … . I must have said something wrong.
a) off
b) round
c) back

959. The officers set a … to catch them.
a) trap
b) plan
c) device

960. The rise in the flat prices … him to sell his for a large profit.
a) achieved
b) enabled
c) managed

961. She enjoyed the dessert so much that she accepted a second … .
a) load
b) pile
c) helping

962. The little boy put a … against the tree and climbed up.
a) scale
b) grade
c) ladder

963. This is one of the London's most … hotels.
a) well-off
b) luxurious
c) rich

964. Some truck drivers expect everyone else to get … their way.
a) away from
b) off
c) out of

965. It's … long time since I last saw you.
a) such a
b) so
c) too

966. The dentist told me to open my mouth … .
a) broad
b) greatly
c) wide

967. Tom left home more than two hours ago. He … be at the office by now.
a) can
b) must
c) would

968. I … you wear the blue coat.
a) say
b) suggest
c) encourage

969. When I was in London I went on a few short day … to tourist sights.
a) travels
b) voyages
c) trips

970. The purple curtains began to … after some time in the sun.
a) fade
b) dissolve
c) melt

971. Our new colleague seems calm enough, but he has a very violent … .
a) mood
b) temper
c) stage

972. It's three years … I went to Cambridge.
a) for
b) last
c) since

973. They can only cure Mary … her illness if they operate on her.
a) of
b) on
c) in

974. I believe … taking my time to finish this project.
a) on
b) in
c) with

975. That man is often extremely rude … people.
a) for
b) with
c) to

976. You demand too much …
him.
a) of
b) for
c) in

977. The branch gave … and the
cat found itself suddenly on the
ground.
a) in
b) way
c) back

978. Mira saw her little sister …
after the dog.
a) run
b) ran
c) runs

979. If you … Harry, tell him to
come and see me.
a) have met
b) meet
c) met

980. Our study … in March if
we receive all feedback.
a) is published
b) published
c) will be published

981. I kept the door open by
putting a … under it.
a) triangle
b) block
c) wedge

982. … from Sarah, all the
employees said they would go.
a) Apart

b) Except
c) Only

983. This cloth … quite thin.
a) touches
b) feels
c) holds

984. The boy says he has got …
in his stomach.
a) hurt
b) pains
c) suffering

985. The drivers are
complaining that their fares are
too … .
a) small
b) little
c) low

986. The terrorist … the pilot to
change direction.
a) forced
b) demanded
c) made

987. As soon as the alarm rang
everyone walked quickly
downstairs, …
gathered in the car park.
a) while
b) then
c) before

988. She has a strong … to see
her town again.
a) liking
b) feeling
c) desire

989. Don't … your drink on the
table. Be careful!
a) spill
b) flood
c) flow

990. This wet weather has lasted for two weeks; … rained every single day.
a) there has
b) it has
c) there was

991. It is a long … from Berlin to Moscow.
a) tour
b) track
c) flight

992. Do you mind not …?
a) to smoke
b) smoke
c) smoking

993. We will have to … sales during the coming year.
a) expand
b) increase
c) extend

994. The meeting, … I was the guest of honour, was enjoyable.
a) by which
b) for which
c) at which

995. That's the woman … daughter I nearly kissed when I was young.
a) whose
b) whom
c) that

996. I am thankful … any advice you could give me.
a) about
b) on
c) for

997. We haven't accused him … anything.
a) by
b) of
c) to

998. The spy surrendered himself … the enemy.
a) in
b) with
c) to

999. This shows continues to … various audiences.
a) enthrall
b) bored
c) catching

1000. The … of supplies and equipment has hampered the progress of medical research for a cure.
a) scarcity
b) rationing
c) discontinuance

1001. In this country home ownership has … rapidly since 1990.
a) raised
b) grown
c) enlarged

1002. Unfortunately, nobody … that airplane crash.
a) lived
b) released
c) survived

1003. We were so late reaching the station that we … missed the train.
a) hardly
b) nearly
c) lately

a) almost

b) already

c) soon

1004. The director didn't offer her the job because of her untidy … .

a) sight

b) presence

c) appearance

1005. You … have seen them yesterday. They're on holiday.

a) mustn't

b) can't

c) needn't

1006. The mansion has been built on the … of a lake.

a) border

b) edge

c) front

1007. Her performance was …; everyone was delighted.

a) faultless

b) unmarked

c) worthless

1008. Please … your bill before you leave the shop.

a) control

b) figure

c) check

1009. I can't even make … where the road is.

a) out

b) up

c) over

1010. I found the articles rather dull; I couldn't read it … .

a) by the end

b) to the end

c) on the end

1011. She has to work hard to keep the house … and tidy.

a) smooth

b) neat

c) plain

1012. How much have you borrowed … me already? Don't you think that's enough?

a) of

b) from

c) on

1013. This coat will protect you … the cold.

a) from

b) about

c) of

1014. Spies may have a number of … names and documents.

a) false

b) artificial

c) synthetic

1015. They were … after working all day.

a) tired out

b) worn out

c) tired down

1016. If I had known about the problem, I … him to go away.

a) told

b) would tell

c) would have told

1017. You … better be careful
not to miss the class.
a) would
b) had
c) should
1018. I hope you don't mind me
… so late at night. It's urgent.
a) telephone
b) telephoning
c) to telephone
1019. As cunning as a … . This
phrase means very clever, very
smart.
a) a fox
b) a leopard
c) an owl
1020. Molecular biology is one
of the most interesting scientific
… .
a) divisions
b) disciplines
c) matters
1021. Take the bus and get … at
Black Lake Road.
a) off
b) down
c) outside
1022. Tom's sister had a baby
daughter yesterday and she is
his first … .
a) cousin
b) relation
c) niece
1023. Will the company be able
to … all their difficulties?
a) overcome
b) dismiss

c) defeat
1024. There was nothing … to
eat in the refrigerator.
a) at last
b) at all
c) at least

1025. The professor was angry
with them because they kept …
talking.
a) up
b) up with
c) on
1026. After going to several
interviews, she … to get a job.
a) managed
b) could
c) achieved
1027. If only he … told the
police the truth in the first place.
a) has
b) would have
c) had
1028. A small … of students
was waiting outside the class.
a) team
b) group
c) gang
1029. Many countries rely on
rice as the … food.
a) capital
b) staple
c) winning
1030. Please take your place in
the … .
a) queue
b) tail

c) file

1031. I like to sit … the river and fish.

a) beside

b) next

c) along

1032. The poor man fell … in front of a train.

a) in full

b) in full cry

c) full length

1033. Her professor brought her some books … art.

a) on

b) for

c) with

1034. I am thinking of looking … a new job.

a) to

b) for

c) after

1035. I've never been good … math.

a) with

b) at

c) in

1036. It's pointless … .

a) asking her for help

b) to ask help from her

c) to ask her of helping

1037. There is no need for you to shout … .

a) at your top voice

b) on top of your voice

c) at the top of your voice

1038. I … him about it for more than two weeks.

a) am asking

b) have been asking

c) asked

1039. They … their success to hard work.

a) attribute

b) aim

c) angle

1040. Prescribed treatments can … the pain but cannot … the patient.

a) palliate/cure

b) alleviate/infect

c) abate/affect

1041. When the police found my wallet, it was … .

a) vacant

b) empty

c) deserted

1042. It was a sad day when the company closed and the employees were all … .

a) paid back

b) paid up

c) paid off

1043. You will become ill … you stop working so hard.

a) until

b) unless

c) if

1044. The sooner we leave this place, the …!

a) preferable

b) better

c) ideal

1045. The weather seems to be
… .

a) clearing up

b) setting up

c) wearing off

1046. After some time you get
used to the people's … of life.

a) habit

b) custom

c) way

1047. I can no longer afford the
cost of … two cars.

a) operating

b) running

c) managing

1048. A soldier has to learn to
carry … orders as soon as they
are given.

a) on

b) off

c) out

1049. Too many players refuse
to … the referee's decisions.

a) accept

b) allow

c) agree

1050. It's not fair that I …
always have to clean the table.

a) should

b) would

c) must

1051. She won't have any
problems. She's a very self-…
young lady.

a) reliable

b) confident

c) trusting

1052. This summer was so hot
that the … in the woods dried
up.

a) bath

b) bowl

c) pond

1053. It's over a year … I
visited the medical doctor.

a) past

b) since

c) when

1054. There's an interesting pc
game … in today's newspaper.

a) advertised

b) informed

c) issued

1055. The lessons usually start
… 8 p.m.

a) with

b) on

c) at

1056. I though you said that you
were … to be in Germany this
month.

a) supposed

b) intended

c) assumed

1057. Motorway traffic was …
after a terrible accident.

a) diverged

b) diverted

c) deflected

1058. She is referred to as a/an
… housewife.

a) only
b) sole
c) mere

1059. I wish she … change her mind so often!
a) shouldn't
b) wouldn't
c) couldn't
1060. The famous woman lived a life thought to be … even by her
contemporaries.
a) exorbitant
b) extraneous
c) extravagant
1061. When I was a child I wanted to … to play the guitar.
a) know
b) learn
c) discover
1062. I really can't make … what's happening here.
a) away
b) over
c) out
1063. Mary has put on so much weight that her clothes don't … her any
more.
a) match
b) fit
c) suit
1064. It's amazing what his mother lets him … away with.
a) get
b) make

c) go
1065. Steve … to the hospital ten minutes before her birth.
a) was
b) got
c) arrived
1066. The man took the stress to write … the complete list for us.
a) out
b) through
c) off

1067. … the papers, the Prime Minister is to give a speech tomorrow.
a) Related to
b) Referring to
c) According to
1068. Clearing the weeds was a much harder … than they had imagined.
a) deed
b) service
c) task
1069. Be careful! It's a minor road and … in places.
a) bending
b) wandering
c) winding
1070. My application was … .
a) turned down
b) let down
c) put down
1071. I am fond of his novels. He is my … author.
a) favourite
b) likely

c) favoured

1072. She studied chemistry at university and … .

a) so did I

b) so I did

c) I did also

1073. Biting one's fingernails is a very bad … .

a) custom

b) habit

c) way

1074. You … be serious about that. I won't do it.

a) mustn't

b) might not

c) can't

1075. He is so keen … learning. He should be encouraged.

a) in

b) on

c) for

1076. Don't blame me … that! It's not my fault.

a) to

b) with

c) for

1077. I don't think she had … me about her problems.

a) tells

b) to tell

c) telling

1078. The judge shouted to counsel on both sides that he would … no argument.

a) hear

b) brook

c) accept

1079. The professor was … out of his job after the scandal.

a) wiped

b) eased

c) wiped

1080. He was unsure that the speech was word … .

a) perfect

b) precise

c) accurate

1081. Mike often … about his expensive car.

a) praises

b) boasts

c) prides

1082. Have you heard? Steven has got married … Susan.

a) to

b) with

c) by

1083. The boy went to bed … very ill.

a) feels

b) having felt

c) feeling

1084. Could you … me fifty dollars? I'll pay you back next Friday.

a) lend

b) take

c) borrow

1085. We hope that one day a cure for cancer will … .

a) find

b) be found

c) been found

1086. We have much pleasure in … the invitation.

a) taking

b) accepting

c) thanking

1087. Tom is a … player. He practises for three hours every morning.

a) keen

b) excited

c) impatient

1088. I had a … that something terrible was going to happen.

a) sense

b) view

c) feeling

1089. If you're trying to lose weight, you should … off fats.

a) eat

b) keep

c) go

1090. Tom decided to … a priest instead of joining the army.

a) train for

b) study for

c) become

1091. Jennifer … drive to the station every day.

a) using to

b) used to

c) had used to

1092. … hard he tries, she never wins at tennis.

a) Wherever

b) Whatever

c) However

1093. When the little boy was hit on the head, he … consciousness.

a) lost

b) fell

c) dropped

1094. The kid got a bad mark because he had … a lot of mistakes in his homework.

a) done

b) committed

c) made

1095. The student who … in his exams was expelled.

a) cheated

b) tricked

c) deceived

1096. The racing car came round the corner … full speed.

a) for

b) at

c) to

1097. I dreamt … you last night.

a) on

b) in

c) of

1098. He … .

a) set off to a stroll

b) set off on a stroll

c) set down to a stroll

1099. If I can't be back on time, she … her dinner alone.

a) has

b) will have

c) would have

1100. As black as … . This phrase means very dirty.

a) the Ace of Spades

b) ink

c) night

.

Answer Key

1.a 2.a 3.c 4.c 5.b 6.c 7.c 8.a 9.c
10.b
11.c 12.c 13.a 14.b 15.c 16.c
17.a 18.c 19.b 20.c
21.a 22.c 23.b 24.c 25.a 26.c
27.a 28.b 29.c 30.a
31.c 32.a 33.b 34.b 35.c 36.a
37.a 38.c 39.c 40.b
41.a 42.c 43.b 44.a 45.c 46.c
47.c 48.b 49.a 50.b
51.b 52.c 53.b 54.a 55.c 56.b
57.b 58.c 59.c 60.a
61.b 62.c 63.a 64.b 65.c 66.c
67.a 68.b 69.c 70.a
71.b 72.b 73.c 74.b 75.a 76.a
77.c 78.c 79.b 80.a
81.c 82.c 83.a 84.b 85.c 86.c
87.b 88.a 89.b 90.c
91.b 92.a 93.c 94.b 95.c 96.b
97.a 98.c 99.b 100.a

101.c 102.c 103.a 104.b 105.c
106.c 107.a 108.b 109.a
110.c 111.b 112.c 113.c 114.a
115.b 116.c 117.a 118.b

119.c 120.a 121.b 122.a 123.c
124.b 125.c 126.b 127.a
128.c 129.c 130.a 131.b 132.c
133.a 134.a 135.c 136.b
137.a 138.b 139.c 140.c 141.c
142.a 143.b 144.c 145.c
146.a 147.a 148.b 149.c 150.b
151.a 152.c 153.c 154.b
155.c 156.a 157.b 158.b 159.c
160.a 161.b 162.c 163.c
164.b 165.a 166.b 167.c 168.a
169.b 170.c 171.c 172.b
173.b 174.c 175.a 176.b 177.a
178.c 179.a 180.b 181.a
182.c 183.b 184.c 185.b 186.c
187.a 188.a 189.c 190.b
191.a 192.c 193.c 194.b 195.c
196.a 197.c 198.b 199.a
200.c 201.b 202.a 203.c 204.b
205.c 206.a 207.c 208.b
209.a 210.c 211.c 212.a 213.b
214.a 215.c 216.b 217.c
218.b 219.b 220.b 221.a 222.c
223.c 224.b 225.c 226.a
227.b 228.c 229.b 230.a 231.c
232.b 233.c 234.a 235.c
236.b 237.c 238.c 239.b 240.a
241.b 242.a 243.c 244.b
245.b 246.b 247.a 248.c 249.b
250.a 251.b 252.c 253.c
254.c 255.a 256.c 257.b 258.c
259.c 260.c 261.b 262.a
263.c 264.a 265.b 266.c 267.a
268.c 269.a 270.b 271.b
272.a 273.b 274.c 275.c 276.a
277.b 278.a 279.c 280.b

281.c 282.c 283.c 284.a 285.c
286.b 287.c 288.b 289.c

290.a 291.a 292.b 293.c 294.c

295.c 296.a 297.b 298.a

299.b 300.a 301.a 302.c 303.c

304.b 305.b 306.b 307.c

308.b 309.a 310.c 311.c 312.c

313.a 314.b 315.c 316.b

317.c 318.a 319.c 320.c 321.a

322.b 323.c 324.c 325.b

326.a 327.c 328.b 329.a 330.c

331.c 332.c 333.a 334.b

335.b 336.a 337.b 338.c 339.a

340.c 341.b 342.a 343.c

344.b 345.b 346.c 347.c 348.b

349.a 350.c 351.b 352.a

353.c 354.a 355.c 356.b 357.b

358.a 359.c 360.b 361.c

362.a 363.c 364.b 365.a 366.c

367.c 368.a 369.b 370.c

371.b 372.a 373.c 374.a 375.b

376.c 377.c 378.a 379.a

380.c 381.a 382.c 383.b 384.b

385.c 386.c 387.a 388.b

389.c 390.c 391.b 392.c 393.a

394.c 395.a 396.c 397.b

398.c 399.a 400.b 401.a 402.b

403.b 404.c 405.c 406.b

407.a 408.a 409.c 410.a 411.c

412.a 413.b 414.b 415.c

416.a 417.c 418.b 419.c 420.a

421.b 422.a 423.c 424.b

425.b 426.a 427.c 428.b 429.b

430.a 431.c 432.c 433.b

434.c 435.c 436.b 437.a 438.c

439.c 440.a 441.b 442.c

443.a 444.b 445.c 446.c 447.b
448.a 449.c 450.b 451.b

452.a 453.c 454.a 455.b 456.c

457.c 458.a 459.c 460.b

461.c 462.b 463.c 464.a 465.c

466.b 467.b 468.c 469.c

470.a 471.a 472.c 473.b 474.b

475.c 476.a 477.b 478.a

479.c 480.b 481.c 482.a 483.b

484.c 485.b 486.c 487.b

488.c 489.a 490.a 491.b 492.c

493.a 494.b 495.a 496.c

497.a 498.c 499.b 500.a 501.a

502.b 503.c 504.a 505.b

506.c 507.a 508.c 509.b 510.a

511.c 512.b 513.a 514.c

515.a 516.c 517.b 518.a 519.b

520.c 521.a 522.c 523.b

524.a 525.c 526.a 527.b 528.a

529.c 530.c 531.b 532.a

533.c 534.b 535.a 536.b 537.b

538.a 539.c 540.a 541.c

542.a 543.c 544.b 545.b 546.c

547.c 548.a 549.c 550.b

551.b 552.b 553.a 554.c 555.c

556.c 557.b 558.b 559.a

560.b 561.c 562.b 563.c 564.a

565.b 566.c 567.b 568.c

569.c 570.a 571.b 572.c 573.b

574.a 575.a 576.c 577.b

578.b 579.c 580.b 581.c 582.a

583.b 584.b 585.a 586.c

587.b 588.c 589.b 590.c 591.b

592.c 593.a 594.b 595.a

596.a 597.c 598.b 599.c 600.a

601.b 602.a 603.c 604.a

605.a 606.c 607.b 608.a 609.c
610.b 611.c 612.c 613.a
614.b 615.a 616.c 617.b 618.c
619.a 620.b 621.c 622.b
623.a 624.b 625.b 626.b 627.a
628.c 629.c 630.a 631.b
632.a 633.c 634.c 635.b 636.b
637.c 638.a 639.a 640.c
641.c 642.a 643.c 644.b 645.b
646.a 647.b 648.b 649.c
650.a 651.b 652.a 653.c 654.c
655.a 656.a 657.b 658.c
659.b 660.c 661.c 662.a 663.c
664.c 665.a 666.b 667.c
668.b 669.a 670.c 671.b 672.a
673.c 674.c 675.a 676.b
677.c 678.c 679.b 680.a 681.a
682.c 683.b 684.b 685.c
686.b 687.c 688.b 689.c 690.c
691.a 692.c 693.b 694.c
695.a 696.b 697.c 698.b 699.c
700.b 701.a 702.c 703.c
704.b 705.a 706.b 707.a 708.b
709.c 710.b 711.b 712.c
713.a 714.c 715.a 716.c 717.a
718.c 719.c 720.b 721.a
722.c 723.b 724.a 725.c 726.c
727.b 728.a 729.c 730.b
731.a 732.b 733.a 734.c 735.b
736.c 737.b 738.a 739.c
740.b 741.b 742.c 743.a 744.b
745.a 746.c 747.b 748.a
749.c 750.b 751.a 752.b 753.c
754.c 755.a 756.b 757.a
758.c 759.c 760.a 761.a 762.c
763.c 764.b 765.b 766.c

767.b 768.c 769.a 770.b 771.b
772.a 773.c 774.b 775.c
776.a 777.c 778.b 779.a 780.c
781.c 782.b 783.a 784.c
785.b 786.c 787.c 788.c 789.a
790.b 791.c 792.b 793.c

794.b 795.c 796.b 797.a 798.b
799.a 800.c 801.b 802.b
803.a 804.c 805.a 806.c 807.b
808.c 809.c 810.b 811.a
812.c 813.b 814.a 815.b 816.a
817.c 818.a 819.b 820.a
821.b 822.b 823.c 824.c 825.a
826.b 827.c 828.a 829.a
830.b 831.a 832.c 833.b 834.a
835.a 836.c 837.b 838.c
839.b 840.b 841.c 842.c 843.a
844.b 845.b 846.a 847.c
848.c 849.b 850.a 851.a 852.b
853.c 854.b 855.c 856.a
857.c 858.c 859.b 860.a 861.c
862.a 863.c 864.c 865.b
866.b 867.c 868.c 869.a 870.b
871.a 872.b 873.b 874.c
875.a 876.b 877.c 878.b 879.c
880.a 881.c 882.b 883.a
884.c 885.b 886.c 887.b 888.a
889.b 890.b 891.b 892.a
893.c 894.c 895.a 896.b 897.c
898.b 899.a 900.c 901.b
902.a 903.c 904.a 905.a 906.c
907.b 908.b 909.c 910.b
911.c 912.a 913.b 914.c 915.a
916.c 917.c 918.a 919.c
920.c 921.c 922.a 923.c 924.b
925.a 926.c 927.b 928.a

929.b 930.c 931.a 932.b 933.c
934.b 935.a 936.a 937.c
938.c 939.b 940.a 941.c 942.c
943.a 944.b 945.b 946.c
947.a 948.b 949.c 950.b 951.a
952.c 953.b 954.c 955.a
956.c 957.a 958.a 959.a 960.b
961.c 962.c 963.b 964.c
965.a 966.c 967.b 968.b 969.c
970.a 971.b 972.c 973.a
974.b 975.c 976.a 977.b 978.a
979.b 980.c 981.c 982.a
983.b 984.b 985.c 986.a 987.b
988.c 989.a 990.b 991.c
992.c 993.b 994.c 995.a 996.c
997.b 998.c 999.a 1000.a
1001.b 1002.c 1003.a 1004.c
1005.b 1006.b 1007.a 1008.c
1009.a
1010.b 1011.b 1012.b 1013.a
1014.a 1015.a 1016.c 1017.b
1018.b
1019.a 1020.b 1021.a 1022.c
1023.a 1024.b 1025.c 1026.a
1027.c
1028.b 1029.b 1030.a 1031.a
1032.c 1033.a 1034.b 1035.b
1036.a
1037.c 1038.b 1039.a 1040.a
1041.b 1042.c 1043.b 1044.b
1045.a
1046.c 1047.b 1048.c 1049.a
1050.a 1051.b 1052.c 1053.b
1054.a
1055.c 1056.a 1057.b 1058.c
1059.b 1060.c 1061.b 1062.c
1063.b

1064.a 1065.b 1066.a 1067.c
1068.c 1069.c 1070.a 1071.a
1072.a
1073.b 1074.c 1075.b 1076.c
1077.b 1078.b 1079.b 1080.a
1081.b
1082.a 1083.c 1084.a 1085.b
1086.b 1087.a 1088.c 1089.b
1090.c
1091.b 1092.c 1093.a 1094.c
1095.a 1096.b 1097.c 1098.b
1099.b
1100.a